A Tale of Two Cities: A Comparison of Air Pollution Governance in the Los Angeles Area of the USA and the Beijing-Tianjin-Hebei Area of China

Energy and Environmental Law and Policy Series

VOLUME 42

Editor

General Editor: Professor Kurt Deketelaere, Professor of Law, University of Leuven, Belgium; Honorary Professor of Law, University of Dundee, UK; Honorary Chief of Staff, Flemish Government; Secretary-General, League of European Research Universities (LERU), Belgium. Kurt's CV – see www.kurtdeketelaere/en/kurt.

Introduction

Environmental protection and energy efficiency/security are important societal challenges. In order to tackle them, policy and legal frameworks are developed at national, regional and global level. Through study and best practices development, the challenges will prove to be solvable.

Contents/Subjects

Environment/Nature/Energy/Climate.

Objective

The aim of this series is to publish works of excellent quality that focus on the study of energy and environmental policy. Through this series the editors:

- contribute to the improvement of the quality of energy/environmental law and policy in general and environmental quality and energy efficiency in particular; increase the access to environmental and energy information for academics, non-governmental organizations, government institutions, and business; and
- facilitate cooperation between academic and non-academic communities in the field of energy and environmental law and policy throughout the world.

Readership

Academics and practitioners in environmental and energy matters.

The titles published in this series are listed at the end of this volume.

A Tale of Two Cities: A Comparison of Air Pollution Governance in the Los Angeles Area of the USA and the Beijing-Tianjin-Hebei Area of China

Wang Xi
Richard Ottinger

Wolters Kluwer

Published by:
Kluwer Law International B.V.
PO Box 316
2400 AH Alphen aan den Rijn
The Netherlands
E-mail: lrs-sales@wolterskluwer.com
Website: www.wolterskluwer.com/en/solutions/kluwerlawinternational

Sold and distributed by:
Wolters Kluwer Legal & Regulatory U.S.
920 Links Avenue
Landisville, PA 17538
United States of America
E-mail: customer.service@wolterskluwer.com

ISBN 978-94-035-4237-9

e-Book: ISBN 978-94-035-4247-8
web-PDF: ISBN 978-94-035-4257-7

About the Authors

Professor Wang Xi is the Director of Platform for Research on Ecological Civilization and Environmental Rule of Law, Kunming University of Science and Technology, and Director of the Environmental and Resources Law Institute, School of Law, Shanghai Jiao Tong University, a principal author and editor of this study.

Professor Richard Ottinger is Dean Emeritus of the Elizabeth Haub School of Law, Pace University, and also a principal author and editor of this study.

Table of Contents

About the Authors v

Preface xiii

Acknowledgments xv

Introduction 1

CHAPTER 1
Comparability: Reasons for Selecting the Targeted Areas 3
1 Comparability in Geographical, Environmental, and Social Conditions 3
2 Comparability in Air Pollution 8
3 Comparability in Improvement of Air Quality 10

CHAPTER 2
Methodology: The Environmental Governance Model 13
1 EG Model as a Whole 14
2 Two Circles 15
3 Equilateral Triangle 15
4 Symbol of Two Overlaying Circles 16
5 Relation Between the Two Circles and the Triangle 17
6 Theoretical Foundation of the EG Model 17
7 Internal Logic 21

CHAPTER 3
Air Pollution Governance in Los Angeles Area 23
1 Political Profile of the United States 23
2 Legal and Ethical Frameworks on Air Pollution Control 25
2.1 Legal Framework 25
2.2 Ethical Framework 27
2.2.1 Development of Environmental Ethic Since the 1950s 28

3 Political Relations in Air Pollution Governance 29
3.1 Relation of Regulation 29
3.1.1 Monitoring Air Pollutants 30
3.1.1.1 Establishment of the Air Quality Monitoring Network 30
3.1.1.2 Establishment of Community Air Protection Program 31
3.1.2 Regulation of Incinerators 31
3.1.3 Regulation of Transportation Sector 33
3.1.3.1 Study of Air Quality 33
3.1.3.2 California Air Resources Board 34
3.1.3.3 First Motor Vehicle Pollution Control Regulations 36
3.1.3.4 California's Smog Check Program 36
3.1.3.5 Low Emission Vehicles Program 37
3.1.3.6 SCAQMD Clean Fleets Program 38
3.1.3.7 Reducing Diesel Exhaust Pollution from Locomotive Transportation 39
3.1.3.8 Regulation of Gasoline 42
3.1.4 Regulation of Ports 43
3.1.4.1 Clean Air Action Plan (2006, 2017) 43
3.1.4.2 Important Elements for the Plan's Success 46
3.1.4.2.1 Action and Clear Responsibilities of the Responsible Agencies 46
3.1.4.2.2 San Pedro Bay Standards 47
3.1.4.2.3 Public Participation 47
3.1.5 Regulation of Building Industry 48
3.1.5.1 California Energy Code 49
3.1.5.2 California Green Building Standards Code 50
3.1.5.3 Energy Efficiency of Buildings 51
3.1.5.4 Economic Building Enterprises 53
3.1.5.5 Water Conservation Ordinance 54
3.1.5.6 Planning and Zoning Code 55
3.1.6 Regulation of Utility Sector 55
3.1.6.1 Power Plant Equipment Improvement and Emission Standards 55
3.1.6.2 Emission Permit System 56
3.1.6.3 Cleaning the Sources of Electricity 57
3.1.7 Regulation of Oil Refineries and Gas Stations 59
3.1.8 Public-Private Partnerships 61
3.1.8.1 Joint Research Council on Power Plant Air Pollution Control 61
3.1.8.2 Urban Forestry Projects 62
3.1.8.3 Partnership Between Government and Organizations-Green Business Certification 63

3.1.8.4 City Energy Project 63
3.1.8.5 Energy Efficiency and Solar Incentive Programs 64
3.1.9 Market-Based Regulations and Policies 65
3.1.9.1 Pollution Trading 65
3.1.9.2 Vehicle Labeling Requirements 66
3.1.9.3 Rebate Program 67
3.1.10 Voluntary Energy Efficiency Programs 67
3.1.10.1 Energy Star 67
3.1.10.2 Leadership in Energy and Environmental Design 67
3.1.10.3 Financial Incentives of the Clean Vehicle Rebate Program 68
3.1.10.4 Nonfinancial Incentives of the Clean Vehicle Rebate Program 69
3.1.11 Governmental Environmental Education 69
3.2 Relation of Supervision Over Regulators 71
3.2.1 Supervision by Federal Government 71
3.2.2 Supervision by Nongovernmental Organizations 71
3.2.3 Supervision by Enterprises 72
3.3 Relation of Supervision Over Enterprises and Other Polluters 74
3.3.1 Media Disclosure and Public Responses 74
3.3.2 NGOs' Participation in Litigations 75
4 Achievements and Challenges 76
4.1 Improvement of Air Quality 76
4.2 Value Change of the Society 76
4.3 Challenges 77

Chapter 4
Air Pollution Governance in BTH Area of China 79
1 Political Profile of China 79
2 Legal and Ethical Frameworks for Air Pollution Control 80
2.1 Legal Frameworks 81
2.1.1 National Framework 81
2.1.2 Local Framework 82
2.2 Ethical Framework 83
2.2.1 Traditional Chinese Environmental Ethics 83
2.2.2 Contemporary Stimulations from International Society 84
2.2.2.1 1972 UN Conference on Human Environment 84
2.2.2.2 1992 UN Conference on Environment and Development 84
2.2.3 Contemporary Chinese Environmental Ethical Ideas 85
2.2.3.1 Scientific Outlook on Development 85
2.2.3.2 Ecological Civilization 86
2.2.3.3 Green Growth 88

2.2.4 Development of Environmental Ethics Since the 1950s 89
3 Political Relations in Air Pollution Governance 90
3.1 Relation of Regulation 90
3.1.1 National Regulatory Measures 90
3.1.1.1 Goals and Targets 90
3.1.1.2 Funding 91
3.1.1.3 Action Plans 91
3.1.1.4 Emission Trading 91
3.1.1.5 Assessment 92
3.1.2 Local Regulatory Measures 92
3.1.2.1 Local Regulations, Plans and Targets 92
3.1.2.2 Emission Permit 92
3.1.2.3 Improving Industrial Structure 93
3.1.2.4 Technology Innovation 93
3.1.2.5 Optimizing Energy Structure 94
3.1.2.6 Regulating of Major Polluting Sources 96
3.1.2.6.1 Automobiles 96
3.1.2.6.2 Port 97
3.1.2.6.3 Dusts 98
3.1.2.7 Phasing out Polluting Industries and Replacement of Employees 98
3.1.2.8 Ban of Open Burning 99
3.1.2.9 Law Enforcement 99
3.2 The Relation of Supervision on Regulators 100
3.2.1 The Supervision of the National Peoples' Congresses 100
3.2.2 Supervision by the Local Peoples' Congresses 100
3.2.3 Ecological and Environmental Inspection 101
3.3 Relation on Supervision Over Enterprises and Other Polluters 104
3.3.1 Supervision by NGOs 104
3.3.1.1 Participating in Governmental Decision-Making Processes 104
3.3.1.2 Reporting 105
3.3.1.3 Public Interest Litigation 105
3.3.2 Supervision by News Media 106
3.3.3 The "Supervision" by Courts 107
4 Achievements and Challenges 107
4.1 Achievements 107
4.1.1 Optimization of Energy Structure and Energy Consumption 107
4.1.1.1 Nationally Optimization 107
4.1.1.2 Optimization in the BTH Area 110
4.1.2 Improvement of Air Quality 111
4.1.3 Air Pollution Governance 115
4.1.3.1 Regulatory Relation 115
4.1.3.2 Relation of Supervision Over Regulators 115

4.1.3.3 Relation of Supervision Over Enterprises and Other Polluters 115
4.2 Value Change in the Society 115
4.3 Challenges 116

Chapter 5
Comparison and Findings 119
1 Macro Comparison 120
1.1 Correlation Between Political Profiles and Air Quality Improvement 120
1.2 Correlation Between Economic Structure and Air Quality Improvement 120
2 Micro Comparison 121
2.1 Comparison of Legal and Ethical Frameworks 121
2.1.1 Comparison of Legal Frameworks 121
2.1.2 Comparison of Ethical Frameworks 122
2.1.2.1 Comparison of Historical Developments of Environmental Ethics in the United States and China 122
2.1.2.1.1 Peak Times 123
2.1.2.1.2 Evolutionary Trends 123
2.1.2.1.3 Driving Forces 124
2.1.3 Comparison of Value Change of Society 125
2.2 Comparison of Regulatory and Other Measures 126
2.2.1 Measures Categorized by Political Relations 127
2.2.2 Measures Categorized by Actors 129
2.2.3 Measures Categorized by Nature 131
2.2.4 Measures Categorized by Function 133
2.2.5 A Summary 134
2.3 Comparison of Governance Processes 134
2.3.1 Comparison of Relation of Regulation 134
2.3.2 Comparison of Relation of Supervision Over Regulators 135
2.3.3 Comparison of Relation of Supervision Over Enterprises and Other Polluters 136
2.3.4 A General Pattern of Air Pollution Governance 137

Chapter 6
Conclusions 139

Bibliography 145

Index 149

Preface

Both the Los Angeles area (LA area) of the U.S. and the Beijing-Tianjin-Hebei area (BTH area) of China have been the focal points of the concerns of the world for air pollution at different times respectively. Both the areas suffered serious air pollution and made great efforts to combat air pollution and achieved remarkable success. This book is the result of a comparative case study on the legal experience of air pollution control in the two areas by an international team consisting of Chinese and American researchers. Based on a Model of Environmental Governance (EG Model), which is developed by the authors and built on the basis of neo-political economy, political science and comparative law, the experience of the air pollution control processes of the two areas is analyzed and compared. Major similarities and differences in the experiences of the areas were identified and analyzed. This study collected a lot of valuable firsthand information from the two areas. This information is not only vivid historical evidence of the air pollution governance processes in the areas but also forms a strong empirical foundation for this comparative study.

The study finds that, firstly, faced with serious health problems caused by air pollution, the mainstream value of the societies of the two areas changed dramatically. Secondly, the changed value of the societies had caused the establishment of a relatively sound legal and ethical framework in the LA area in the 1970s and in the BTH area in the 2010s, respectively. Thirdly, under the legal and ethical frameworks, there were mainly three political relations in the air pollution governance processes of the two areas. These relations are: (1) regulatory relation between the regulators and the regulated communities; (2) supervisory relation between the supervisors such as legislatures and residents and the public in general on one side, and the governmental regulators on the other side; and (3) another supervisory relation between the legislatures, news media and civil society on one side and the polluters on the other side. Fourthly, by comparing the "legal formants" such as the change of mainstream social values, the legal and ethical frameworks, and the three political relations in the air pollution governance processes of the two areas, as well as the numerous and various measures applied in the processes, the study finds that the political profiles of the two countries are not determinative factors for the success of air pollution control.

Instead, the substantive capabilities of a state are the determinative factors. The substantive capabilities demonstrated by the legal and policy experience of air pollution control of the two areas are: (1) the capability of environmental ethical support; (2) the capability of legal framework building; (3) the capability of good governance. These findings possibly are useful enlighteners to other countries that suffered air pollution and engaged in combats against air pollution problems.

Acknowledgments

Los Angeles Area

The Los Angeles area part of this study could not have been done without the superb help of Angelina Galiteva, who was herself a key player in all of the formative Los Angeles area decarbonization and air pollution control initiatives. She guided this research, and during a week I spent in the LA area to learn about these events, assembled for me all the other principal players in the LA area achievements, both governmental and non-governmental organization. The time she spent on this project and the effort of her colleagues to make sure I got a full and accurate picture of the background for these accomplishments were invaluable. A superstar Pace Law School JD and LL.M graduate, Angelina so impressed David Freeman, the General Manager of the Los Angeles Department of Water and Power (the LA electric utility), that he hired her to head its Environmental Department at which, under her guidance, Los Angeles became a national leader in utility renewable energy and environmental protection innovation. She then was promoted to head its Green LA, Environmental Affairs and New Product Development Organization. She was appointed by Governor Brown and later reappointed by Governor Newsom to the California Independent System Operator Board of Governors, becoming the first female Chair of the Board and helping to achieve the recent milestone achievement of operating the grid on 100% renewable energy. Angelina has been instrumental in ensuring that the State remains on track to achieve its precedent-setting legislation requiring the deep decarbonization of California's economy by 2045.

Warmest thanks to all the following people with whom Angelina arranged for me to meet. They were all incredibly generous in providing me with the details and documents of the accomplishments and travails that led to the substantial cleanup of Los Angeles area air pollution:

> Mayor of Santa Anna, Miguel Pulido Los Angeles Department of Water & Power (ILAWPD)
> Nancy Sutley, Sustainability Chief, Economic Development Officer (former CEQ Chair)

Air Quality Management Board (AQMD)
Mark Abramowitz, Governing Board Member
Bara Baird, Chief Deputy Counsel
Tracy Goss, Planning and rules Manger & P.E. (presented AQMB materials)
Bill Kelly
Activists Groups
Joseph Lyou, President & CEO, Coalition for Clean Air (Convenor)
Diane Moss, Director, Renewables 100 Policy Institute
Gary Polakovic, President, MakeOverEarth (former *LA Times* air quality reporter)
Peter Greenwald, former AQMD General Counsel
Susana Reyes, LA Mayor's Sustainability and & Climate Team
Nicholas Burant, Coalition for Clean Air Office Manager & Policy Associate
Mark Abromowitz (AQMD Board)

Without the generous help of these extraordinary people, the LA portion of the paper could never have included so many of the background facts underlying the LA pollution cleanup.

Particular thanks also to the Research Assistants from the Elisabeth Haub School of Law at Pace University who performed much of the research and writing of this study and continued with the editing even after they graduated: Pianpian Wang, Radina Valova, and Kristen Motel; also to recognize Haub/ Pace graduate Samantha Perlmutter, and students, Zachery Heberer and Jack Ventura who undertook to accommodate the footnote references to the OSCOLA reference requirements.

Beijing-Tianjin-Hebei (BTH) Area

Wang Xi, one of the authors of this book, would like to dedicate this book to the following professors for their great support, encouragement and guidance in his legal training:

Han Depei, Professor of Wuhan University Law School, who was the Academic Supervisor for Wang Xi's Master's in Law study at that school.
Liang Xi, Professor of Wuhan University Law School, who was the Academic Supervisor for Wang Xi's PhD (law) study at that school;
William Jones, Professor of Washington University Law School (at St. Louis), who was the Academic Supervisor for Wang Xi's Master's Degree (law) study at that school.

Warmest thanks to all the following people for their tireless support to this study:

Guo Xiang, Ph.D. candidate, Grade 2021, School of Environmental Science and Engineering, Kunming University of Science and Technology.
Zhang Chujia, Ph.D. candidate, Grade 2015, Law School of Shanghai Jiao Tong University, and now a Dr. and Lecturer in the Law School of Nanjing Normal University.

Zhang Haoyu, graduate student, Grade 2021, School of Law, Kunming University of Science and Technology.

Special thanks to Professor Nicholas Robinson from both Professor Richard Ottinger and Professor Wang Xi for his longtime support of this and other environmental law studies of the authors.

Special thanks to Professor Emeritus Ben Boer, Law School of the University of Sydney, for his review and suggestions on the draft of this book.

Introduction

This study targets the Los Angeles (hereinafter referred to as "LA") of the United States and the Beijing-Tianjin-Hebei area (hereinafter referred to as "BTH area") of China. Both areas are particularly important to the U.S. and China in terms of economic, environmental and social development. Despite the stark differences in their political systems, both areas had suffered from severe air pollution problems in the past. The LA area suffered serious haze in the 1940s and 1950s. The BTH area was similarly experiencing a record world level of air pollution in the 2010s.[1] In 2014, all the major air pollution indexes, such as $PM_{2.5}$, PM_{10}, SO_2 and NO_2, exceeded the national air quality standards highly. A serious haze that originated in the BTH area had extended to cover a large size of the territory of the country.

Both the areas made great efforts to combat air pollution and achieved remarkably. This study explores the major legal and policy measures taken by the two areas and tries to see how people there gradually reduced air pollution and made the areas better places to live; particularly, what are the governance processes established for combatting air pollution and how the major actors worked together in the processes. Major similarities and differences in the legal and policy experiences of the two areas are identified and analyzed so as to have an in-depth understanding of the experience of the two areas.

In addition to this introduction, this study consists of six parts. Chapter 1 is dedicated to reasons for the selection of the two areas for this study. Chapter 2 presents

1. In 2014, the annual average concentration of $PM_{2.5}$ in 13 prefecture-level and above cities in the BTH area was 93 micrograms per cubic meter, with only Zhangjiakou City meeting the $PM_{2.5}$ standard and 12 other cities exceeding the standard; the annual average concentration of PM_{10} was 158 micrograms per cubic meter, with 13 cities exceeding the standard; the annual average concentration of SO_2 was 52 micrograms per cubic meter, with four cities exceeding the standard; the annual average concentration of NO_2 was 49 micrograms per cubic meter, with 10 cities exceeded the standard. The annual average $PM_{2.5}$ concentration in Beijing was 85.9 micrograms per cubic meter. The annual average $PM_{2.5}$ concentration in Tianjin was 83 micrograms per cubic meter. The annual average $PM_{2.5}$ concentration in Shijiazhuang was 124 micrograms per cubic meter. *See* Ministry of Ecology and Environment, "Bulletin on Environmental Situation" (2014), http://www.mee.gov.cn/qwjs2019/?searchword=2014%E5%B9%B4%E5%85%AC%E6%8A%A5, accessed October 6, 2021.

an Environmental Governance Model (the EG model) and illustrates the basic methodology of this comparative study. Chapter 3 introduces the legal and policy experience of air pollution in the LA area. Chapter 4 introduces the same experience in the BTH area. Chapter 5, through the application of the EG Model and the empirical information introduced in Chapter 3 and Chapter 4, presents a comparison of the air pollution governance processes in both areas, along with some in-depth observations and findings. Chapter 6 concludes the study by presenting some theoretical insights.

CHAPTER 1

Comparability: Reasons for Selecting the Targeted Areas

Comparative environmental law is a branch of social science dedicated to the comparative study of environmental law, environmental law practice and environmental jurisprudence in various countries (including the constituent parts of a country with different legal systems and federal countries), and to the understanding and elaboration of the general laws of environmental law and environmental legal phenomena from their similarities and differences.[2] Comparability is a precondition for any comparative study, including comparative environmental law. We believe that, for this study, the experience of the legal and policy control of air pollution in the LA area and the BTH area are comparable in many aspects.

1 COMPARABILITY IN GEOGRAPHICAL, ENVIRONMENTAL, AND SOCIAL CONDITIONS

The LA and BTH areas are geographically comparable. Los Angeles is in the State of California, USA, on the shoreline of the Pacific Ocean. The Los Angeles area includes the City of Los Angeles and surrounding communities. The area of Lost Angeles County covered in this study is depicted on the following map:

2. Wang Xi, A Preliminary Study of Comparative Environmental Law in China, Law Review, Law School of Wuhan University, 1984, 4.

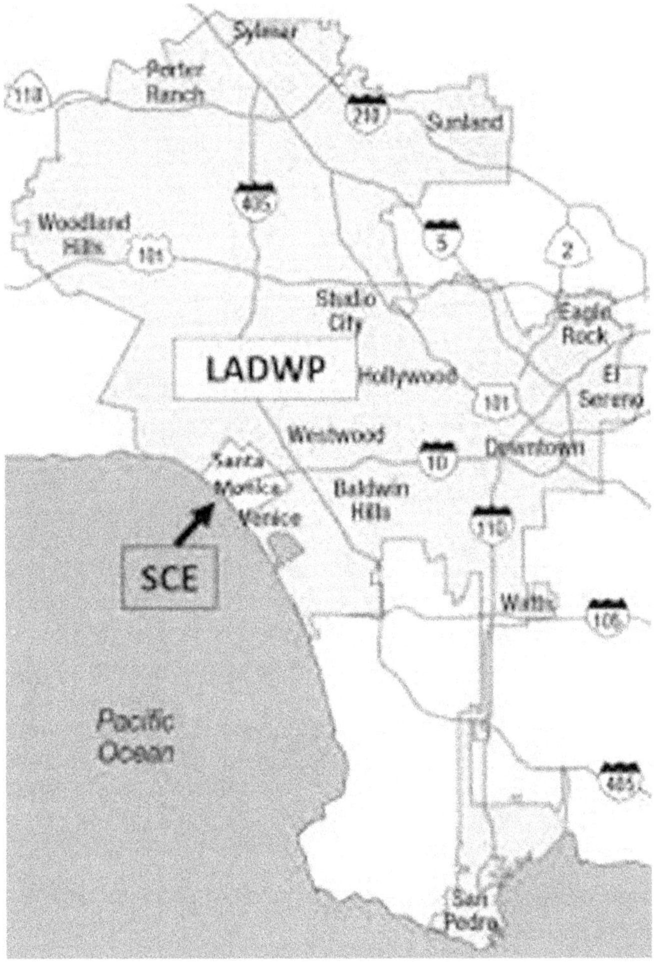

As shown in the topologic map below, Los Angeles is bordered by San Pedro Bay and Santa Monica Bay on the eastern side of the vast Pacific Ocean, backed by the majestic San Antonio Mountains, and set in an open basin surrounded by mountains on three sides and the sea on one side. This geographic condition contains air within the area.[3] This leads to the generation of ozone that occurs when these air pollutants are "cooked" by heat and sunlight:[4]

3. Nate Berg, "Why Does California's Central Valley Have Such Bad Air Pollution?" (*The Atlantic*, September 28, 2011), www.citylab.com/weather/2011/09/behind-pollution-californias-central-valley/207/, accessed March 4, 2022.
4. Tony Barboza, "New federal EPA Smog Standard Angers Both Sides of the Issue" *The Los Angeles Times* (Los Angeles, October 1, 2015), www.latimes.com/nation/la-na-epa-adopts-stricter-smog-standard-but-disappoints-environmentalists-20151-story.html, accessed March 4, 2022.

As the following map shows, the BTH area is located in the central northeast part of China:

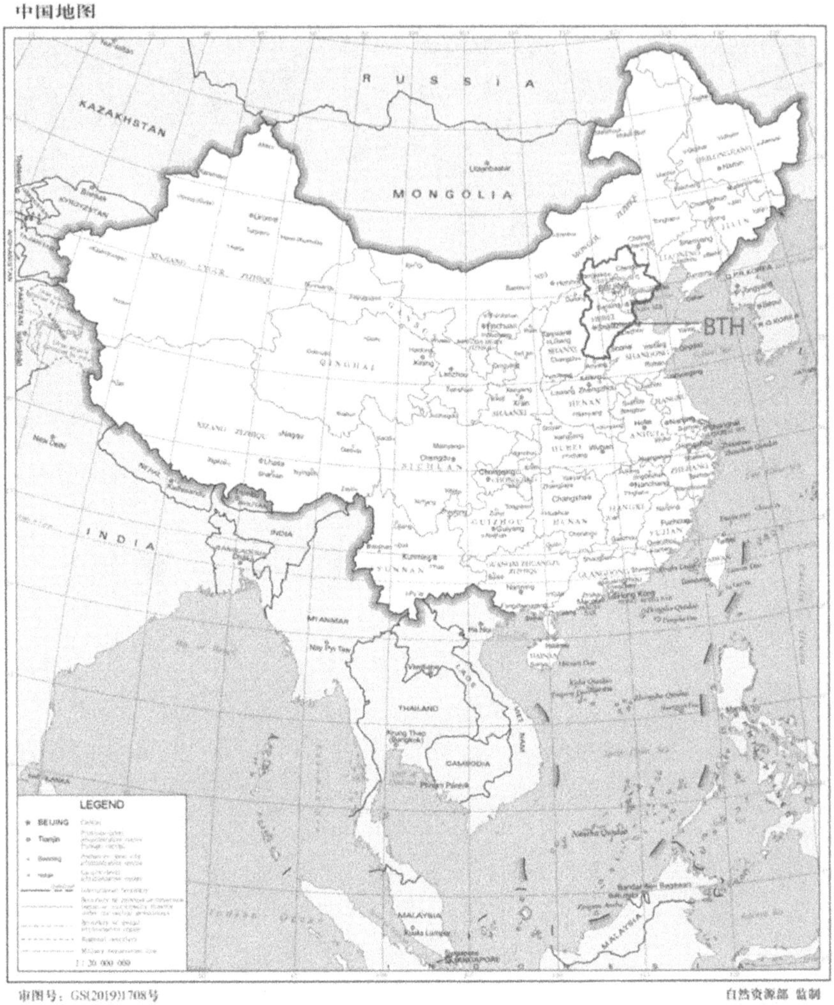

The location of the BTH area in China

The following map shows that the BTH area covers Beijing City, Tianjin City, and 26 cities in Hebei Province, Shanxi Province, Shangdong Province and Henan Province.[5] Therefore, the area is also called "2 plus 26 cities." Beijing City, the capital city of China, is located in the center of the BTH area. Tianjin City, one of four large cities

5. Those cities are, Shijiazhuang, Tangshan, Handan, Xintai, Baoding, Langfang, Hengshui, Xiong An New Area in Hebei Province; Taiyuan, Yangquan, Changzhi, Jincheng in Shanxi Province; Jinan, Zibo, Jining, Dezhou, Liaocheng, Bingzhou, Heze in Shandong Province; and Zhengzhou, Kaifeng, Anyang, Hebi, Xinxiang, Jiaozuo and Puyang in Henan Province. *See* City Government of Beijing, "A three-year action plan for Beijing to win the battle for blue sky," September 14, 2018, http://www.beijing.gov.cn/zhengce/zhengcefagui/201905/t20190522_61552.html, accessed October 28, 2021.

under the direct leadership of the Central Government of China, is located on the east side of Beijing, with its east side open to the Bohai Bay. The two cities are surrounded by the Hebei Province. The area is surrounded by Yanshan Mountains, Jibei Mountains, and Taihang Mountains on three sides and facing the Bohai Bay on one side:

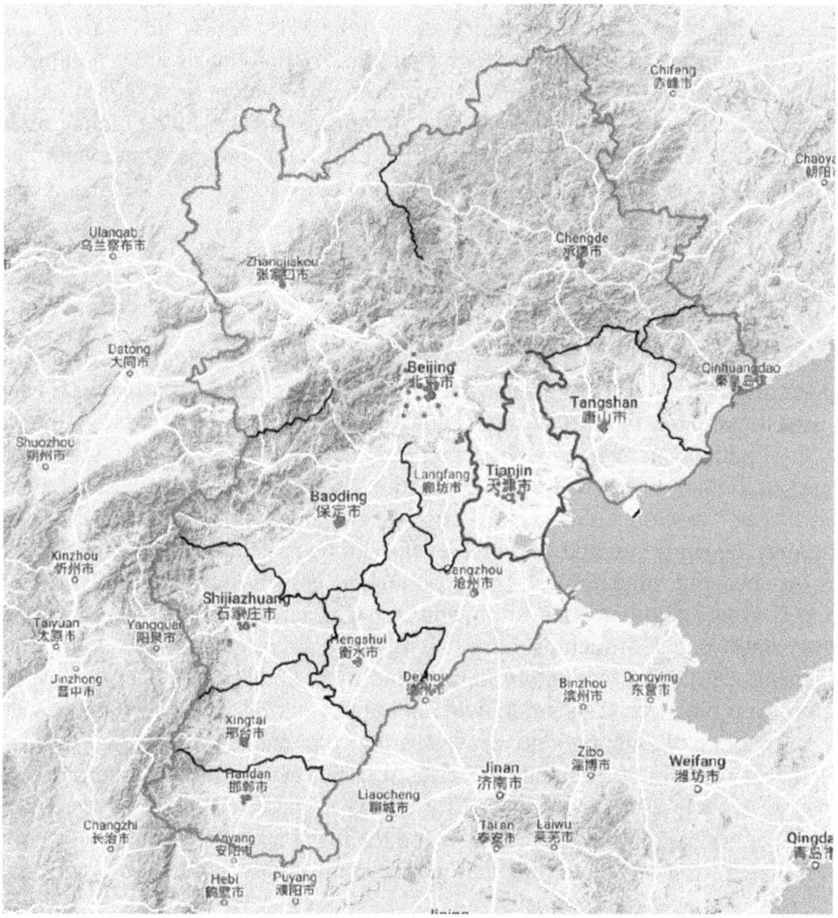

Geographic condition of the BTH area

In terms of industrialization, the two areas are comparable. With the rapid growth of the American automobile industry and the outbreak of the Pacific War in the early 1940s, Los Angeles and its surroundings were booming, with an influx of factories and people making it the area with the highest number of cars in the country. Los Angeles had 2.5 million cars in the 1940s and consumed approximately 1,100 tons of gasoline per day. In addition, other industries such as oil drilling, refineries and building industry. The Los Angeles area's population had grown rapidly from 900,000 before World War II to 3.7 million today. The Southern California area, centered in Los

Angeles, is the largest automotive market in the world, with an average of 1.8 cars per licensed Los Angeles citizen.

The BTH area is one of the most industrialized areas in China.[6] The imbalanced industrial structure with a high proportion of secondary industries and a coal-based energy structure makes Hebei Province a source of heavy air pollution. Both Beijing and Tianjin are industrialized cities with a well-developed tertiary industry. Motor vehicles are the main means of transportation in the BTH area. The BTH area is an area with a high density of population. For example, by the end of 2018, Beijing had a resident population of 21.54 million, a Gross Domestic Production (GDP) of RMB 3,032 billion, a motor vehicle fleet of 6,084,000 and a total annual energy consumption of 73.2 million tons of standard coal. Compared to 2013, the total economic volume grew by 53.1%, motor vehicle ownership by 11.9%, energy consumption by 8.9% and the population increased by 1.9%.[7]

2 COMPARABILITY IN AIR POLLUTION

Both the LA area and the BTH area suffered serious air pollution historically. In the early summer of 1943, Los Angeles was first hit by serious smoggy weather. The entire city was surrounded by a thick, light blue smog. Although there was a surge in the number of patients going to the city's medical centers for treatment of eye and throat diseases, it did not attract widespread attention. Initially, some health experts insisted that it was an "absolute coincidence," but the smog did not dissipate. On July 26 of the same year, the smog reached its worst level, with news reports stating that "the nasty smog has become unbearable." These pollutants usually have harmful side effects, such as causing coughing, congestion, and throat and chest pain, eventually leading to asthma, emphysema, bronchitis, lung cancer, and even death.[8] In 1955, more than 400 people aged 65 died of respiratory failure, and in 1970, about 75% of the population suffered from pink eye. This smog, which contains ozone, nitrogen oxides, acetaldehyde and other oxidants, not only caused serious damage to the health of Los Angeles area citizens and serious damage to agriculture but also led to big number of traffic accidents. In early 2015, the greater City of Los Angeles, California was revealed to have the highest level of ozone pollution and the fifth highest level of particle pollution of any American city in an annual, nationwide study conducted by the American Lung

6. In 2020, the total GDP was RMB 3,610,255 million for Beijing, RMB 3,620,690 million for Hebei and RMB 140,873 million for Tianjin, with a total RMB 8,639,318 million (about USD 1.34082215 trillion based on the exchange rate of October 5, 2021). The GDP of iron and steel industry occupied 28.1% of the iron and steel GDP of the whole country. The national steel output in 2020 was 1.324892 million tons. Among them, Beijing produced 1.8442 million tons of steel, Tianjin 57,240,500 tons and Hebei province 313,201,200 tons. Steel production in the BTH accounted for 28.1% of national output. The State Statistics Bureau, https://data.stats.gov.cn/search.htm, accessed September 28, 2021.
7. Ministry of Ecology and Environment, "History of Air pollution control in Beijing from 2013 to 2018" (September 24, 2019), http://www.mee.gov.cn/xxgk2018/xxgk/xxgk15/201909/t20190924_735251.html, accessed October 6, 2021.
8. *United States Census Bureau* (Quick Facts, Los Angeles, California), https://www.census.gov/quickfacts/table/PST045215/0644000, accessed March 4, 2022, at p. 95.

Association.[9] Ozone and particulate matter are two of the criteria air pollutants designated by the Environmental Protection Agency (EPA) that pose significant health risks to urban populations.[10]

These pollutants arose from a wide variety of sources. The transportation sector was the prime pollution contributor. It introduced a disproportionate volume of nitrous oxides and ozone into the Los Angeles air. Los Angeles has been home to both the largest domestic manufacturing center and the nation's largest port in terms of value of goods handled and tonnage,[11] both of which led to increased air pollution because of the increased transportation required to process and ship those goods.[12] A relatively high population density of 3,990 people per square mile,[13] a ratio of 0.54 vehicles per person,[14] and concentration of 2,161 vehicles per square mile,[15] all help to explain why the transportation sector is significantly more important to air pollution in Los Angeles than other cities in the country. Inefficient buildings in Los Angeles were the second largest source of air pollution in the city,[16] due to the additional energy required to operate the electricity, heating, cooling and water within the building. Increased energy requirements were met by increased energy generation, that causes increased air pollution. The industrial and utilities sectors collectively contributed largely to the greenhouse gases found in the Los Angeles atmosphere,[17] that also led to Los Angeles having been ranked second in the Top 20 United States of carbon-emitting counties in 2008.[18] It was noted that "ignorance and apathy" of residents was a primary problem in the LA area in the 1940s.[19]

The BTH area suffered serious air pollution in the first decade of the twenty-first century. According to the 2013 National Report on Air Quality of Key Cities, in the first half of 2013, the average percentage of days that the air quality met the standard was

9. American Lung Association, "State of the Air 2015" (2015), http://www.stateoftheair.org/2015/city-rankings/most-polluted-cities.html, accessed August 20, 2015.
10. United States Environmental Protection Agency, "Criteria Air Pollutants," http://www.epa.gov/air/criteria.html, accessed March 24, 2022.
11. "City-Data" (Los Angeles: Economy), http://www.city-data.com/us-cities/The-West/Los-Angeles-Economy.html, accessed March 4, 2022.
12. "City-Data" (Los Angeles: Economy), http://www.city-data.com/us-cities/The-West/Los-Angeles-Economy.html, accessed March 4, 2022.
13. Damien Newton, "Density, Car Ownership, and What It Means for the Future of Los Angeles" (*Streetsblog LA*, December 13, 2010), http://la.streetsblog.org/2010/12/13/density-car-ownership-and-what-it-means-for-the-future-of-los-angeles/, accessed March 4, 2022.
14. Damien Newton, "Density, Car Ownership, and What It Means for the Future of Los Angeles" (*Streetsblog LA*, December 13, 2010), http://la.streetsblog.org/2010/12/13/density-car-ownership-and-what-it-means-for-the-future-of-los-angeles/, accessed March 4, 2022.
15. Damien Newton, "Density, Car Ownership, and What It Means for the Future of Los Angeles" (*Streetsblog LA*, December 13, 2010), http://la.streetsblog.org/2010/12/13/density-car-ownership-and-what-it-means-for-the-future-of-los-angeles/, accessed March 4, 2022.
16. "Energy Efficient Buildings," https://d3n8a8pro7vhmx.cloudfront.net/mayorofla/pages/17003/attachments/original/1428427253/environment-energy-efficient-buildings.pdf?1428427253, accessed March 8, 2022.
17. *See*: https://ww2.arb.ca.gov/our-work/programs/local-actions-climate-change/local-government-actions-climate-change, accessed August 8, 2022.
18. "Earth Observatory NASA" (American Carbon), https://earthobservatory.nasa.gov/features/AmericanCarbon, accessed March 9, 2022.
19. Toward Clean Air, https://milesfinney.net/334/articles/la_history.htm#Early_Smog_Control_Efforts, accessed March 26, 2023.

31.0% in the BTH area, with 26.2% of days with heavy pollution, 15.9% points higher than the national average for major cities.[20] In terms of pollutant concentrations, the average $PM_{2.5}$ concentration in the first half of 2013 was 115 micrograms per cubic meter, with all cities in the area exceeding the secondary standard for the annual average value of $PM_{2.5}$; only four cities in the area—Beijing, Chengde, Zhangjiakou and Langfang—met the secondary standard for the annual average value of SO_2; only three cities—Cangzhou, Zhangjiakou and Chengde—met the secondary standard for the annual average value of NO_2.[21] In the first half of the year, Beijing accounted for 23.3% of the heavily polluted days and 61.1% of the days exceeding the standard; Tianjin accounted for 19.9% of the heavily polluted days and 61.1% of the days exceeding the standard; and Shijiazhuang accounted for 51.9% of the heavily polluted days and 90.1% of the days exceeding the standard in the first half of the year.[22] The main pollutants are sulfur dioxide (SO_2), nitrogen dioxide (NO_2), inhalable particles (PM_{10}, $PM_{2.5}$), carbonic oxide (CO) and ozone (O_3) in the area.[23] As for pollutant sources, motor vehicles are the main air pollution source for Beijing. The main air pollution source for Hebei Province is coal, and for Tianjin, it is dust, mobile exhausts and industrial air emissions.[24]

3 COMPARABILITY IN IMPROVEMENT OF AIR QUALITY

The two areas are comparable in terms of improvement of air quality. As will be introduced in detail in Chapter 3 and Chapter 4, respectively, both the LA area and the BTH area have made remarkable achievements in improving their air quality.

In short, in terms of geographic conditions, level of industrialization, size of population, seriousness of air pollution, and improvement in air quality, the legal and policy experience of the two areas are comparable. Those commonalities are something like the "legal formants" proposed by Rodolfo Sacco, a well-known Italian comparative law scholar.[25] Professor Jorge E. Vinuales, Cambridge University,

20. Ministry of Environmental Protection, "Bulletin on the State of China's Environment" (2013), https://www.mee.gov.cn/hjzl/sthjzk/zghjzkgb/201605/P020160526564151497131.pdf, accessed October 29, 2021.
21. Ministry of Environmental Protection, "Bulletin on the State of China's Environment" (2013), https://www.mee.gov.cn/hjzl/sthjzk/zghjzkgb/201605/P020160526564151497131.pdf, accessed October 29, 2021.
22. Ministry of Environmental Protection, "Bulletin on the State of China's Environment" (2013), https://www.mee.gov.cn/hjzl/sthjzk/zghjzkgb/201605/P020160526564151497131.pdf, accessed October 29, 2021.
23. Li He, "338 Cities Are Going to Release the Air Monitoring Data in 2015" (*Chinese Academy of Social Sciences*, 2015), https://www.gov.cn/xinwen/2014-12/31/content_2798735.htm, accessed May 7, 2016.
24. Liu Shixin, "China Has Completed the Analysis of Atmospheric Pollution Sources of 9 Cities in BTH" (April 1, 2015), http://www.xinhuanet.com/politics/2015-04/01/c_1114836965.htm, accessed October 29, 2021.
25. *See*: R. Sacco, Legal Formants: A Dynamic Approach to Comparative Law (Installment I of II) (1991), 39 American Journal of Comparative Law 1 DOI: 10.2307/840669.

summarized and listed six approaches of comparative law research.[26] The "legal formants" is one of them. According to Professor Jorge E. Vinuales, the "legal formants" approach focuses on the factual operation of law.[27] It is just what we are doing in this study. There are many "legal formants" in the legal and policy experience of air pollution control in the two areas. We hope that the comparative study of those "legal formants" will result in insights into air pollution governance.

26. *See*: Emma Lees & Jorge E. Vinuales (eds.), The Oxford Handbook of Comparative Environmental Law, Oxford University Press, 2019, pp. 10-16.
27. *See*: Emma Lees & Jorge E. Vinuales (eds.), The Oxford Handbook of Comparative Environmental Law, Oxford University Press, 2019, p. 14.

CHAPTER 2

Methodology: The Environmental Governance Model

A conceptual model—the Environmental Governance Model (hereinafter referred to as "EG Model")—is applied for this comparative study.[20] Since the model provides an analytical framework for this study, it would be helpful to introduce it at the beginning of this study.

Here, the concept of "governance" comes from political science. According to the definition provided by the Global Governance Committee, the concept of "governance" means "the sum total of the many ways in which various public and private individuals and institutions manage their common affairs. It is an ongoing process by which conflicting or different interests are reconciled and joint action taken. This includes both political institutions and rules that have the power to compel obedience and informal institutional arrangements that people agree to or think are in their interests. It has four characteristics: governance is not a set of rules, nor an activity, but a process; The basis of the governance process is not control, but coordination; Governance involves both the public and private sectors; Governance is not a formal system,

28. This model is in its latest version. It was developed and improved from its English original version and modified versions. The English original version of model was called "IPPEP Model." It was released, for the first time, in an article in English entitled "Assessing Environmental Governance of the Hudson River Valley: Application of the IPPEP Model," jointly written by W. Xi, et al., (Winter 2014) 31 Pace Environmental Law Review 1. The second English version of this model was published in Emma Lees & Jorge E. Vinuales (eds.), The Oxford Handbook of Comparative Environmental Law, Oxford University Press, 2019, as the Chapter Six entitled "People's Republic of China" written by Wang Xi, pp. 128-148. The model introduced here is a further development based on the second English version. Compared with its second version, the major change in the model is the addition of a symbol of value choice in the center of the equilateral triangle. The idea of the symbol was inspired by an article written by D. Tarlock, Is There a There There in Environmental Law (2004), 19 Journal of Land Use and Environmental Law 213 and an article written by T.S. Aagaard, Environmental Law as a Legal Field: An Inquiry in Legal Taxonomy (2010), 95 Cornell Law Review 2.

but an ongoing interaction."[29] We define the concept of "environmental governance" as a political process in which all actors or stakeholders, including public and private entities, collaborate towards achieving the goal of environmental protection within specific legal and ethical frameworks in their respective societies.

1 EG MODEL AS A WHOLE

As shown in the figure below, the EG Model consists of four parts when viewed from an outside-in perspective. The first part is a solid line circle representing laws and regulations, i.e., the legal framework for environmental governance processes. The second part is a dotted line circle representing environmental ethics, i.e., the ethical framework for environmental governance processes. The third part is an equilateral triangle in the center of the two circles, which represent the major three political relations in an environmental governance process. The fourth part is a symbol consisting of an overlay of two solid circles located at the center of the equilateral triangle. The symbol represents the choice or balance of values in environmental decision-making processes. As a whole, the equilateral triangle represents an ideal situation of environmental governance in which all the major parties or actors interact and form favorable political relations for making correct decisions on the utilization of natural resources and the environment under favorable legal and ethical frameworks:

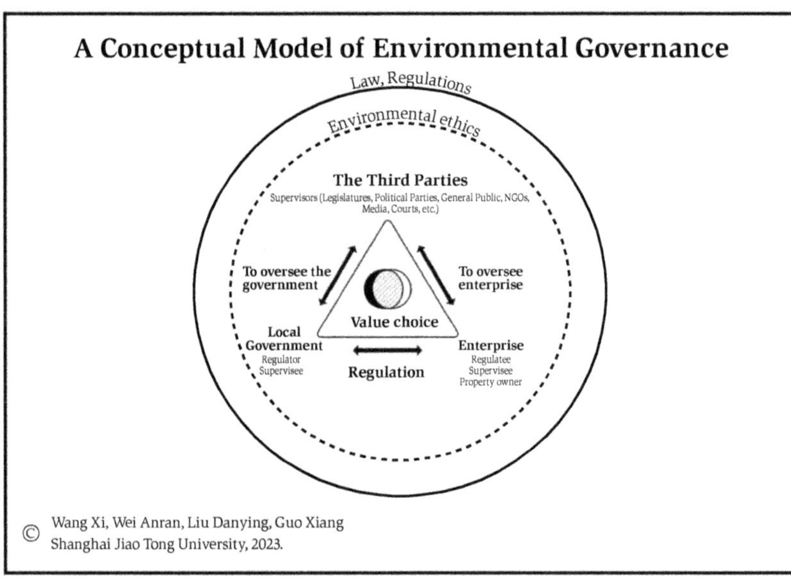

29. *See* Global Governance Committee: Our Global partnership, Oxford University Press, 1995, p. 23. This paragraph is quote and translate from Yu Keping (ed.), Governance and Good Governance, (in Chinese), China Social Science Press, 2000, pp. 4-5.

2 TWO CIRCLES

The two circles surrounding the triangle represent the frameworks for the operation of the three basic political relations in the environmental governance process. The inner circle represents the moral or ethical framework for a process of environmental governance. It consists of the principles, norms, and rules of environmental ethics prevailing in a society. The outer circle represents the framework of law, including all the statutory laws and regulations and common laws on environmental matters. Law is the ultimate norm safeguarding the normal exercise of the legitimate rights of all the three groups of major actors represented by the three corners of the triangle. They are the baseline code of conduct for people to deal with the environment. Violation of them must result in legal sanctions. When the inner circle is not sufficient to regulate people's conduct towards the environment, it is the outer circle that provides the restriction. Therefore, no effort must be spared to maintain the integrity of this circle.

3 EQUILATERAL TRIANGLE

In the center of the model, there is an equilateral triangle. The three corners of the triangle represent three groups of major actors or stakeholders in the environmental governance process. The left corner represents governments (the executive or administrative authorities), including all levels of the governments. The roles of governments play in the process of environmental governance are mainly two. One is as a regulator, i.e., to regulate environmental-related activities of enterprises and others. The other is to be supervised or supervisee, i.e., to be supervised by all the supervisors in the process of environmental governance. The right corner of the triangle represents enterprises and other polluters. The role they play in the process of environmental governance is mainly two. One is to be regulated by the governments. In addition, as lawful property owners, they have the legal right to maintain and protect their property, including the rights to utilize their property lawfully and to take lawful actions against any illegal infringement of their property. Under these circumstances, they are a supervisor and are against any illegal infringement of their property from either the governments or the other actors in the process of environmental governance. The top corner of the triangle represents a group of the "third-parties" actors, including legislatures, citizens, non-governmental organizations (hereinafter refers to NGOs, news media, courts and all the regulated entities or regulatees). They are the supervisors in the process of environmental governance. They have a common role to play in the process—to supervise the environmentally related activities of the other two groups of actors-government and enterprises and other polluters. Because of their different legal status, each of them has to follow different legal channels designed for their supervision.

There are three equivalent straight lines connecting the three corners of the triangle. They are the three sides of the triangle. Each of the sides represents a major political relation in the process of environmental governance. The left side is a line connecting the top corner with the left corner, which represents a relation of supervision over the governments (regulators) between all the third-party actors and the governments. The right side is a line connecting the top corner with the right corner, which represents a relation of supervision over enterprises and other polluters between all the third-party actors and enterprises and other polluters. At the bottom of the triangle, there is a line connecting the left corner with the right corner, which represents a relation of regulation between the government and enterprises and other polluters. Among the three relations represented by the three equivalent straight lines, the regulatory relation represented by the bottom line of the triangle is more fundamental to the other two relations represented by the left and right lines in the triangle. It is more fundamental because it represents the fundamental purpose or goal of a process of environmental governance. The remaining two relations, no matter whether they have a relation with the government or a supervisory relation with polluters, all aim to achieve what environmental regulations intend to accomplish.

4 SYMBOL OF TWO OVERLAYING CIRCLES

In the center of the triangle, there is a symbol made up of a crossing overlap by two circles. The symbol means a choice of value between the value of economy and the value of environment. While the black circle represents the value of economy, the white circle represents the value of environment. The overlap part of the symbol, filled with Oblique lines, represents a final result of decision-making by all the actors or stakeholders in an environmental governance process, which is an ideal choice of values and an ideal compromise or integration of the value of economy and the value of environment. Why is the symbol located in the center of the triangle? It is because the process of environmental governance ultimately aims to make decisions on how human beings should exploit natural resources and the environment. This decision-making is central to any process of environmental governance. It is the purpose of the major three political relations among the major three groups of actors or stakeholders in environmental governance processes.

The idea about this symbol was inspired by Professor Dan Tarlock, Kent Law School of the Illinois Institute of Technology, USA. He may be the first American law professor who proposed to identify the "content" of the field of environmental law. In 2004, he asked an important question on what is there in the field of American environmental law.[30] His answer to the question is that "the extremely complex and evolving moral and scientific nature of environmental problems ensures that, for the foreseeable future, environmental law will be a law about the process of decision rather than a process of evolving decision rules."[31] He pointed out further that the decision-making processes "must be rational processes constrained as a set of principles that ensure that they are responding to our understanding of what makes a problem environmental. Decision processes equally must be more than ad hoc, open-ended,

30. D. Tarlock, Is There a There There in Environmental Law (2004), 19 Florida State University Journal of Land Use and Environmental Law 2.
31. D. Tarlock, Is There a There There in Environmental Law (2004), 19 Florida State University Journal of Land Use and Environmental Law 2, pp. 219-220.

stakeholder negotiations."[32] We agree with Dan Tarlock's theory and visualize the core as such a symbol.

5 RELATION BETWEEN THE TWO CIRCLES AND THE TRIANGLE

The relation between the triangle and the circles is a relation between the legal and ethical framework and the three major political relations. It is a relation between restraining and being restrained. The two circles regulate the conduct of the three groups of major actors or stakeholders in the major three political relations in environmental governance. As a whole, the equilateral triangle encompasses all major activities and political relations in the process of environmental governance. The equilaterality of the triangle represents an ideal scenario for environmental governance, wherein all actors or stakeholders can fully exercise their legal rights while simultaneously fulfilling their duties. It is worth noting that this relation eventually focuses on the decision-making on how human beings should exploit natural resources and environment, a critical value choice between the value of economy and the value of environment.

6 THEORETICAL FOUNDATION OF THE EG MODEL

The EG Model is premised on a multiple theoretical basis. It is supported by microeconomics, political economics, political science, law and ethics or moral philosophy.

The two circles surrounding the triangle, representing the legal and ethical frameworks, are justified by the basic principles of law and ethics. Ethics work through people's introspection and self-restraint. Unless it becomes a unanimously accepted rule of conduct, moral restraint will not be reliable and predictable. However, when an ethical rule is accepted by a society, it will effectively regulate or normalize people's conduct without any cost for forcing them to do so. This is the most important advantage of ethics or moral norms. In addition, the development of ethical norms usually takes a long time. It sometimes lags behind the need to deal with the urgent challenges of rapidly developing societies. Therefore, ethics alone is not sufficient to protect a society from the various challenges of rapidly developing societies, such as the challenges brought about by industrialization. Thus, there is a need for law, including legislation and common law. Legislation is the process of law-making. One of the advantages of law-making is to fill in the gaps left by the gradual development of ethics. In front of the social challenges with which ethics is slow to deal, legislation is the only and effective choice. All, the modern societies of the world are facing various challenges from the rapid development of industrialization, such as pollution. To deal with and overcome the challenges, people have to adjust their behavior toward nature and the environment. Environmental ethics and environmental law provide them with ethical norms and legal standards of conduct, respectively.

32. D. Tarlock, Is There a There There in Environmental Law (2004), 19 Florida State University Journal of Land Use and Environmental Law 2, p. 220.

The bottom side of the triangle, which represents the relation of regulation, is justified by microeconomics. Microeconomics suggests that there is an "externality" when there is "an activity that imposes involuntary costs or benefits on others, or an activity whose effects are not fully reflected in prices ad market transactions."[33] When there is an externality, the market will be a failure as far as that externality is concerned. Externality includes a positive one and a negative one. Pollution is a negative externality that imposes involuntary costs and negative effects such as harm and damage to the health and welfare of the people to the people and those costs and effects are not fully reflected in prices and market transactions. Facing the challenges of negative environmental externalities, the major measure taken by all countries of the world is governmental intervention. The classical microeconomics suggested that "as our society has become more densely populated and as the production of energy, chemicals, and other materials increases, negative externalities or spillover effects have grown from minor nuisances into major threats. This is where governments come in. Government regulations are designed to control externalities like air and water pollution, damage from strip mining, hazardous wastes, unsafe drugs and foods, and radioactive materials."[34] For enterprises, the major potential polluters, one thing that is common for them is that when there is a flaw or loophole in environmental regulation, they will generally try to make use of that flaw or loophole to reduce production costs and make extra profits or benefits at the cost of the environment. To correct this problem, unfortunately, it is not sufficient to rely on their environmental morality or ethics. There must be a public regulator to regulate them by implementing and enforcing environmental law. As the book will show later, the theories on externality and regulation apply well in explaining the air pollution problem and the necessity of regulation of air pollution.

The left side of the triangle, representing the relation of supervision over regulators, is justified by the Public Choice Theory of political economics, which is a theoretical crystal at the junction of economics and political science. Professor James Buchannan, the leading scholar of the theory and the laureate of the Robel Prize of Economics (1987), pointed out that "individual behavior in collective choice is likely to reflect shorter time horizons than comparable behavior in private or individualized choice, and for individually rational reasons."[35] He illustrates this position by three examples taken from the operation of the Government of the U.S. such as "the high tax trap," "the inflation trap," and "the public-debt trap."[36] In all of those examples, federal governmental officials fall into the traps "because of the necessary attenuation of individually identifiable rights or shares in the fruits of collective or governmental

33. Paul A. Samuelson & William D. Nordhaus (eds.), Xiao Chen & Jiang Jingyuan translated and noted, Economics, the Eighteenth Edition, (English and Chinese), The People's Posts and Telecommunications Press, May 2011, p. 36.
34. Paul A. Samuelson & William D. Nordhaus (eds.), Xiao Chen & Jiang Jingyuan translated and noted, Economics, the Eighteenth Edition, (English and Chinese), The People's Posts and Telecommunications Press, May 2011, pp. 36-37.
35. Geoffrey Brennan & James M. Buchanan, The Reasons of Rules, Liberty Fund, Inc., Cambridge University Press, 2000, p. 92.
36. Geoffrey Brennan & James M. Buchanan, The Reasons of Rules, Liberty Fund, Inc., Cambridge University Press, 2000, pp. 94-106.

'investment', individual time horizons in politics are shortened."[37] He further pointed out that "if this underlying hypothesis is valid, it would follow that as modern societies have become increasingly collectivized or politicized, there has been a shift toward a higher discount rate implicit in the allocation of the economy's resources."[38] He concluded that "... through the use of three applications from macro-economic policy, we have tried to demonstrate in practical and relevant terms the basic logic of, or reason for the imposition of binding constraints or rules on the activities of collective units or government. ... In short, the results produced by the short-time perspective in modern politics may be 'Pareto pessimal'."[39] Constrained by the time periods (their terms of service), the votes of their constituencies, and the maximization of their personal utilities, governmental officials easily fall into the various "traps" when they carry out their public duties because they tend to pursue the short-time accomplishments in their terms of office rather than to work on something for a long-term effect, i.e., something which becomes the achievements of an un-known official after his term of office, in the future. In order to help governments to overcome the problem of short-sighted decisions, that result in an unreasonable and disproportionate discount of social resources, the Public Choice Theory suggests imposing "binding constraints or rules on the activities of collective units or governments."[40] Only under constant and effective supervision can the governments faithfully and diligently carry out their environmental regulatory responsibilities. Where there is a lack of supervision over governments, they usually tend to be slack in carrying out their public duties, including environmental regulation. If there is a failure of regulation, the "market failure" represented by pollution and ecological destruction will persist and grow. As the book will show later, both the experience of serious air pollution in Los Angeles after World War II and in the BTH area of China in the 2010s demonstrated that the problems of short-time perspective of the local governments and the "Pareto pessimal" existed the two areas. Therefore, as the Public Choice Theory suggests, the countermeasure for correcting the short-time perspective and the "Pareto pessimal" is "to impose binding constraints or rules on the activities of collective units or governments." This is exactly what the two areas did in the 1970s and 2010s.

The right side of the triangle, representing the relation of supervision over enterprises and other polluters, is justified by journalism, ethics and law. The role of journalism is justified by Principle 10 of the Rio Declaration on Environment and Development, which says that "environmental issues are best handled with the participation of all concerned citizens, at the relevant level. At the national level, each individual shall have appropriate access to information concerning the environment that is held by public authorities, including information on hazardous materials and

37. Geoffrey Brennan & James M. Buchanan, The Reasons of Rules, Liberty Fund, Inc., Cambridge University Press, 2000, p. 92.
38. Geoffrey Brennan & James M. Buchanan, The Reasons of Rules, Liberty Fund, Inc., Cambridge University Press, 2000, p. 92.
39. Geoffrey Brennan & James M. Buchanan, The Reasons of Rules, Liberty Fund, Inc., Cambridge University Press, 2000, p. 107.
40. Geoffrey Brennan & James M. Buchanan, The Reasons of Rules, Liberty Fund, Inc., Cambridge University Press, 2000, p. 107.

activities in their communities, and the opportunity to participate in decision-making processes. States shall facilitate and encourage public awareness and participation by making information widely available. Effective access to judicial and administrative proceedings, including redress and remedy, shall be provided."[41] The theory of journalism demonstrates that one unique function of the media is to discover and distribute information on pollution through their networks by printing or digitally. The distribution of information by media can significantly magnify the information so that it usually awakes people and society from the matter reported. In this way, the media plays a key role in promoting environmental ethics and environmental education. Enterprises and other polluters will be under great moral pressure if they are identified and reported by the media. However, the supervision of media depends on the mainstream ethics of the society in which the media works. Without a minimum level of support from environmental ethics, the reports of media cannot have a good role in environmental education, so there will be no pressure on enterprises and other polluters. Therefore, ethics come in and play an essential role in environmental governance. Ethics and media work together and mutually reinforce environmental governance. In addition to the supervisory roles of media and ethics, litigation for public environmental interests also plays a role in supervision of enterprises and other polluters. In addition to providing legal remedies to the plaintiffs, the litigation may deter other potential violators of environmental law. Here comes one of the roles of law—deterrence. The deterrence is another special kind of supervision over enterprises and other polluters. As this book will show later, all those theories apply well in explaining the experience of air pollution control in Los Angeles and the BTH area.

The symbol of value choice in the center of the triangle is justified by the theory of environmental economics. For example, Mr. Lester Brown, a well-known environmentalist, and the Director of the Earth Policy Institute, U.S.A., has pointed out the critical importance of compromising and integration of the economic value and the value of environment. He pointed out that "the ecological economy—an economy that can sustain the environment, requires the formation of economic policies based on the framework established by ecological principles."[42] He called for the decision-makers to integrate the value of economy with the value of environment. He correctly suggested that when facing the problem of environmental externality, "one remedy for this would be for environmental scientists and economists to work together to calculate the costs of climate change, acid rain and air pollution, and then add them to the current price as a tax on electricity generated from burning coal to give the full cost of coal use. This comprehensive cost accounting means that all economic decision-makers—government and private consumers—have the information they need to make more informed and ecologically responsible decisions."[43] The idea of integrating the value of economy and the value of environment had been formally accepted by all

41. United Nations Conference on Environment and Development, Rio Declaration on Environment and Development, http://www.un-documents.net/rio-dec.htm, accessed July 9, 2023.
42. Lester R. Brown ed., Lin Zixin, etc., translate, Eco-Economy: Building and Economy for the Earth, (in Chinese), Dongfang Publishing House, 2002, p. 2.
43. Lester R. Brown ed., Lin Zixin, etc., translate, Eco-Economy: Building and Economy for the Earth, (in Chinese), Dongfang Publishing House, 2002, p. 23.

countries of the world at the UN Conference on Environment and Development in Johannesburg, Brazil, in 1992. The Principle Four of the Declaration of Environment and Development adopted by the conference declared that "in order to achieve sustainable development, environmental protection shall constitute an integral part of the development process and cannot be considered in isolation from it."[44] This principle is a worldwide consensus. It provides strong support for the symbol of value choice in the EG model. So the symbol is actually a symbol of integration of environment and development as declared by the Principle Four.

7 INTERNAL LOGIC

The EG Model reflects a logic which dominates the operation of environmental governance. The following graph is a generalization and a geometry expression of this logic:

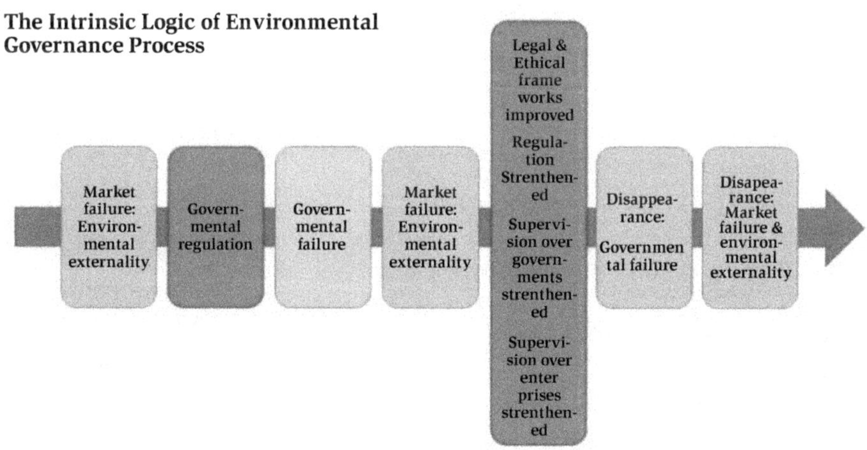

Wang Xi, Kunming U. Science & Technology, 13 Feb 2023

This logic can be translated into the following sequence of phrases:

(1) The existence of market failure is represented by an environmental externality.
(2) Governmental regulation is needed in order to overcome the market failure.
(3) Governmental regulation may fail due to the laziness of regulators or even "regulatory capture."
(4) When governmental failure exists, the market failure represented by the environmental externality remains.

44. A/CONF.151/26 (Vol. I) Report of the United Nations Conference on Environment and Development, https://www.un.org/en/development/desa/population/migration/generalassembly/docs/globalcompact/A_CONF.151_26_Vol.I_Declaration.pdf, accessed July 2, 2023.

(5) In order to overcome the market failure represented by environmental externality under the situation of governmental failure, improving the legal and ethical frameworks, under which the environmental governance process operated, is needed.
(6) When the legal and ethical frameworks are improved and the process of environmental governance operates properly, both the market failure and the governmental failure disappear.

In 2014, Professor Nicholas Robinson of Pace University gave the original version of the EG Model[45] a mathematical expression as the following.[46] It is another expression of the ideas that the EG Model wishes to deliver and be helpful to understand the EG model:

A Formula Expression of the IPPEP Model

1. (R) + (− E) = G
2. (− R) +(− E) = (− G)
3. (− R) + (− E) + (NGO , changing R) = G
4. (− R) + (− E) + (NGO + J , changing R) = G
5. (− R) + (− E) + (− NGO) + (− J) = − G
6. (− R) + (− E) + NGO + C (changing R or law) = G

R: Strong environmental regulator
− R: Weak environmental regulator
− E: Polluting enterprise
J: Court in favor of environment
− J: Court not in favor of environment
− NGO: Ineffective NGO participation or no NGOs at all
G: Good environmental governance
− G: Poor environmental governance
C: Environmental Congress

* These formulae are Jointly designed by Nicholas Robinson (Pace U. USA), Wang Xi (SJTU, CN), Richard Ottinger (Pace U. USA), and Wang Pianpian (Pace U. USA) in July 2013.

Therefore, the EG Model is a crystal of multi-disciplines and has an intrinsic self-sustained theoretical logic. Practically, it can serve as a useful tool to investigate the situation of environmental governance of a country or a particular area or society. With this model, the legal and policy experience of air pollution control in the LA and BTH areas are compared and analyzed. This model and its underlying theory provide a useful method and a solid theoretical basis for the subsequent comparative study.

45. By that time, it was called the Model of Interactions between Parties in Process of Environmental Protection (the IPPEP Model).
46. W. Xi, et al., Assessing Environmental Governance of the Hudson River Valley: Application of the IPPEP Model (Winter 2014) 31 Pace Environmental Law Review 1, p. 101.

CHAPTER 3

Air Pollution Governance in Los Angeles Area

In this part, the legal and policy experience of air pollution control in the LA area will be introduced. Section 1 introduces the legal and ethical frameworks. Section 2 explores the basic political relations in air pollution governance. Section 3 summarizes the achievements and challenges in air pollution control in the area. The rich data and information introduced in this part are not only helpful for the readers to understand the air pollution governance processes of the LA area but also provide a strong basis for the comparative study of Chapter 5.

1 POLITICAL PROFILE OF THE UNITED STATES

For this comparative legal study, a brief survey of the political profile of the United States is a good start. This study focuses on three aspects of the political profiles of the United States and China. The three aspects are the form of state structure, the form of organization of the state powers, and the system of political parties. They lay down the basic background of the political system of a country.

In terms of the form of state structure, the United States applies a federal system. It is governed by federal, state and local governments. The federal government consists of three parts: (1) the Executive Branch led by the President, also Head of State, who is elected every four years; (2) the Congress consisting of Representatives in the House of Representatives elected for two-year terms, their numbers determined by the population of each state, and the Senate, two Senators from each state elected for six-year terms; and (3) the Supreme Court and federal courts, appointed by the President and confirmed by the Senate with lifetime terms. The three governance bodies are designed to perform a check and balance to prevent deviances from the basic tenants of the Constitution. The Constitution with its 30 amendments is "the supreme law of the land." It sets forth the basic principles guiding U.S. governance and the responsibilities of each of the Executive, Congress and the federal courts. The tenth amendment declares that "The powers not delegated to the United States by the Constitution, nor prohibited by it to the States, are reserved to the States respectively, or to the people." Therefore, the states still have considerable authority. There are 50 states, each with its own Governor, state legislature and state courts, elected as provided in state constitutions and laws, and likewise for city and local governments each with their elected mayors, city councils and local courts.

In terms of the form of organization of the state powers, the United States applies a system of presidential republic. The President appoints and supervises the various departments of the government, with principal appointments subject to confirmation by the Senate. The departments administer the programs of the government pursuant to legislative directions provided by the Congress. The President and his appointees also make legislative proposals and the federal budget to the Congress. The Congress then approves, modifies or rejects the actions of the Congress. Legislation passed by the Congress can be vetoed by the President, subject to an override by a two-third vote of both Houses. Passed legislation can be rejected or altered by the courts if they find anything in it to be contrary to the Constitution. The public may have a say in the legislative process if the legislation is referred for hearings and markup to the appropriate committees in the House and Senate, though frequently of late, the legislative process is bypassed and omnibus legislation is passed without hearings at the end of a congressional session.[47]

In terms of the system of political party, the United States is basically a two-party system of Republicans and Democrats; there have been third parties seeking election in the history of the country, but they almost never have succeeded, but sometimes have determined the outcome of elections, but sometimes have determined the outcome of elections as they divided the vote of a party that otherwise would have won.

The Congress operated quite efficiently until the early 1990s. Legislation generally was written by Members and was referred to congressional committees where it was subjected to hearings at which both Republican and Democratic members could select witnesses; then it received subcommittee and then full Committee "mark ups" at which all Committee Members could offer amendments. The resulting bills were then referred to the full House of Representatives or Senate for consideration, usually with "open rules" at which any Member could offer amendments, after which the bill passed by the House or Senate was referred to a Conference Committee if the versions differed; then the conference bill was passed again by both houses of the Congress. This orderly process went sour with the election of a super-conservative Speaker of the House of Representatives and the influence of a super-conservative Republican organization known as the "Tea Party" movement which sought successfully to bypass procedure, wrote the giant end-of-year legislation, and insert their priorities.

As relates to support for the environment, however, until the mid-1990s, Congressional support was bipartisan. Most of the basic U.S. environmental legislation (Clean Water and Clean Air Acts, Toxic Substances Act, etc.) was passed with strong bipartisan support and signed into law by Republican President, Richard Nixon. With

47. *See*: The Government Affairs Institute, Georgetown University, gai.georgetown.edu, accessed November 6, 2023.

the election of 2016, all the systems of government broke down. The Republican Senate Majority Leader was able to garner total control of the Senate Republicans, all Republicans voting as a block, making it virtually impossible to pass any legislation without his support in an evenly divided Senate. President Trump systematically issued executive orders undermining the important environmental provisions that had been passed by the previous Congress and regulations that had been instituted by the EPA for protection and climate change mitigation. The President was able to stack the Supreme Court with three additional conservative justices, and thus eliminate its important role as a nonpartisan institution and a constructive check on the Executive. Indeed, the Supreme Court became a tool for support and passage of the Republican political party agenda. The current President has performed miracles of restoring order to the government and getting passed significant legislation, even with an evenly divided Senate and biased courts. With respect to the environment and climate change mitigation, his administration has restored many of the environmental regulations enacted by the previous administration and eliminated by the successor Administration. Most significantly, the current President enacted the important climate mitigation initiatives in The Inflation Reduction Act of August 2022,[48] but without a single minority party vote in either house of Congress.

2 LEGAL AND ETHICAL FRAMEWORKS ON AIR POLLUTION CONTROL

As the two circles of the EG Model show, the air pollution control in the LA area is under a legal framework and an ethical framework. Those frameworks consist of legal and ethical rules which provide standards of conduct for all the major actors and the political relations among them in the air pollution governance processes.

2.1 Legal Framework

The legal framework on air pollution control in the LA area consists of federal law of the United States, state law of California, and city ordinances.

The United States has formed a large legal system for air pollution prevention and control. The system consists of the federal constitution, state constitutions, federal statutes, state statutes, local ordinances, federal and state administrative regulations, local government actions, judicial interpretations of the above-enacted laws by the courts and common law, as well as international treaties ratified by the U.S. Congress. The 1970 amendments to the U.S. Clean Air Act (CAA) set out the basic approach for air pollution control in the U.S. Two further amendments to the Act were adopted in 1977 and 1990. In terms of the federal-state relationship, the Act embodies "cooperative federalism," whereby federal ambient air quality standards and air pollutant emission standards are set by federal government and usually are stated to be

48. Text-H.R. 5376-117th Congress (2021-2022), https://www.irs.gov/inflation-reduction-act-of-2022, accessed October 23, 2022.

implemented by the states through their implementation plans which sometimes are submitted to and approved by federal government. In order to strengthen the control of air pollution in nonattainment areas, the U.S. Congress added specific provisions for air pollution control in these areas when it amended the CAA in 1977. The major new measures include deadlines for compliance with ambient air quality standards, permits for new source construction and operations, and mandatory vehicle inspections and maintenance.[49] In the mid-1970s, EPA introduced market-based measures such as a "bubble policy," "emissions trading" and "emissions banking." For air pollution control in vulnerable clean air areas, the CAA had specific provisions for the Prevention of Significant Deterioration and Visibility Protection. The CAA was amended in 1990 to include a chapter on "permits," which strengthen the requirements for emitting air pollutants.[50] The CAA specifically provides for the control of air pollution from mobile sources. It covers the control of emissions from new and existing vehicles, aircraft, city buses, etc. It also provides for the regulation of fuels.

Under the federal CAA, the U.S. EPA is required to designate nonattainment areas for certain air pollutants. This designation indicates that air pollution in the area exceeds federal standards by a large margin and poses a risk to public health. However, air pollution in California reached such highs that the CAA authorized the EPA to issue a waiver allowing an express exception permitting California to promulgate its own new-vehicle emission standards above and beyond those mandated under the CAA. More specifically, the CAA adopted a provision permitting California to exceed the federal motor vehicle emission requirements, with a preemption waiver from the EPA under section 209(a) of the CAA, and permitted other states to adopt the California standards.[51] California can obtain, and had obtained a waiver from the EPA in order to issue its own emissions standards,[52] in response to the exceptionally poor air quality in the state.[53] However, the Trump administration initiated action to cancel the waiver and maintain only reduced federal standards for California; but the Biden EPA took action to restore these regulations.[54]

To combat air pollution, California has developed a four-tiered regulatory system comprising the federal government, the State of California, California's air management districts and local governments, as well as a legal system comprising the federal and California State "Clean Air Acts" as the basic law, including the federal Air

49. *See*: https://www.epa.gov/clean-air-act-overview/evolution-clean-air-act#caa77.
50. *See*: https://www.epa.gov/clean-air-act-overview/clean-air-act-highlights-1990-amendments.
51. 42 USC § 7543.
52. 42 USC § 7543.
53. It should be noted that other states under the challenged waiver were permitted to adopt California's standards, so long as their standards are "identical" to those of California. 42 USC § 7507. General information regarding the waiver program can be found at U.S. EPA, California Waivers and Authorizations United States EPA (Vehicle Emissions and California Waivers and Authorizations), https://www.epa.gov/state-and-local-transportation/vehicle-emissions-california-waivers-and-authorizations, accessed March 4, 2022.
54. KT LA 5 Morning News (Biden administration proposes restoring California's right to set own emission standards, April 22, 2021), https://ktla.com/news/california/biden-administration-proposes-restoring-californias-right-to-set-own-emission-standards/, accessed March 4, 2022.

Pollution Control Act and the Air Quality Standards Act.[55] A variety of local, state and federal regulatory agencies were involved.

The City of Los Angeles began to investigate the air pollution problem in the 1940s. In 1945, its investigation led to development of an ordinance that set limits on smoke emissions from any single source. A Bureau of Smoke Control, established in the City's Health Department, had the responsibility of enforcing the ordinance. This ordinance only applied to its municipal boundaries. Also in 1945, Los Angeles County passed ordinances establishing a Division of Air Pollution Control and setting emission standards applicable also to the unincorporated areas of the County. However, these two ordinances did not cover all of the places in the smog area and could only ease some of the fragmented problems. As the knowledge of air pollution grew over time, local governments in Los Angeles areas realized that a more comprehensive management path was needed to target industrial sources, fumes, smoke, and sulphur compounds, and thus the Los Angeles County Air Pollution Control District (LAPCD) was established in 1947 under state legislation that authorized the Board of Supervisors of any county in California to commence operation of a countywide air pollution control district.[56]

2.2 Ethical Framework

The new environmental ethic that emerged in the 1960s provided a strong philosophical foundation and framework for environmental law. As summarized by Mr. Rice Odell in 1980, "in brief, environmentalism is based in a fundamental way on feelings that stress the importance of nature and all its diverse parts. This importance is expressed in terms of necessity, respect, reverence, or love. Together they add up to a strong negation of the long accepted cultural machismo by which nature is fair game to be denigrated or destroyed in the pursuit of other goals."[57] Professor Steven Ferry of Suffolk University pointed out that "beginning in the 1960s, much of the American public recognized that protection of the environment was imperative to preserving its social and cultural values, as well as the nation's natural resources."[58] The new environmental ethic was reflected by the environmental statutes in the 1970s and 1980s. For example, Article 2 of the National Environmental Policy Act declares that the purposes of the Act are: "to declare a national policy which will encourage protective and enjoyable harmony between man and his environment; to promote efforts which will prevent or eliminate damage to the environment and biosphere and

55. *See*: Hou Jiaru & Wang Qian: California Air Pollution Prevention and Control Experience, Environmental Education, 2014, 4, pp. 94-95.
56. D.H. Willick & T.J. Windle, Rule Enforcement by the Los Angeles County Air Pollution Control District (1973), 3 Ecology Law Quarterly 508 accessed March 8, 2022.
57. Rice Odell, Environmental Awakening: A New Revolution to Protect the Earth, published by the Conservation Foundation, 1980, at p. 6. Rice Odell (1947-2020) was a member of the Conservation Foundation since 1967. He was the editor of the Conservation Foundation Letter. The Letter is an eight-page monthly newsletter, focusing on analyzing a single environmental topic.
58. Steven Ferrey, Environmental Law, Seventh Edition, published by Wolters Kluwer in New York, 2016, p. 6.

stimulate the health and welfare of men … ."[59] It is one of many general statements on the new environmental ethic developed since the 1960s in the United States.

2.2.1 Development of Environmental Ethic Since the 1950s

The following graph shows the development of the American environmental ethic since the 1950s:[60]

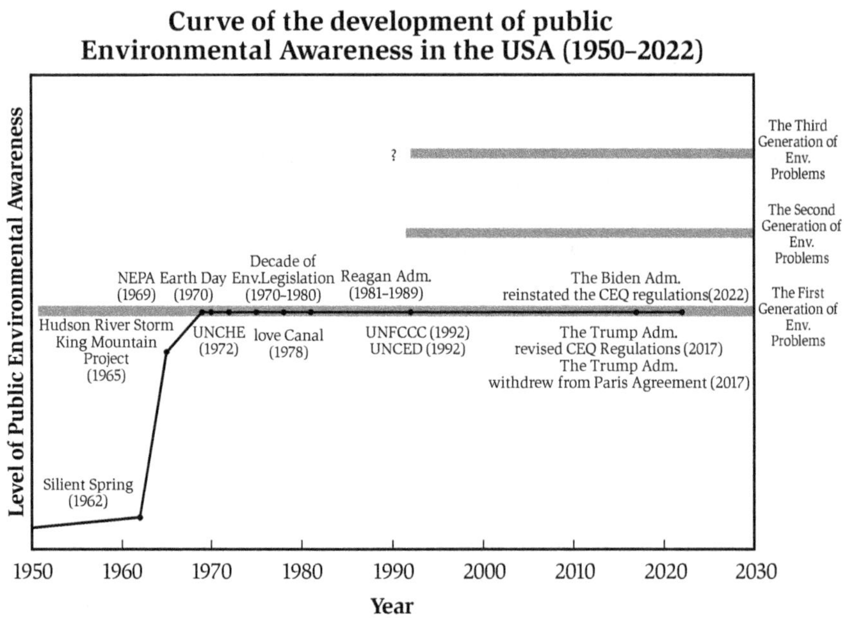

It is noted that the curve had a sudden rise and reached a high point in the period of the late 1960s and early 1970s. The first nationwide celebration of Earth Day on April 22, 1970, indicated the new high point of the development of the environmental ethic of the American people since 1950. The first Earth Day celebration awakened the people and made them think about what are the causes of environmental crises and how to overcome them.[61] In addition, it is noted that the curve keeps horizontal and without any fluctuation since the 1970s. That means there was no remarkable rise in the environmental ethic of the people in general. Considering the need to cope with the

59. Section 4321, Congressional declaration of purpose, (NEPA section 2), Chapter 55-National Environmental Policy Act, 42 U.S.C.A. 4321 to 4370f. Selected Environmental Law Statutes, West, A Thomson Reuters business, 2009, p. 714.
60. The graph was published in Chinese for the first time in W. Xi, A Comparison of the Political and Cultural Background of Environmental Legislation Between China and the United States: From the Perspective of the Evolution of Public Environmental Consciousness (2022), 44 Environmental Impact Assessment 4 pp. 30-37, at p. 32.
61. For details, *see* Barry Commoner, The Closing Circle, Bantam Books, Inc., 1976, at pp. 1-6.

second generation of environmental problems such as climate change, the standstill of the curve is worrisome.

Unfortunately, the new environmental ethic is not universally shared today in the United States. One party views the preservation of the environment and addressing the threats of climate change are the basic ethic to be preserved, while the other party views the costs of these measures to be excessive and result in large loss of fossil fuel jobs and economic disruption. If the latter views prevail in the 2024 elections, air pollution will certainly suffer greatly, (perceiving environmental protection as harmful to the economy). They vigorously support the continued use of coal, oil and gas for energy, rejecting the scientific findings of climate threats as simply weather. In the previous Administration, they sought to weaken or remove all measures to address climate change, remove scientists from policy review boards, propose removal of the funding for environmental agencies, and appoint to environmental agencies people who opposed the policies of the agencies for which they were appointed to serve. Fortunately, the current Administration has proposed and adopted strong climate legislation and administrative measures.

3 POLITICAL RELATIONS IN AIR POLLUTION GOVERNANCE

As represented by the three sides of triangle in the EG model, there are three basic political relations in the air pollution governance of the LA area. Those data and information are not only valuable as historical records but also valuable for the comparative study in Chapter 5. As time goes on, the value of those data and information will increase.

3.1 Relation of Regulation

Faced with serious air pollution, the first thing done by the governments of the LA area was to establish regulations on air pollution sources, often implementing federal legislation. The relationship between the local regulators and the enterprise and other polluters for air pollution control is the fundamental political relation in the air pollution process of the LA area. As this section shows, the scope of the relation is broad. It covers all the industrial sectors that emit air pollutants, such as incinerators, transportation, building industry, utilities, oil refineries, and gas stations. In addition to direct regulation, there are many indirect regulatory programs and activities, such as public-private partnerships, market-based regulations and policies, voluntary energy efficiency programs, and governmental environmental education. The following is an introduction to those regulatory relations by sectors of industries.[62]

62. The introduction is lengthy and detailed for at least three reasons. The first is that it is not easy to collect those data and stories. Thanks to the unique and competent international team of this research, we are fortunately be able to collect those detailed and valuable data and information in the United States and China. The second is that the data and stories introduced here and next Part are very valuable for historical reasons. They can be a good information basis for any related

3.1.1 *Monitoring Air Pollutants*

3.1.1.1 Establishment of the Air Quality Monitoring Network

The U.S. EPA requires that local agencies perform an assessment of their air quality surveillance systems every five years to determine, at a minimum, if the network meets the monitoring objectives defined in the Code of Federal Regulations.[63] Agencies must report whether new sites are needed, whether existing sites are no longer needed and can be terminated, and whether new technologies are appropriate for incorporation into the Ambient Air Monitoring Network.

As the local air pollution control agency, South Coast Air Quality Management District (SCAQMD) is responsible for controlling air quality emissions from various sources to meet National Ambient Air Quality Standards (NAAQS) as well as ambient air quality standards established by the California Air Resources Board (CARB). Every three years, an Air Quality Management Plan (AQMP) is developed and adopted by the SCAQMD Board that determines what actions will be taken to bring the South Coast Air Basin (SCAB) into compliance with state and federal clean air standards. To assess compliance with state and federal standards, a surveillance network of 38 permanent air monitoring sites and five single-pollutant source impact lead (Pb) air monitoring sites are maintained to measure criteria pollutants.[64] In order to better position the monitoring sites, the SCAQMD staff conducted an extensive review of the air monitoring sites in the SCAB in late 1980.[65] In the early 1990s, in the City of Los Angeles alone, it had six air quality monitoring stations throughout the city.[66] By 2016, the Los Angeles County had 26 air monitoring stations.[67] These stations collect data on the air quality and serve as an important tool for air quality management. This network not only provides air quality information to the agencies for monitoring but also serves as a key data source to make sound and up-to-date policies and regulations.

---

future studies. Thirdly and most importantly, they will be categorized, compared and analyzed for a better understanding of the air pollution governance processes of the LA area and BTH area in Chapter 5.

63. 40 CFR § 10 (2021).
64. Rene M. Bermudez, Brian Vlasich & Jason Low, "Annual Air Quality Monitoring Network Plan" (*South Coast Air Quality Management District*, May 2, 2016), www.aqmd.gov/docs/default-source/clean-air-plans/air-quality-monitoring-network-plan/annual-air-quality-monitoring-network-plan.pdf?sfvrsn = 13, accessed March 4, 2022.
65. Rene M. Bermudez, Brian Vlasich & Jason Low, "Annual Air Quality Monitoring Network Plan" (*South Coast Air Quality Management District*, May 2, 2016), www.aqmd.gov/docs/default-source/clean-air-plans/air-quality-monitoring-network-plan/annual-air-quality-monitoring-network-plan.pdf?sfvrsn = 13, accessed March 4, 2022.
66. The City Planning Commission, "Air Quality Element" (1992), http://planning.lacity.org/cwd/gnlpln/AQltyElt.pdf, accessed March 4, 2022.
67. California Air Resources Board, "Quality Assurance Air Monitoring Sites by County," https://ww3.arb.ca.gov/qaweb/countyselect.php?c_arb_code = 21, accessed March 8, 2022.

3.1.1.2 *Establishment of Community Air Protection Program*

To reduce exposure in communities most impacted by air pollution, the CARB established the Community Air Protection Program (CAPP) in 2018 under the California Assembly Bill AB 617.[68] The Program began with a small number of communities that were considered to be highly burdened economically and was to expand as the Program moved on.[69] Most of the first selected communities in late September 2018 were located in Southern California.[70] CARB's responsibilities under the CAPP include identifying impacted communities, establishing the criteria for air monitoring and local emissions reduction programs, and developing statewide strategies for reducing emissions.[71] The local air districts are the primary level for implementing the CAPP program, including establishing air monitoring campaigns, developing and implementing community emissions reduction programs, evaluating sources of data and local knowledge that may be available in refining, prioritizing their lists of recommended communities for the purpose of public health, and conducting outreach with communities under consideration to help inform their recommendations.[72] The core of the CAPP program aims to create a close partnership and coordination with local governments, land use commissions, transportation agencies, and other relevant parties, and thus to better utilize existing air quality control and monitoring efforts as well as to develop a comprehensive emission reduction approach addressing local land use decision-making.[73]

3.1.2 ***Regulation of Incinerators***

In the late 1940s and early 1950s, air pollution officials made significant strides in reducing smoke and fumes, including banning backyard incinerators that "brought the

68. California Air Resources Board, "Community Air Protection Program" https://ww2.arb.ca.gov/capp, accessed March 8, 2022.
69. California Air Resources Board, "Community Air Protection Program Framework-Concept Paper" (February 7, 2018), https://ww2.arb.ca.gov/sites/default/files/2018-02/capp_concept_paper_february_2018.pdf, accessed March 8, 2022.
70. Tony Barboza, "California Counters Trump on Car Emissions Standards, Expands Other Climate Rules" (*LA Times,* September 28, 2018), www.latimes.com/local/lanow/la-me-carbon-fuels-20180928-story.html, accessed March 4, 2022.
71. California Air Resources Board, "Community Air Protection Program Framework: Concept Paper" (February 7, 2018), https://ww2.arb.ca.gov/sites/default/files/2020-05/capp_concept_paper_february_2018_acc.pdf, accessed March 4, 2022 OR California Air Resources Board (n 307).
72. California Air Resources Board, "Community Air Protection Program Framework: Concept Paper" (February 7, 2018), https://ww2.arb.ca.gov/sites/default/files/2020-05/capp_concept_paper_february_2018_acc.pdf, accessed March 4, 2022 OR California Air Resources Board (n 307), at p. 8.
73. California Air Resources Board, "Community Air Protection Program Framework: Concept Paper" (February 7, 2018), https://ww2.arb.ca.gov/sites/default/files/2020-05/capp_concept_paper_february_2018_acc.pdf, accessed March 4, 2022 OR California Air Resources Board (n 307), at pp. 9-11.

smog war to the home front."[74] In 1944, the City of Los Angeles's main incinerator fell into disrepair and was permanently closed that led to establishment of the use of home backyard incinerators.[75] As a solution to deal with the trash that could not be burned in the city incinerator, the City approved an increase in the daily hours of rubbish burning.[76] After the smog attack of 1943, officers of Los Angeles County, together with scholars, studied the problem during 1945-1947 and identified that backyard incinerators were one of the main sources of smog, and they suggested that incinerators should be prohibited.[77] Many residents fiercely opposed plans to ban backyard incinerators, believing that oil refineries were the true cause of smog and that refineries should be regulated first.[78] A 1956 poll of 3,000 county residents was conducted that showed that 40% of respondents blamed industry for smog, and about 30% of respondents thought cars have the responsibility, while only 5% of people thought that home incinerators were the cause.[79] However, some residents began attributing high smog levels and poor health quality to the smoke from the backyard incinerators and complained to their local governments.[80]

At the beginning, in 1954, the City tried to adjust the burning hours to ease the smog problem, but residents complained about the inconvenience.[81] The public still depended on backyard incinerators with no other options to get rid of trash, even though they did realize the disadvantage of the units. The smog problem remained, and more concrete actions were needed. In 1955, Mayor Norris Poulson of the City of Los Angeles proposed "a new tax-funded municipal garbage collection program for the entire city that would assure the availability of city-owned landfills and collection trucks for years to come."[82] This provided a new way to deal with trash and thus reduce the opposition from the public. By the summer of 1956, the city had started to phase in

74. "The Southland's War on Smog: Fifty Years of Progress Towards Clean Air" (*South Coast AQMD*), www.aqmd.gov/home/research/publications/50-years-of-progress, accessed March 8, 2022.
75. "History Keepers: Backyard Residential Incinerator" (*California Historical Society*, August 10, 2016), http://californiahistoricalsociety.blogspot.com/2016/08/history-keepers-backyard-reslb id.ential.html, accessed March 4, 2022.
76. "History Keepers: Backyard Residential Incinerator" (*California Historical Society*, August 10, 2016), http://californiahistoricalsociety.org, accessed March 4, 2022.
77. "History Keepers: Backyard Residential Incinerator" (*California Historical Society*, August 10, 2016), http://californiahistoricalsociety.blogspot.com/2016/08/history-keepers-backyard-reslb id.ential.html, accessed March 4, 2022, at p. 333.
78. "History Keepers: Backyard Residential Incinerator" (*California Historical Society*, August 10, 2016), http://californiahistoricalsociety.blogspot.com/2016/08/history-keepers-backyard-reslb id.ential.html, accessed March 4, 2022.
79. Michael Holland, "City Archives Show How LA Banned Incinerators to Fight Smog" (Off-Ramp, March 13, 2014), https://archive.kpcc.org/programs/offramp/2014/03/13/36466/city-archive s-show-how-la-banned-incinerators-to-f/, accessed April 1, 2022.
80. Michael Holland, "City Archives Show How LA Banned Incinerators to Fight Smog" (Off-Ramp, March 13, 2014), https://archive.kpcc.org/programs/offramp/2014/03/13/36466/city-archive s-show-how-la-banned-incinerators-to-f/, accessed April 1, 2022, at p. 334.
81. Michael Holland, "City Archives Show How LA Banned Incinerators to Fight Smog" (Off-Ramp, March 13, 2014), https://archive.kpcc.org/programs/offramp/2014/03/13/36466/city-archive s-show-how-la-banned-incinerators-to-f/, accessed April 1, 2022, at p. 334.
82. Michael Holland, "City Archives Show How LA Banned Incinerators to Fight Smog" (Off-Ramp, March 13, 2014), https://archive.kpcc.org/programs/offramp/2014/03/13/36466/city-archive s-show-how-la-banned-incinerators-to-f/, accessed April 1, 2022, at p. 334.

trash collection in areas where incinerator use was being slowly phased out.[83] More than a decade after the problem was first identified, trash collection programs were established, and backyard incinerators were finally banned in 1957. Finally, in 2003, the CARB adopted a regulation banning all outdoor residential waste burning in California. The regulation went into effect January 1, 2004.[84] The history of abolishing incinerators in Los Angeles is an interesting example to show the limitation of public participation when the public lacked sufficient education and could not consider a problem beyond its own interests—and how the government finally prevailed.

3.1.3 Regulation of Transportation Sector

3.1.3.1 Study of Air Quality

Transportation-focused air quality legislation and regulations in California have been guided heavily by scientific studies of the impacts of air pollutants on public health. Research and publicly accessible measurements of air pollution have been part of California's strategy from the outset.

In 1952, Dr. Arie Haagen-Smit considered the "father of air pollution control," discovered that ozone is created by the chemical interaction of industrial and automobile exhaust and sunlight.[85] Dr. Haagen-Smit was hired by the LAPCD to conduct the research; however, simultaneously, the oil industry—specifically, the Western Oil and Gas Association, through the Stanford Research Institute, funded research that attempted to downplay the role of the oil industry in air pollution, asserting that the blame was almost exclusively on automobiles.[86] The battle between the researchers was resolved, in part, by concurrent research conducted by the Air Pollution Foundation (AFP), that found that automobiles were a major cause.[87] The AFP, that existed from 1954-1961,[88] was formed by various industries, including automobile manufacturers, with the understanding that "their future, in part, depended upon continued economic growth in Los Angeles," and economic growth could be hampered by air pollution.[89]

83. Michael Holland, "City Archives Show How LA Banned Incinerators to Fight Smog" (Off-Ramp, March 13, 2014), https://archive.kpcc.org/programs/offramp/2014/03/13/36466/city-archives-show-how-la-banned-incinerators-to-f/, accessed April 1, 2022, at p. 334.
84. California Air Resources Board, "About: History," https://ww2.arb.ca.gov/about/history, accessed March 8, 2022.
85. California Air Resources Board, "About: History," https://ww2.arb.ca.gov/about/history, accessed March 8, 2022.
86. George Gonzalez, Politics of Air Pollution, Urban Growth, Ecological Modernization, and Symbolic Inclusion, SUNY Press Albany, 2012.
87. George Gonzalez, Politics of Air Pollution, Urban Growth, Ecological Modernization, and Symbolic Inclusion, SUNY Press Albany, 2012, at p. 85.
88. George Gonzalez, Politics of Air Pollution, Urban Growth, Ecological Modernization, and Symbolic Inclusion, SUNY Press Albany, 2012, at p. 81.
89. George Gonzalez, Politics of Air Pollution, Urban Growth, Ecological Modernization, and Symbolic Inclusion, SUNY Press Albany, 2012, at p. 80.

In 1983, the California Legislature mandated that the CARB study the health effects of toxic air contaminants.[90] As a result, the CARB has conducted periodic studies of carcinogenic toxic air pollutants. One report, the SCAB Multiple Air Toxics Exposure Study (MATES), estimates carcinogenic risk across the South Coast area by geographic location and provides a useful interactive map to highlight particularly troubled areas.[91] First published in 1998 as MATES I, the study found that particulate matter from diesel exhaust is a principal toxic air contaminant. In response, the CARB developed the Diesel Risk Reduction Plan that spells out the process by which California would reduce the health risks of diesel emissions particulate matter.[92] MATES II, completed in 2000, confirmed that diesel particulate emissions were a major contributor to local toxic air pollution. This finding prompted the development of the SCAQMD's Clean Fleets Program[93] that is aimed at significantly reducing air pollution and safeguarding public health by mandating that commercial fleet operators purchase new vehicles with cleaner-burning engines where existing engines exceed the standards.[94] MATES V is currently underway and includes a focus on fixed-site monitoring "to characterize long-term areal air toxics levels in residential and commercial areas."[95]

3.1.3.2 California Air Resources Board

Following the "Great Smog" of London in 1952,[96] during which several thousand people died, California Governor Goodwin J. Knight established a committee to develop air pollution controls for Los Angeles to prevent such a disaster from happening in California, and he appointed Arnold O. Beckman, a prominent researcher, as the chair of what was known as the "Beckman Committee." The Committee ultimately recommended that, among other things, emissions from automobiles and diesel trucks be strongly regulated.[97] Consequently, the Los Angeles County Motor Vehicle Pollution Control Laboratory was established as part of the

90. California Air Resources Board (Risk Reduction Plan to Reduce Particulate Matter Emissions from Diesel-Fueled Engines and Vehicles, October 2000), https://ww2.arb.ca.gov/sites/default/files/classic/diesel/documents/rrpfinal.pdf, accessed March 8, 2022.
91. *South Coast Air Quality Management District* (Multiple Air Toxics Exposure Study, May 1, 2015), https://www.aqmd.gov/home/air-quality/air-quality-studies/health-studies/mates-iv, accessed March 8, 2022.
92. Mike Bogdanoff, South Coast Aqmd Clean Transportation Programs, https://www.energy.gov/sites/prod/files/2014/03/f9/deer_2003_bogdanoff.pdf, accessed November 8, 2023.
93. Mike Bogdanoff, South Coast Aqmd Clean Transportation Programs, https://www.energy.gov/sites/prod/files/2014/03/f9/deer_2003_bogdanoff.pdf, accessed November 8, 2023.
94. South Coast Air Quality Management District (MATES V Multiple Air Toxics Exposure Study), https://www.4cleanair.org/wp-content/uploads/NACAA-MATES-V.pdf, accessed November 8, 2023.
95. South Coast Air Quality Management District (MATES V Multiple Air Toxics Exposure Study), https://www.4cleanair.org/wp-content/uploads/NACAA-MATES-V.pdf, accessed November 8, 2023.
96. *Met Office* (The Great Smoke of 1952), http://www.metoffice.gov.uk/learning/learn-about-the-weather/weather-phenomena/case-studies/great-smog, accessed March 4, 2022.
97. *Met Office* (The Great Smoke of 1952), http://www.metoffice.gov.uk/learning/learn-about-the-weather/weather-phenomena/case-studies/great-smog, accessed March 4, 2022, at p. 143.

LAPCD in 1955, and in 1955 and 1966, respectively, the California Bureau of Air Sanitation and the Motor Vehicle Pollution Control Board were established and were eventually brought together in 1967 to create the CARB that remains to this day the state agency with primary responsibility over air pollution from mobile sources.[98] The CARB was created in order to develop air pollution standards based on scientific evidence and to "enable a group of professionals and experts to observe conditions, synthesize the science and make recommendations to a citizen board on how to abate or mitigate poor air quality,"[99] and is meant to provide an intensive, coordinated state, Regional, and local effort to protect and enhance the ambient air quality of the state,[100] notably enabling a decision of the CARB that explicitly recognizes that "air pollution knows no political boundaries," and that "a Regional approach to the problem should be encouraged whenever possible."[101] The CARB has, from its inception, followed in the footsteps of its first Chairman, Dr. Haagen-Smit, by using research on the causes and health effects of air pollution to guide its policymaking.

The CARB's mission balances public health, environmental, and economic concerns. Its policies have required automobile manufacturers to increase vehicle fuel efficiency, reduce emissions, and produce a certain number of Zero Emission Vehicles.[102] The CARB has also focused on assisting consumers by providing incentives for the purchase of alternative fuel and electric passenger vehicles, as well as for heavier-duty truck owners to improve engine performance and reduce emissions, among other initiatives.[103]

Of the regional air pollution agencies created under the CARB described above, the SCAQMD is the largest. It covers nearly half of California's total population and has jurisdiction covering more than 10,000 square miles, including all of Orange County, as well as the urban sections of Los Angeles, Riverside, and San Bernardino counties—the geographic area covered by this study.[104] The SCAQMD was responsible for the "only area in the United States classified by the [U.S.] Environmental Protection Agency as an extreme nonattainment area for ozone" and "one of only five areas designated as a serious non-attainment area for small particulate matter."[105]

Several recent occurrences importantly affect California transportation regulations. First, in 2022, the Supreme Court issued a decision[106] limiting EPA's authority to regulate climate change on the ground that Congress didn't authorize such regulations

98. California Air Resources Board (History), https://ww2.CARB.ca.gov/about/history, accessed March 4, 2022.
99. State News Service, Briefing Report: Legislature's Large CARB Footprint (April 21, 2010).
100. Cal Health & Safety Code § 39001 (West 2014).
101. Cal Health & Safety Code § 39001 (West 2014).
102. Cal Health & Safety Code § 39001 (West 2014).
103. California Air Resources Board (History), https://ww2.CARB.ca.gov/about/history, accessed March 4, 2022.
104. South Coast Air Quality Management District (Map of Monitoring Areas), http://www.SCAQMD.gov/docs/default-source/default-document-library/map-of-monitoring-areas.pdf, accessed March 4, 2022.
105. *California Division of Transportation Planning* (Federal Nonattainment Areas Table), http://www.dot.ca.gov/env/air/nonattainment-areas-table.html, accessed March 4, 2022.
106. *West Virginia v. EPA*, https://www.supremecourt.gov/opinions/21pdf/20-1530_n758.pdf, last accessed on January 8, 2022.

with sufficient specificity that may affect these regulations; however, the recently passed Inflation Reduction Act attempts to meet the Supreme Court objections,[107] a conclusion that some states have promised to challenge. Second, the California CARB passed a regulation to prohibit the sale of automobiles that release carbon into the air, applicable to 35% of the cars sold by 2025 and 68% of the cars sold by 2030. Since California is the largest auto market in the country, and its auto efficiency standards can be adopted by a dozen other large states, if passed this measure could have an enormous influence on reducing carbon releases from automobile and truck sources both in California and the rest of the country, perhaps other countries as well.[108] Although the Los Angeles area's air quality improved markedly since it began its effort to curb air pollution, it remained in a nonattainment zone for ozone and particulate matter,[109] and thus the work of the various actors in curbing emissions, while being effectively addressed, may not yet be done.

3.1.3.3 First Motor Vehicle Pollution Control Regulations

The 1960s marked the very first motor vehicle pollution control regulations in the U.S. They initially focused on tailpipe emissions control technology. In 1961, what was at the time the California Motor Vehicle Pollution Control Board, promulgated the nation's first passenger car pollution regulations when it mandated that passenger vehicles sold in California be equipped with "positive crankcase ventilation," that is a technology that controls hydrocarbon crankcase emissions.[110] In 1966, the Motor Vehicle Pollution Control Board mandated the nation's first tailpipe emissions standards for hydrocarbons (HC) and Carbon monoxide (CO), and for NOx in 1971,[111] and the U.S. Congress followed suit by setting minimum national federal emissions controls standards for HC, CO, and NO_X in 1970.[112]

3.1.3.4 California's Smog Check Program

Another significant contributor to reducing air pollution has been California's Smog Check Program that entered into effect in 1984[113] under which vehicles older than six

107. https://www.weforum.org/agenda/2022/08/why-the-u-s-inflation-reduction-act-is-an-important-step-in-the-transition-to-clean-energy/.
108. https://www.npr.org/2022/08/25/1119456396/california-is-set-to-ban-sales-of-new-gasoline-powered-cars-by-2035#:~:text=los%20angeles%20%E2%80%94%20California%20air, accessed August 29, 2022.
109. Mark Gold et al., "2015 Environmental Report Card for Los Angeles County" (*UCLA Institute of Environment & Sustainability*, 2015), ioes.ucla.edu/project/2015-environmental-report-card-for-los-angeles-county, accessed March 8, 2022.
110. *Bay Area Air Quality Management District* (History of the Air District, December 20, 2021), www.baaqmd.gov/about-the-air-district/history-of-air-district, accessed March 4, 2022.
111. *Bay Area Air Quality Management District* (History of the Air District, December 20, 2021), www.baaqmd.gov/about-the-air-district/history-of-air-district, accessed March 4, 2022.
112. *U.S. Environmental Protection Agency* (Milestones in Mobile Source Pollution Control and Regulations), https://www.epa.gov/fueleconomy, accessed November 6, 2023.
113. *Bay Area Air Quality Management District* (History of the Air District, December 20, 2021), www.baaqmd.gov/about-the-air-district/history-of-air-district, accessed March 4, 2022.

years must undergo a biennial smog test and receive a smog certification. Compliance requires payment of a USD 20 annual abatement fee. The rule applies equally to all vehicles, whether or not purchased in California. New California residents cannot receive a Department of Motor Vehicles registration unless their vehicles undergo the smog test and receive the required certificate. California does not accept any other state's smog certification as proof of compliance.[114]

Certain vehicles are exempt from the smog check inspection requirements, including older models (pre-1975 for gasoline and pre-1997 for diesel engines), diesel-fueled and natural gas-powered vehicles weighing more than 14,000 lbs., and hybrid and electric vehicles.[115] To assist in enforcement, the CARB has set up a telephone "hotline" to allow people to call its Pollution Complaints Program and report smoking vehicles. Citizens can also report idling commercial vehicles, locomotives at rail yards, and school buses or vehicles idling near schools.[116]

In order to provide flexibility for complying with the smog check requirements, the CARB developed the Consumer Assistance Program that is operated by the California Bureau of Automotive Repair. Under this program, car owners whose vehicles fail the smog test can sell their noncompliant vehicles to the State for up to USD 1,500 if they are unwilling or unable to bring their vehicles into compliance with smog requirements. Additionally, qualified consumers whose vehicles fail the smog check can receive up to USD 500 to finance repairs that would reduce tailpipe emissions.[117] The CARB mandated that all 1988 and later model-year vehicles be equipped with computers that monitor emissions and signal alerts when emission limits are exceeded.[118]

3.1.3.5 Low Emission Vehicles Program

Another important vehicle emission reduction initiative by the CARB is the Low Emission Vehicles (LEV) program. The LEV Program regulations were first conceived in 1990 with mandates that ran through 2003, and were subsequently amended in 1998 (LEV II) and 2012 (LEV III), with increasingly stringent emissions standards designed to help California meet the air pollution reduction goals that were then required by the federal government.[119] The LEV program covers passenger cars, light-duty trucks, and

114. *California Department of Motor Vehicles* (Smog Information), https://www.dmv.ca.gov/portal/dmv/detail/vr/smogfaq, accessed March 8, 2022.
115. *California Department of Motor Vehicles* (Smog Information), https://www.dmv.ca.gov/portal/dmv/detail/vr/smogfaq, accessed March 8, 2022.
116. California Air Resources Board (Air Pollution Complaints), https://ww2.arb.ca.gov/, accessed November 6, 2023.
117. California Bureau of Automotive Repairs (Consumer Assistance Program), https://www.bar.ca.gov/Consumer/Consumer_Assistance_Program/, accessed March 4, 2022.
118. California Air Resources Board (OnBoard Diagnostic II (OBD II) Systems—Fact Sheet/FAQs, September 19, 2019), https://ww2.arb.ca.gov/resources/fact-sheets/board-diagnostic-ii-obd-ii-systems-fact-sheet, accessed March 8, 2022.
119. LEV I regulations are found at 13 CCR 1960, LEVII at 13 CCR 1961, and LEVIII at 13 CCR 1961.2. Further information on the LEV program can be found at California Air Resources Board (Low

medium-duty vehicles and regulates non-methane hydrocarbons, CO, NOx, formaldehyde, and particulates, as well as carbon dioxide, methane, nitrous oxide, and hydrofluorocarbons. Given the stringent standards, both federally and within California, as well as for states adopting California's standards, it was important to address the auto manufacturing industry's concerns and how they are designed to make the compliance process as streamlined and efficient as possible. The CARB and U.S. EPA thus developed the Compliance Assurance Program or "CAP 2000" under the federal CAA. The CAP 2000 regulations streamlined certification procedures for manufacturers and required them to test 2,000 vehicles each year at one and four years of age to make certain that their fleets are meeting the federal (and California) emissions standards.[120]

3.1.3.6 *SCAQMD Clean Fleets Program*

Following the MATES I and II studies, the SCAQMD promulgated seven "fleet rules" to reduce diesel fuel emissions and other toxic air pollutants and criteria pollutants from the vehicles of public and private fleet operators.[121] The rules cover street sweepers; light- and medium-duty public fleet vehicles; on-road transit buses; residential and commercial refuse collection vehicles; commercial airport vehicles, such as taxis and shuttle buses; school buses; and heavy-duty vehicles. While the details of each rule vary, in general, the seven rules cover "any federal, state, county, city or governmental department or agency, any special district such as water, air, sanitation, transit, and school districts, or private individual firm, association, franchise, contractor, user or owner who provides sweeping services to a government agency that owns or leases 15 or more vehicles."[122] Any time a covered fleet operator wishes to add vehicles to its fleet, it must purchase either lower-emission or alternative fuel vehicles. Lower-emission vehicles are those that run on low-sulfur diesel fuel, that has a maximum sulfur content of 15 parts per million, and have their engines outfitted with an exhaust control device approved by the Air Resources Board. Uncovered alternative fuel vehicles include those that run on liquefied natural I gas, liquefied petroleum gas (propane), methanol, electricity, or fuel cells.[123] The rules are designed to gradually transition covered operators to fewer polluting fleets over time—they do not require that operators switch out their fleets within a given timeframe. Furthermore, not all

Emission Vehicles Program), https://ww2.arb.ca.gov/our-work/programs/low-emission-vehicle-program, accessed November 8, 2023.

120. U.S. Environmental Protection Agency (Regulatory Announcement: Compliance Assurance Program CAP 2000, March 1999), https://nepis.epa.gov/Exe/ZyPDF.cgi/P1009Z20.PDF?Dockey=P1009Z20.PDF, accessed March 8, 2022.

121. Criteria pollutants are six common air pollutants found across the U.S. and include ground-level ozone, carbon monoxide, sulfur oxide, nitrous oxide, and lead. They are designated under the CAA, and the EPA is responsible for setting national ambient air quality standards for each pollutant. United States Environmental Protection Agency, "What Are the Six Common Air Pollutants?," https://www.epa.gov/criteria-air-pollutants, accessed March 8, 2022.

122. The language is the same for each of the rules. Less-Polluting Sweepers Rule 1186.1(b) (January 9, 2009), aqmd.gov/docs/default-source/rule-study/reg-xi/rule-1186-1-less-polluting-sweepers.pdf?sfvrsn=4, accessed April 12, 2022.

123. Cal. Code Regs. Tit. 13, § 2025(f) (2021).

fleet operators must comply—the program generally targets operators who own 15 or more vehicles, and each individual rule includes certain exemptions.[124]

The Clean Fleets Program applies only within the jurisdiction of the SCAQMD. The CARB has promulgated its own set of regulations to govern diesel emissions from heavy-duty on-road vehicles, enacted pursuant to the CAA's requirement that California meet its NAAQS as part of California's State Implementation Plan.[125] The CARB's heavy-duty vehicle regulations are designed to reduce emissions of diesel particulate matter (PM), nitrogen oxides, and various other criteria pollutants.[126] They apply to owners, operators and retailers of subject vehicle fleets, and not only to on-road vehicles but also to yard trucks with off-road engines used in agriculture, street sweepers, and school buses (but only to vehicles with a manufacturer's gross vehicle weight above 14,000 pounds).[127] The regulations have various start dates, ranging from 2012-2023, and offer some flexibility for compliance. Lighter vehicles must be equipped with a 2010 model-year emission equivalent engine.[128] Heavier vehicles must meet PM's best available control technology (BACT) requirements by either installing the highest level Verified Retrofits for Off-Road Diesel Vehicle System (VDECS) or equipping the engines with an original equipment manufacturer diesel particulate filter.[129] Heavier vehicles must also have a 2010 model-year emissions equivalent engine and may meet this requirement by either replacing the engine, retrofitting it with an Off-Road Vehicle System (VDECS) that achieves 2010 model-year equivalent emissions, or temporarily delaying compliance.[130] Covered fleet owners, operators and retailers are required to meet detailed reporting and record-keeping requirements, and civil and criminal penalties are levied for noncompliance, that is determined by the CARB's Executive Officer by examining such factors as the "willfulness of the violation, the length of time of noncompliance, whether the fleet made any attempt to comply, and the magnitude of noncompliance."[131]

3.1.3.7 Reducing Diesel Exhaust Pollution from Locomotive Transportation

Taken together, the CARB and U.S. EPA's rules provide a robust regulatory regime for locomotives. Recognizing the health risks associated with diesel exhaust, in 2005, the CARB entered into the "CARB/Railroad Statewide Agreement" with the Union Pacific and Burlington Northern Rail Roads (hereinafter referred to as the "Railroad Agreement"),[132] and through separate rulemaking also mandates diesel fuel standards for

124. Cal. Code Regs. Tit. 13, § 2025(f) (2021).
125. *California Dump Truck Owners Assoc. v. Nichols*, 784 F.3d 500, 503 (9th Cir. 2015).
126. Cal. Code Regs. Tit. 13, § 2025(a) (2021).
127. Cal. Code Regs. Tit. 13, § 2025(b) (2021).
128. Cal. Code Regs. Tit. 13, § 2025(f) (2021).
129. Cal. Code Regs. Tit. 13, § 2025(d)(47) (2021).
130. Cal. Code Regs. Tit. 13, § 2025(g) (2021).
131. Cal. Code Regs. Tit. 13, § 2025(z) 2021.
132. California Air Resources Board, "CARB/Railroad Statewide Agreement: Particulate Emissions Reduction Program at California Rail Yards" (June 2005), https://ww2.arb.ca.gov/resources/documents/2005-statewide-railyard-agreement, accessed November 6, 2023.

locomotives, as further explained below. Additionally, under a separate CARB rule-making, starting from January 2007, diesel fuel sold for refueling intrastate trains in California had to meet the specifications of CARB diesel fuel,[133] though there are exceptions, such as for locomotives that meet certain EPA emission standards.[134] Diesel fuel had to meet certain minimum requirements as to the sulfur and aromatic hydrocarbon content, as well as its lubricity, or friction. Train owners or operators were allowed alternately to comply by submitting an "alternative emissions reduction plan" that provides for using substitute fuels and/or emission control strategies.[135]

In 1998, the U.S. EPA promulgated its first emissions regulations for trains.[136] The regulations were updated in 2008, with stricter emissions standards for newly-built locomotives and existing trains that are "remanufactured." Trains were required to be outfitted with "currently available technologies" that reduce diesel PM and NOx emissions. From 2015 onward, new locomotives had to include high-efficiency catalytic after-treatment technology.[137] Finally, the rules require that all new and most remanufactured trains be equipped with "idle reduction technology," that, similar to the Railroad Agreement between the CARB and railroad companies, automatically shuts off a train's engine when it idles unnecessarily.[138] The U.S. EPA's rules were estimated to reduce annual NOX emissions by 800,000 tons and annual diesel PM emissions by 27,000 tons across the nation.

Under the 2008 Railroad Agreement updates, railroads were required to reduce diesel emissions through a variety of measures. The first is reducing train idling at rail yards.—Under the agreement, trains outfitted with AIR devices cannot idle for more than 15 consecutive minutes and all intrastate trains, whether outfitted with the devices or not, are prohibited from idling for more than 60 minutes. There are exceptions to this requirement, such as when compliance is not feasible because the train's engine would be at risk of damage or when maintenance is being conducted.[139] Railroads were also required to reduce visible emissions from their locomotives by

---

More information on the CARB's locomotives programs is available at, https://www.epa.gov/regulations-emissions-vehicles-and-engines/regulations-emissions-locomotives, accessed November 6, 2023.

133. Cal. Code Reg. Tit. 13, § 2299(a) (2005).
134. Cal. Code Reg. Tit. 13, § 2299(b)(5)(B) (2005).
135. Cal. Code Reg. Tit. 13, § 2299(b)(5)(B) (2005).
136. United States Environmental Protection Agency, "Non-Road Engines, Equipment and Vehicles: Locomotives," https://www.epa.gov/regulations-emissions-vehicles-and-engines/regulations-emissions-locomotives, accessed November 6, 2023.
137. U.S. Environmental Protection Agency, "EPA Finalizes More Stringent Emissions Standards for Locomotives and Marine Compression-Ignition Engines" (*Regulatory Announcement*, March 2008), https://nepis.epa.gov/Exe/ZyPDF.cgi/P100094D.PDF?Dockey=P100094D.PDF, accessed March 4, 2022.
138. U.S. Environmental Protection Agency, "Office of Transportation and Air Quality, Control of Emissions from Idling Locomotives" (*Emission Facts*, December 2013), https://nepis.epa.gov/Exe/ZyPDF.cgi/P100HP4Q.PDF?Dockey=P100HP4Q.PDF, accessed March 8, 2022.
139. California Air Resources Board, "ARB/Railroad Statewide Agreement: Particulate Emissions Reduction Program at California Rail Yards" (June 2005), https://ww2.arb.ca.gov/sites/default/files/2020-06/2005%20mou%20remediated%2003102020.pdf, accessed March 4, 2022, at p. 3.

repairing those trains that emit excessive exhaust.[140] At a minimum, they must perform annual inspections of each locomotive in their fleet and measure visible emissions either with an opacity meter or a visible emissions evaluator. Locomotives that are found to have excessive visible emissions must be routed to the nearest repair facility within 96 hours or as expeditiously as possible.[141] The Railroad Agreement included specific provisions for involving community members and local air districts in the emissions reduction process through annual meetings.[142] Railroads were also required to evaluate what feasible changes could be undertaken to reduce pollution, and recommended actions include increasing the buffer zone between the railway and the community; tailoring the idling requirements to each community's unique conditions; and undertaking various efficiency measures.[143] Railroads were required to gather data, such as railroad activity and emissions inventories, based on which the CARB completes health risk assessments, following which a determination is made whether additional actions are needed to reduce pollution.[144] This is another example of the CARB turning to scientific measurements and data in crafting air pollution reduction programs. Another notable feature of the Railroad Agreement was that it expressly listed possible funding sources for the mitigation measures it contemplated, including both public and private funds.[145] Finally, the Railroad Agreement had "teeth"—it included financial penalties for violations, ranging from USD 400-USD 1,200 for individual instances of violations to as high as USD 10,000-USD 40,000, depending on the number of months of noncompliance and for more egregious violations, such as not implementing the necessary steps to meet the program requirements.[146]

---

140. California Air Resources Board, "ARB/Railroad Statewide Agreement: Particulate Emissions Reduction Program at California Rail Yards" (June 2005), https://ww2.arb.ca.gov/sites/default/files/2020-06/2005%20mou%20remediated%2003102020.pdf, accessed March 4, 2022, at p. 6.
141. California Air Resources Board, "ARB/Railroad Statewide Agreement: Particulate Emissions Reduction Program at California Rail Yards" (June 2005), https://ww2.arb.ca.gov/sites/default/files/2020-06/2005%20mou%20remediated%2003102020.pdf, accessed March 4, 2022.
142. California Air Resources Board, "ARB/Railroad Statewide Agreement: Particulate Emissions Reduction Program at California Rail Yards" (June 2005), https://ww2.arb.ca.gov/sites/default/files/2020-06/2005%20mou%20remediated%2003102020.pdf, accessed March 4, 2022, at p. 8.
143. California Air Resources Board, "ARB/Railroad Statewide Agreement: Particulate Emissions Reduction Program at California Rail Yards" (June 2005), https://ww2.arb.ca.gov/sites/default/files/2020-06/2005%20mou%20remediated%2003102020.pdf, accessed March 4, 2022, at p. 9.
144. California Air Resources Board, "ARB/Railroad Statewide Agreement: Particulate Emissions Reduction Program at California Rail Yards" (June 2005), https://ww2.arb.ca.gov/sites/default/files/2020-06/2005%20mou%20remediated%2003102020.pdf, accessed March 4, 2022, at p.10.
145. California Air Resources Board, "ARB/Railroad Statewide Agreement: Particulate Emissions Reduction Program at California Rail Yards" (June 2005), https://ww2.arb.ca.gov/sites/default/files/2020-06/2005%20mou%20remediated%2003102020.pdf, accessed March 4, 2022, at p.11.
146. California Air Resources Board, "ARB/Railroad Statewide Agreement: Particulate Emissions Reduction Program at California Rail Yards" (June 2005), https://www.epa.gov/regulations-emissions-vehicles-and-engines/regulations-emissions-locomotives, accessed November 6, 2023, at p.13.

3.1.3.8 *Regulation of Gasoline*

Regulations governing the composition of gasoline are set at both the federal level pursuant to the CAA, and by the state of California that are more stringent than the federal standards. Under federal law, the CAA requires states with "nonattainment areas" (those parts of the country that do not meet ambient air quality standards for a given pollutant)[147] to promulgate programs that reduce carbon dioxide (CO_2) emissions during winter months, when those areas are likely to have higher CO_2 concentrations. Under these programs, the oxygen content of gasoline must be increased, typically by adding a chemical compound.[148] Doing so allows the gasoline to burn more completely and thus emit less CO_2. The burden of compliance falls on gasoline refiners, who originally could choose which oxygenate to add, either methyl tertiary-butyl ether (MTBE) or ethanol.[149]

The LA area is one of two areas in California that, due to its extremely poor air quality, is considered a "nonattainment" zone and must comply with the CAA's oxygenated gasoline requirements. Accordingly, California initiated its Wintertime Oxygenates Program in 1992 to comply with the CAA mandate.[150] When concerns arose that MTBE might contribute to groundwater pollution, California began the process of phasing it out and then banning it.[151] It has met the CAA's requirements by instituting its own gasoline requirements that are far more stringent than those at the federal level.[152] More specifically, under California's Reformulated Gasoline (RFG) Program, gasoline producers and importers[153] must meet stringent requirements as to the following contents and qualities of their fuel: Reid Vapor Pressure (RVP), sulfur, benzene, aromatics, olefins, oxygen, T50, and T90.[154] The RFG program has a very wide reach, as it applies to "all sales, supplies, offers or movements of California gasoline, including transactions directly involving the fueling of motor vehicles at a retail or bulk purchase-consumer facility."[155] Specific test methods and sampling procedures must be used for each covered additive in order to determine compliance. For example, the regulations specify the type of containers that must be used in collecting motor fuel samples; the type of sampling apparatus to be used; the time and

147. CAA § 7407(d)(1)(A)(i).
148. California Air Resources Board (Oxygenates, MTBE, Ethanol and Other Information), http://www.CARB.ca.gov/fuels/gasoline/oxy/oxy.htm, accessed March 4, 2022.
149. California Air Resources Board (MTBE: Gasoline), https://ww2.arb.ca.gov/resources/documents/gasoline-oxygenates, accessed March 8, 2022.
150. California Air Resources Board "Gasoline Oxygenates" (Oxygenates, MTBE, Ethanol and Related Information), https://ww2.arb.ca.gov/resources/documents/gasoline-oxygenates, accessed November 6, 2023.
151. CCR 2262.2. MTBE was subsequently banned in a number of other states and has been mostly phased out of use in gasoline nationally; *See* U.S. (*Environmental Protection Agency* "MTGE" (Overview, February 20, 2016), https://archive.epa.gov/mtbe/web/html/faq.html, accessed March 4, 2022.
152. U.S. (Environmental Protection Agency "MTGE" (Overview, February 20, 2016), https://archive.epa.gov/mtbe/web/html/faq.html, accessed March 4, 2022.
153. Cal. Code Regs. Tit 13, § 2261 (Barclays through 2022 Register 8).
154. Cal. Code Regs. Tit 13, § 2262 (Barclays through 2022 Register 8).
155. Cal. Code Regs. Tit 13, § 2261(a)(1)(A)(2). (Barclays through 2022 Register 8).

place that sampling is to be conducted (e.g., samples must be taken from both shipping and receiving tanks when loading or discharging motor fuel); and labeling and shipping requirements.[156]

3.1.4 Regulation of Ports

The Port of Los Angeles (POLA) and the Port of Long Beach (POLB), together with the stationary sources (power plants, oil refineries and other large factories) have generated significant amounts of pollutants in the Los Angeles area. As America's premier gateway for goods and services and a bustling center for global commerce, the POLA encompasses 7,500 acres of land and water along 43 miles of waterfront. It features 27 passenger and cargo terminals, including automobile, breakbulk, container, dry and liquid bulk, multi-use, and warehouse facilities that handle billions of dollars worth of cargo each year.[157] Along with the POLB, the POLA contemporaneously facilitates 14.1 million containers annually, earning the title of the fifth-largest seaport in the world in 2005.[158] However, the economic prosperity of the two ports comes with their contribution to the serious degrading of LA air quality. They are the single largest fixed sources of air pollution in the entire Los Angeles basin[159] and they emit as much diesel exhaust as 16,000 trucks running for 24 hours straight.[160] Fortunately, air pollution associated with operations at the Ports has been consistently reduced since the ports adopted a Clean Air Action Plan to reduce emissions in 2005, according to reports of POLA and POLB's Inventory of Air Emissions review.[161]

3.1.4.1 Clean Air Action Plan (2006, 2017)

The Clean Air Action Plan serves as the basis of control measures incorporated into the State Implementation Plan (SIP) through the SCAQMD's AQMP, by targeting the port-related sources that were identified in the emissions inventories prepared by the Ports of Long Beach and Los Angeles with advanced technologies and innovative initiatives.[162] Participation in this plan-development process is led by the Ports, is voluntary, and is not intended to supplant federal, state, or local air quality standards.[163] Under the Plan, there are seven programs that focus on all the key aspects

156. Cal. Code Regs. Tit 13, § 2263 (Barclays through 2022 Register 8).
157. *The Port of Los Angeles* (About the Port), https://www.portoflosangeles.org/about/. > accessed March 8, 2022.
158. Gilbert Estrada, "*KCE*" (Brief History of the Ports of Los Angeles and Long Beach," January 24, 2014), https://www.pbssocal.org/shows/departures/brief-history-of-the-ports-of-los-angeles-and-long-beach, accessed November 6, 2023.
159. https://www.aqmd.gov/nav/about/initiatives/clean-port, assessed August 8, 2022.
160. https://www.aqmd.gov/nav/about/initiatives/clean-port, assessed August 8, 2022, at p. 414.
161. https://www.portoflosangeles.org/environment/air-quality/air-emissions-inventory, assessed August 8, 2022.
162. https://www.portoflosangeles.org/environment/air-quality/air-emissions-inventory, assessed August 8, 2022.
163. *The Port of Long Beach* (San Pedro Bay Ports: Clean Air Action Plan (Overview) FORWARD, 2006), https://www.portoflosangeles.org/environment/air-quality/san-pedro-bay-ports-clean-air-action-plan, accessed November 6, 2023.

of port operations, including ocean-going vessels, trucks, cargo handling equipment, harbor craft, and rail (railroad transportation related to the Ports). Also included was a Technology Advancement Program (to oversee general technology improvement) and Bay wide Standards (general standards for the Ports' activities).[164] For example, through an Ocean-Going Vessels program, ships can earn financial incentives by sending their cleanest vessels.[165] The Harbor Department of POLA pays a monetary reward ranging from USD 250 to USD 1,250 to vessel operators quarterly if the vessel's engines meet the requirements of International Maritime Organization (IMO) standards, or if the vessel operators demonstrate an emission reduction technology that reduces specified levels of Diesel Particulate Matter (DPM) and NOx emissions.[166] This measure, in part, is aimed to encourage vessel operators to send their newest, cleanest vessels to the Port as well as discourage vessels from using bunker fuel, the dirtiest fuel distilled from crude oil.[167]

Furthermore, the Clean Air Action Plan governs small aspects of harbor operation. In the past, a ship ran its engines even when it was loading or unloading. Under the Alternative Marine Power (AMP) program, a unique air quality program that was launched in 2004 to reduce emissions from container vessels docked at the Port of Los Angeles (POLA), vessel operators relying on shore power were required by January 1, 2014, to shut down their auxiliary engines at-berth for 50% of the fleet's vessel visits and also reduce their onboard auxiliary engine power generation by 50%, in order to comply with 2007 container ship emissions abatement regulations.[168] Shipping lines have to retrofit their ships to comply with the new technology, a process that costs them USD 500,000 to USD 1.5 million per vessel.[169] Program participation increased from 54% of total port calls in 2014 to 72% in 2016.[170]

In recognition of the groundbreaking work and commitment by both Ports, several awards and recognitions have been delivered, including the 8th Annual National EPA Clean Air Excellence Award in 2007.[171]

In the announced refuting of the Trump administration's announced exit from the Paris Climate Agreement, Los Angeles Mayor Eric Garcetti and Long Beach Mayor

164. https://cleanairactionplan.org, accessed August 8, 2022.
165. The Port of Los Angeles (Ocean-Going Vessels Emission reduction), www.portoflosangeles.org/environment/ogv.asp, accessed March 6, 2022.
166. https://cleanairactionplan.org, accessed August 8, 2022.
167. https://cleanairactionplan.org, accessed August 8, 2022.
168. *Port of Los Angeles* (Alternative Motor Power), www.portoflosangeles.org/environment/amp.asp, accessed March 6, 2022.
169. *Port of Los Angeles* (Port of Los Angeles Ready to Meet California's Shore-Side Power Requirement, January 8, 2014), www.portoflosangeles.org/references/news_10814_amp-shoreside_power_requirements, accessed March 8, 2022.
170. *Port of Los Angeles* (AMP Operator Summary Report 2014 and 2016), www.portoflosangeles.org/environment/amp.asp, accessed March 6, 2022.
171. "About the Clean Air Action Plan" (*San Pedro Bay Ports-Clean Air Action Plan*), https://www.portoflosangeles.org/environment/air-quality/san-pedro-bay-ports-clean-air-action-plan, accessed November 6, 2023.

Robert Garcia signed an agreement to update the Clean Air Action Plan in June 2017.[172] The updated Plan included the following new requirements:[173]

- cargo handling equipment, rail, and harbor craft, outlining specific, detailed strategies, including implementation deadlines to reduce emissions and to move toward zero emissions.
- of the infrastructure necessary for near-zero and zero-emissions goods movement.).
- of system-wide changes.
- of Zero-Emissions and Freight Efficiency goals, supporting the zero-emissions and freight efficiency targets set by the state and other agencies and containing a new focus on greenhouse gas reductions with 2030 and 2050—reduction targets.[174]
- of Funding and viable technologies, as two big challenges, were posed to the port officials when the updated Plan was revealed.[175]

The state government is a major funding source, and funds also contribute to technology development. The California Energy Commission provided a USD 8 million grant to support the first phase of a transition to zero-emissions at Total Terminals In international's container terminal at Pier T that is the port's largest terminal, through a Port Advanced Vehicle Electrification Project (PAVE).[176] It is noted that the PAVE Project was the first in the world to demonstrate a heavy-duty, off-road, direct current fast-charging system in a seaport environment.[177] The CARB made a preliminary grant of USD 41 million to the Port of Los Angeles (POLA) to reduce emissions from drayage trucking.[178]

172. Rachel Dovey, "California Mayors Sign Zero Emissions Pact for Ports" (*Next City*, June 15, 2017), https://www.universalcargo.com/mayors-sign-pact-for-zero-emissions-at-ports-of-los-angeles-long-beach/, accessed November 6, 2023.
173. "Clean Air Action Plan Update Factsheet" (*San Pedro Bay Ports-Clean Air Action Plan*, October 2017), https://www.portoflosangeles.org/environment/air-quality/san-pedro-bay-ports-clean-air-action-plan/, accessed November 6, 2023.
174. "Clean Air Action Plan Update Factsheet" (*San Pedro Bay Ports-Clean Air Action Plan*, October 2017), www.cleanairactionplan.org/documents/2017-clean-air-action-plan-update-fact-sheet-10-23-17.pdf/, accessed March 6, 2022.
175. Tony Barboza, "*LA Times*" (Plan Calls for L.A., Long Beach Ports to Go to Zero-Emissions Technology; Cost Could Hit USD 14 billion), www.latimes.com/local/lanow/la-me-ports-clean-air-20170719-story.html, accessed March 6, 2022.
176. *Captain* (Grant Supports Zero-Emission Cargo Handling at Port of Long Beach, June 22, 2018), https://gcaptain.com/grant-supports-zero-emission-cargo-handling-at-port-of-long-beach/, accessed March 6, 2022.
177. *Captain* (Grant Supports Zero-Emission Cargo Handling at Port of Long Beach, June 22, 2018), https://gcaptain.com/grant-supports-zero-emission-cargo-handling-at-port-of-long-beach/, accessed March 6, 2022.
178. *Michael Angell* (Kenworth Part of USD 82 Million Project at Port of Los Angeles for Zero-Emissions Trucking, September 14, 2018) *Freight Waves* (Kenworth Part of USD 82 Million Project at Port of Los Angeles for Zero-Emissions Trucking), www.freightwaves.com/news/port-los-angeles-kenworth-zero-emissions, accessed March 6, 2022.

3.1.4.2 Important Elements for the Plan's Success

3.1.4.2.1 Action and Clear Responsibilities of the Responsible Agencies

The Ports, in particular the POLA, as the directly responsible agencies, have played a central role in the Clean Air Action Plan, gathering financial support and technical guidance from the EPA, the SCAQMD and the CARB.

In 2000, the SCAQMD released a Multiple Air Toxic Exposure Study regarding pollution from ships, trucks and trains in the vicinity of the POLA and POLB and major transportation corridors. This study raised concerns about the impact of emissions from on-road and off-road vehicles' port-related activities. Since then, both Ports have had terminal development plans challenged and delayed due to concerns about the adequacy of environmental mitigation.[179] With the pressure of environmental issues, POLA and POLB positioned themselves to "assure that companies engaged in goods movement pay their fair share of the cost of cleaning up our air and protecting our citizens."[180] Meanwhile, the Ports also "recognized that their ability to accommodate the projected growth in trade would depend upon their ability to address adverse environmental impacts (and, in particular, air quality impacts) that result from such trade."[181] Therefore, POLA and POLB had to act proactively to help the ports reduce their air pollution. First, the Ports urged CARB to make the Clean Air Action Plan a standard that all California ports must meet and encouraged EPA to make it a standard that all ports in the United States must meet.[182] Second, the Ports organized a panel discussion for the drafting process by working with other agencies and stakeholders as well as providing a draft in multi-languages for public comments.[183]

SCAQMD provided significant funding to support the Clean Air Action Plan's first five-year Port requirements.[184] Also, CARB, SCAQMD, and EPA have been deeply involved in the Plan's development. Apart from financial support, CARB, SCAQMD and

179. The Port of Long Beach, "San Pedro Bay Ports: Clean Air Action Plan (Overview)" (*The Port of Los Angeles*, 2006), https://www.portoflosangeles.org/environment/air-quality/san-pedro-bay-ports-clean-air-action-plan/, accessed November 6, 2023.
180. *The Port of Los Angeles* (Statements of the Presidents of the Los Angeles Board of Harbor Commissioners and the Long Beach Board of Harbor Commissioners), https://kentico.portoflosangeles.org/getmedia/1ac86737-3ebd-4279-adc8-b82492753858/1-13-22-regular-meeting-minutes_draft.
181. *The Port of Los Angeles* (Statements of the Presidents of the Los Angeles Board of Harbor Commissioners and the Long Beach Board of Harbor Commissioners), https://kentico.portoflosangeles.org/getmedia/1ac86737-3ebd-4279-adc8-b82492753858/1-13-22-regular-meeting-minutes_draft, at p. 13.
182. *The Port of Los Angeles* (Statements of the Presidents of the Los Angeles Board of Harbor Commissioners and the Long Beach Board of Harbor Commissioners), https://kentico.portoflosangeles.org/getmedia/1ac86737-3ebd-4279-adc8-b82492753858/1-13-22-regular-meeting-minutes_draft, at p. 14.
183. *The Port of Los Angeles* (Statements of the Presidents of the Los Angeles Board of Harbor Commissioners and the Long Beach Board of Harbor Commissioners), https://kentico.portoflosangeles.org/getmedia/1ac86737-3ebd-4279-adc8-b82492753858/1-13-22-regular-meeting-minutes_draft, at p. 15.
184. Regular Meeting Minutes Thursday, January 13, 2022 AT 9:00 a.m., Board of Harbor Commissioners https://kentico.portoflosangeles.org/getmedia/1ac86737-3ebd-4279-adc8-b82492753858/1-13-22-regular-meeting-minutes_draft, accessed November 6, 2023.

EPA helped the Ports to develop procedures by which early actions would be considered when evaluating projects under both the health risk and "fair share" criteria for emissions reduction standards.[185] For example, some standards require tenants of the Ports to follow the most effective equipment/technologies verified by the CARB.

3.1.4.2.2 San Pedro Bay Standards

As part of the Clean Air Action Plan, the Ports, along with an inter-agency Technical Working Group (TWG) comprised of EPA, CARB and the SCAQMD staff, developed the San Pedro Bay Standards to focus on five categories: On-road heavy-duty trucks, ocean-going vessels, cargo handling equipment, harbor craft and railroad locomotives, that are the hotspots of air pollution of port-related activities. The San Pedro Bay Standards consist of two components: reducing health risks and mass reduction of polluting emissions.[186] The Standards are updated regularly to include and reflect new regulations and targets in other requirements. Methods are also developed to evaluate if new port-related projects are consistent with the components of the Standards.[187]

3.1.4.2.3 Public Participation

Good public participation is not only required in the comment period of the plan-development stage but also can be enforced by well-organized lawsuits brought by citizen organizations that help shape and monitor the Clean Air Action Plan at the plan-implementation stage. According to the published comments invited by the Ports, four public meetings "were held, were very well attended, and the Ports received hundreds of written comments in addition to the oral comments received at the meetings."[188] Furthermore, NGOs got involved with the Plan's development with the other agencies. The Natural Resources Defense Council (NRDC) helped the Ports develop the Clean Air Action Plan and its Clean Truck Program (CTP) between 2005 and 2008 with a focus on protecting local communities.[189] The Port of Los Angeles' Board devised a concession agreement to govern the relationship between the POLA and drayage companies under the CTP. The agreement required a company to affix a placard on each truck, with a phone number for reporting concerns, and to submit a plan listing off-street parking locations for each truck, and other requirements, in order

185. Port of Los Angeles "San Pedro Bay Ports" (clean air action plan overview), https://kentico.portoflosangeles.og/getmedia/68ad1b1f-2241-4edb-8bf2-d9621af288b2/2010_caap_update_final.
186. Port of Los Angeles "San Pedro Bay Ports" (clean air action plan overview), https://kentico.portoflosangeles.og/getmedia/68ad1b1f-2241-4edb-8bf2-d9621af288b2/2010_caap_update_final, at p. 32.
187. Port of Los Angeles "San Pedro Bay Ports" (clean air action plan overview), https://www.portoflosangeles.org/environment/air-quality/san-pedro-bay-ports-clean-air-action-plan, at pp. 45-49.
188. https://www.epa.gov/sites/default/files/2021-03/documents/420r21011.pdf, accessed August 8, 2022.
189. Natural Resources Defense Council, Cleaning up Southern California's Air, www.nrdc.org/air/diesel-exhaust/california-air-quality.asp, accessed March 6, 2022.

to ease the increasing traffic congestion and air pollution in the POLA's surrounding area. The agreement also set out penalties for violation, including possible suspension or revocation of the right to provide drayage services.

The American Trucking Association Inc. (ATA), the largest national trade association for the trucking industry,[190] unsuccessfully sued POLA on behalf of the drayage companies in 2009, claiming that the Federal Aviation Administration Authorization Act of 1994 (FAAAA) expressly preempted two of the agreement's provisions, regarding off-street parking plan and display of designated placards on the vehicles.[191] POLA's primary argument focused on motives rather than means regarding environmental concerns.[192] Environmental groups such as the NRDC, Sierra Club and Coalition for Clean Air, Inc. acted as supporters of POLA in this lawsuit.[193] It is notable that the Clean Air Action Plan has obtained assistance from these NGOs during the implementation stage. Besides defending the City of Los Angeles' CTP against legal attack by the trucking industry, NRDC's legal team also "assure[d] that the [CTP] has robust enforcement so that only motor carriers that meet the Port's environmental standards are granted the privilege of doing port business, and that port-serving trucks are well-maintained."[194]

3.1.5 Regulation of Building Industry

California incorporated energy requirements into the State's building code in 1940 to address inefficient use of electricity, heat, cooling and water in buildings that result in air pollution. Many of the buildings in Los Angeles were built before California's Building Energy Efficiency Standards were enacted to eliminate wasteful use of energy. The City's buildings are the second largest source of air pollution and the leading user of energy and water.[195] The energy generated from power plants is used to supply water, heating and cooling, and electricity to homes and buildings. Reducing energy usage decreases the demand for power generation, resulting in less air pollution. To reduce air pollution within Los Angeles, the City has focused on enacting energy and water conservation measures and controlling greenhouse gas emissions to reduce air pollution and climate change mitigation. The City expected to create over 17,000 jobs through its energy efficiency programs by 2020.[196] The Mayor of Los Angeles, Eric Garcetti, introduced a plan to increase energy efficiency eliminating 15% of the City's

190. American Trucking Associations (About), https://www.trucking.org/about-ata, accessed November 6, 2023.
191. *Am Trucking Ass'n v. City of Los Angeles*, 569 US 641 (2013).
192. *Am Trucking Ass'n v. City of Los Angeles*, 569 US 641 (2013), at p. 2098.
193. These groups got involved by sending lawyers to be part of the Respondent team. *Am Trucking Ass'n v. City of Los Angeles*, 569 US 641 (2013), at p. 2098 at p. 2009.
194. *Am Trucking Ass'n v. City of Los Angeles*, 569 US 641 (2013), at p. 2098 at p. 495.
195. "Energy Efficient Buildings" (*Los Angeles*), https://d3n8a8pro7vhmx.cloudfront.net/mayorofla/pages/17003/attachments/original/1428427253/environment-energy-efficient-buildings.pdf?1428427253, accessed March 4, 2022.
196. DeShazo, J.R. et al., "Efficiently Energizing Job Creation in Los Angeles" (*UCLA & LA DWP*, 2014), https://luskin.ucla.edu/publication/efficiently-energizing-job-creation-in-los-angeles, accessed March 8, 2022.

total energy demand, that includes reducing water use per capita by 20% by 2034 and reducing energy use of all buildings by 30% per square foot by 2035.[197] The Mayor also set goals for reducing the importation of water by 50% by 2025, aiming to source 50% of its water locally by 2035.[198]

There are several principal parties with regulatory authority over building energy efficiency, water conservation, and waste disposal practices. The State of California has enacted laws aimed at improving building energy efficiency within the State. The California Energy Commission is the State's primary energy policy and planning agency and has adopted Building Energy Efficiency Standards that aim to reduce building energy consumption.[199] The Commission is responsible for setting the state's energy efficiency standards. The CARB is part of the State's EPA and is dedicated to addressing all aspects of air pollution.[200] It is governed by a board comprised of scientific experts and elected officials representing air pollution concerns from all areas of the state.[201] The CARB implements policies aimed at improving public health and minimizing environmental impacts.[202] Finally, the SCAQMD is the smog-control agency for Southern California, including Los Angeles. All deal with promoting building energy efficiency and reducing air pollution.

The City of Los Angeles, subject to the control of the State, develops its own local ordinances to regulate residential and nonresidential buildings within City limits, *inter alia*. The City Council is the governing legislative body and enacts the relevant ordinances that are subject to approval by the Mayor.[203] The City must comply with State Energy Efficiency Standards but can also adopt its own initiatives and regulations that exceed minimum state standards. Local jurisdictions wishing to enforce local energy standards must submit an application and materials to the California Energy Commission for approval

3.1.5.1 California Energy Code

California's Building Standards Commission enacted the California Energy Code to reduce the state's energy consumption. The Energy Code contains efficiency standards for new and altered homes, as well as for Commercial buildings. Implementation of these standards reduced energy across the state that resulted in cost-saving for building

197. "Energy Efficient Buildings" (*Los Angeles*), https://d3n8a8pro7vhmx.cloudfront.net/mayorofla/pages/17003/attachments/original/1428427253/environment-energy-efficient-buildings.pdf?1428427253, accessed March 4, 2022.
198. Eric Garcetti, "PLAN Transforming Los Angeles" (Los Angeles Office of Mayor), https://d3n8a8pro7vhmx.cloudfront.net/mayorofla/pages/17002/attachments/original/1428470093/pLAn.pdf?1428470093, accessed March 8, 2022.
199. https://www.energy.ca.gov/about/core-responsibility-fact-sheets, accessed August 8, 2022.
200. "CARB Mission and Goals" (*CA Air Resources Board*, March 27, 2012), https.www.carb.ca.gov/html/mission.htm, accessed November 6, 2023.
201. "About Our Board" (*CA Air Resources Board*, August 10, 2015), https://ww2.arb.ca.gov/about, accessed March 8, 2022.
202. *CA Air Resources Board*, https://ww2.arb.ca.gov/, accessed November 6, 2023.
203. "Los Angeles 'City Council'" (General Information and Meetings), https://lacity.gov/government/elected-officials/city-council, accessed November 6, 2023.

owners, encouraged a healthy economy, stabilized the energy market, and protected the environment.[204] In 2015, the Commission voted unanimously to approve updated building efficiency standards designed to cut energy use in residential homes by 28%. These also set a goal of accomplishing zero net energy use for new homes in California by 2020.[205] Energy savings to achieve this goal include high-performance insulation for attics and walls, instantaneous water heaters, high-efficiency lighting, and on-site solar or other renewable generation.[206]

3.1.5.2 California Green Building Standards Code

The California Energy Commission enacted the California Green Building Standards Code, commonly known as "CAL Green" in 2008.[207] CAL Green is part of the CA Building Standards Code and was adopted to improve public health and safety by encouraging energy-efficient buildings. The CARB, the Department of Public Health, the Department of Water Resources, and many other administrative agencies were involved in formulating the code. CAL Green sets mandatory conservation requirements for new and renovated buildings, as well as more stringent optional provisions that allow existing buildings to meet heightened standards. The Green Building Code requires new dwellings to have electric vehicle charging capability and energy-efficient lighting, appliances, and heating and cooling and also must be solar power ready. Plumbing fixtures must reduce water use by at least 20% of the maximum flow rate for the fixture[208] and irrigation systems must have controls like soil moisture meters and rainfall monitors. Every building sold needs to have its own Operation and Maintenance Manual defining green measures such as its water reuse systems and public transportation in the area.[209] In response to feedback from stakeholders, Los Angeles established a Green Building Team comprised of administrators from various city agencies. This team was responsible for holding monthly public meetings to examine proposals, address suggestions for modifications to the code, establish and maintain city staff education, provide a public outreach program, and address any unforeseen issues that could arise.[210]

---

204. *See*: https://www.energy.ca.gov/programs-and-topics/programs/building-energy-efficiency-standards.
205. *NRDC* (New California Building Efficiency Standards Set the Stage for Zero Net Energy Homes by 2020, June 10, 2015), https://www.nrdc.org/bio/meg-waltner/new-california-building-efficiency-standards-set-stage-zero-net-energy-homes-2020, accessed November 6, 2023.
206. *California Public Utilities Commission* (2020 Planning and Information for California Zero Net Energy Homes, 2013), http://www.californiaznehomes.com/#!links-and-resources/c19bx, accessed March 4, 2022.
207. Cal. Code Regs. Tit. 24, Part 11 (2013).
208. California Department of Housing and Community Development "A Guide to the California Green Building Standards Code" (Low-Rise Residential, June 2012), www.hcd.ca.gov/codes/state-housing-law/calgreengulbid.e.
209. California Department of Housing and Community Development, "GUIDE TO The 2016 California Green Building Standards Code—Residential," https://shop.iccsafe.org/media/wysiwyg/material/4571S16-TOC.pdf, accessed November 6, 2023.
210. Los Angeles City Planning (Building a Green Los Angeles', May 2008), http://cityplanning.lacity.org/code_studies/GreenLa/Brochure.pdf, accessed March 4, 2022.

3.1.5.3 Energy Efficiency of Buildings

The Los Angeles Department of Water and Power (LADWP) has several programs to help small businesses that are less likely to be able to upgrade to efficient equipment, conserve energy and minimize their contribution to air pollution because of costs. For example, the LADWP Commercial Lighting Incentive Program helps businesses replace standard lighting fixtures with high-performance lighting.[211] Small businesses receive free energy-efficient lighting assessments, equipment, rebates, and installation services. Additionally, the Small Business Direct Install Program[212] provides a free assessment of commercial buildings to identify energy-saving opportunities and then develops a plan to improve energy efficiency. Each business that participates can receive free lighting upgrades and the option to purchase efficient materials at discounted rates.

The LADWP offers residential property owners and businesses an incentive to buy and install solar power through the Commercial Solar Incentive Program.[213] This program gives customers the opportunity to install solar energy at 30% to 40% of the cost, in addition to available tax credits. Additionally, when the rooftop system generates more power than the building requires, the State provides for net metering—the owner's electricity meter runs backward, and the excess energy supplied to the utility is reflected as a bill credit.[214] This feature was recently discontinued, however because of the inequity of requiring low-income households to pay for the savings by wealthier solar installation owners, and it was replaced by incentives for solar installations by low-income households.[215]

The SCAQMD provides resources on its website to assist homeowners in making choices to minimize air pollution, such as offering information on low-VOC (Volatile Organic Compound) paints, cleaning solvents, home improvement supplies, certified residential water heaters, healthy hearths,[216,217] lawn and garden equipment,[218] and

211. LADWP "CLIP" (How to Save-Small Businesses, December 30, 2016), https://www.ladwp.com/ladwp/faces/wcnav_externalId/c-sm-lighting?_adf.ctrl-state=105k1evolb_4&_afrLoop=289188208978818&_afrWindowMode=0&_afrWindowId=duoesfmas#%40%3F_afrWindowId%3Dduoesfmas%26_afrLoop%3D289188208978818%26_afrWindowMode%3D0%26_adf.ctrl-state%3Dsipc2nb7a_79, accessed March 8, 2022.
212. LADWP (Rebates and Programs-Commercial Direct Install Program), www.ladwp.com/ladwp/faces/ladwp/commercial/c-savemoney/c-sm-rebatesandprograms/c-sm-rp-sbdi?_afrLoop=255929794581651&_afrWindowMode=0&_afrWindow Ibid.=null#%40%3F_afrWindow Ibid.%3Dnull%26_afrLoop%3D255929794581651%26_afrWindowMode%3D0%26_adf.ctrl-state%3Dbl9zeoh6b, accessed March 4, 2022.
213. LA DWP (Solar Incentive Program), https://ladwp.com/ladwp/faces/ladwp/res Ibid.ential/r-gogreen/r-gg-installsolar/r-gg-sip-aboutprogram?adf.ctrl-state=8wbacyoq1_4&_afrLoop=245855266088846, accessed March 4, 2022.
214. LA DWP (Solar Incentive Program), https://www.ladwp.com/ladwp/faces/Search?_adf.ctrl-state=sipc2nb7a_117&_afrLoop=289525825707918, accessed March 8, 2022.
215. *See* Newsletter: Everything you need to know about California's plan to slash solar incentives, https://www.latimes.com/environment/newsletter/2021-12-16/california-plan-to-cut-solar-incentives-boiling-point, accessed November 7, 2023.
216. South Coast AQMD (Program), www.aqmd.gov/home/programs, accessed March 4, 2022.
217. South Coast AQMD (Green Painters Program), www.aqmd.gov/home/programs/community/community-detail?title=green-painter, accessed March 4, 2022.

wood stove and fireplace change-out incentives.[219] Additionally, SCAQMD offers discounts and, in some cases, free fireplace and woodstove updates for income-qualified residents.[220] Wood smoke is a significant source of fine particulate matter and contains toxic air contaminants. Under the program, residents can get a voucher that can be used at a participating retailer to get a discounted price on the purchase and installation of a qualified pollution control device.

In 2014, the Los Angeles Green Building Code was amended to require residential buildings to have cool roofs by using roofing materials that meet threshold values for reflectance and thermal emittance. The Cool Roof Ordinance[221] was passed after the city held a cool roof conference in 2013, at which stakeholders, researchers, and policy makers met to exchange information.[222] During this conference, the benefits of cool roofs, such as reducing smog formation, decreasing air pollution-related illnesses, and energy savings, were explained. After the conference, the City Council unanimously approved a residential cool roof requirement as part of the LA Green Building Code.[223] Cool roofs are constructed with material that reflects sunlight and absorbs less heat, that lowers roof temperatures and consequently, lowers energy use, smog production and ambient air temperature.[224] The CA Energy Commission estimates that on a warm afternoon in Los Angeles, each 1.8°F decrease in the daily maximum temperature lowers peak demand for electric power by approximately 2% to 4%, and each 1 Kelvin (light intensity measurement) decrease reduces smog by 5%.[225] It can also produce significant financial savings.[226] Rebates are available for single and multi-family residential homeowners to install cool roofs.[227]

Replacing dark surfaces with vegetation, as well as with cool roofs, lessens the urban heat island effect,that occurs when dark surfaces absorb solar radiation and radiate it as heat energy, causing reduction of hot air temperatures that speed the formation of smog and increase the temperature in the city, and raise the demand for energy.[228] Lighter surfaces or vegetated surfaces reflect UV radiation and cool the air

---

218. South Coast AQMD (Lawn Equipment), www.aqmd.gov/home/programs/community/community-detail?title=lawn-equipment, accessed March 4, 2022.
219. South Coast AQMD "Incentives & Programs" (Wood Stove & Fireplace Change-Out Incentive Program), www.aqmd.gov/home/programs/community/community-detail?title=wood-device-incentive-program, accessed March 4, 2022.
220. AQMD "Check before You Burn" (Important Information on Buring Wood During Winter, November 2013), www.aqmd.gov/docs/default-source/planning/Wood-Burning-Device/cbybflyer_nov2013.pdf?sfvrsn=0, accessed March 4, 2022.
221. LA, Cal, Ordinance 183149 (July 11, 2014).
222. LA Dep't of Building and Safety, Cool Roofs (What you need to know about LADWP Rebates and Building Code Requirements, March 2015), http://ladbs.org/LADBSWeb/green-bldg.jsf, accessed March 4, 2022.
223. LA Dep't of Building and Safety, Cool Roofs (What you need to know about LADWP Rebates and Building Code Requirements, March 2015), http://ladbs.org/LADBSWeb/green-bldg.jsf, accessed March 4, 2022.
224. https://escholarship.org/uc/item/9484d9wr, assessed August 8, 2022.
225. https://escholarship.org/uc/item/9484d9wr, assessed August 8, 2022.
226. https://escholarship.org/uc/item/9484d9wr, assessed August 8, 2022.
227. LADWP (Cool Roofs What You Need to Know about Rebates and Building Code Requirements, March 2015), www.ladbs.org/docs/default-source/publications/ordinances/cool-roof-fact-sheet-and-faq.pdf?sfvrsn=10, accessed March 4, 2022.
228. Heat Island Effects, https://www.epa.gov/heatislands, accessed November 6, 2023.

temperature through evapotranspiration and shading. Los Angeles has 900 miles of alleyways that line the back of homes and buildings that could benefit from such measures.[229] In response, the City initiated a program to resurface its 900 miles of alleys with porous materials and to create gardens in the alleys.[230]

3.1.5.4 Economic Building Enterprises

As defined in this section, "economic building enterprises" that impact energy and air quality in Los Angeles include commercial and residential building owners, building management companies and individual managers, and architects and engineers. The largest expense of operating a commercial property often is for building energy use, comprising, on average, 30% of building costs.[231] Commercial building owners have a financial interest in conserving energy to lower the building's operation cost and increase profits from rentals or offer lower rents. Both residential and commercial building owners must comply with City regulations, like the Los Angeles Green Buildings Code and the City's Water Use Ordinance. Building owners and homeowners must comply with the ordinances or risk fines, hearings, or even utility service shut-off.[232] Building management companies also have responsibility for assuring the buildings they manage comply with City ordinances. Building management companies also may improve commercial properties to save the building owners money and make the space attractive to tenants. The more energy these buildings can save, the more likely it is that building owners will hire the management company.

In the early 1990s, the City of Los Angeles recognized the need to incorporate energy efficiency into municipal projects but faced significant barriers, including a lack of information and institutional resistance.[233] To overcome these barriers, the City formed a Sustainable Design Task Force to "incorporate environmentally sensitive design features into the city's new construction and remodeling projects." The Task Force was chaired by the City Architect and had a volunteer advisory group comprised of city employees and local experts in design, engineering, waste management, and construction. To put the Task Force's recommendations into action, the City formed the Sustainable Design Implementation Program (SDIP) under the Bureau of Engineering, that was implemented by three designated city employees. SDIP pursues grant funding, provides training and seminars on green buildings for City staff, and incorporates sustainable designs into city projects.[234] Also, the City now requires Energy Star compliant roofing materials to be used on all municipal facilities with new or replaced roofing.[235] Additionally, the City Council adopted the Leadership in Energy

229. Heat Island Effects, https://www.epa.gov/heatislands, accessed November 6, 2023.
230. El Nasser, Haya, USA Today "Cities Cleaning," ("Greening" Urban Alleys), http://environmentla.org/pdf/USA%20Today%20Green%20Alleys.pdf, accessed March 4, 2022.
231. EPA (Energy Efficiency in Nongovernmental Buildings), https://www.epa.gov/statelocalclimate/local/topics/commercial-industrial.html, accessed November 7, 2023.
232. https://www.greeneconome.com/, accessed August 8, 2022.
233. https://www.energy.ca.gov› download, accessed August 8, 2022.
234. https://www.energy.ca.gov› download, accessed August 8, 2022.
235. https://www.energy.ca.gov› download, accessed August 8, 2022.

and Environmental Design (LEED) rating system, and the LEED silver level certification is required for all new LA Department of Public Works construction projects that are 7,500 square feet or larger.

3.1.5.5 Water Conservation Ordinance

Water supply energy consumption has a direct correlation with air pollution.[236] Energy is used in five stages of the water cycle, starting with extracting water from its source and conveying it to storage facilities:Supplying and conveying water from its source is one of the most energy-intensive parts of the water delivery chain;[237] treating the water and transporting it to end users; circulating, pressurizing, and heating or cooling the water;[238] and pumping wastewater out of buildings and into treatment plants all consume a lot of energy. Accordingly, decreasing water usage can dramatically reduce energy consumption and, consequently, lessen air pollution. The Water Conservation Ordinance[239] regulates how and when consumers may use water (e.g., watering lawns).[240] A special response unit within the LADWP enforces compliance with the Ordinance. Repeated failure to comply can result in penalties ranging from a citation letter or a written warning to monetary fines or water service shut-off. To help customers comply with the ordinance, the LADWP provides a water use calculator,[241] along with brochures and information on weather-friendly landscaping.[242]

236. U.S. Dep't Energy ("Report to Congress on the Interdependency of Energy and Water, Chapter III: Supplying Water Requires Energy" p. 25, 2006), https://www.epa.gov/statelocalenergy, accessed November 7, 2023; *Natural Resource Defense Council* ("Energy Down the Drain—The Hidden Costs of California's Water Supply" pp. 1, 7, 2004), https://www.nrdc.org/sites/default/files/edrain.pdf, accessed March 4, 2022.
237. U.S. Dep't Energy, "Report to Congress on the Interdependency of Energy and Water" (Chapter III: Supplying Water Requires Energy, p. 25, 2006), https://energy.sandia.gov/wp-content//gallery/uploads/dlm_uploads/121-RptToCongress-EWwEIAcomments-FINAL.pdf, accessed March 4, 2022.
238. U.S. Dep't Energy, "Report to Congress on the Interdependency of Energy and Water" (Chapter III: Supplying Water Requires Energy, p. 25, 2006), https://energy.sandia.gov/wp-content//gallery/uploads/dlm_uploads/121-RptToCongress-EWwEIAcomments-FINAL.pdf, accessed March 4, 2022.at p. 413.
239. LA, Cal, Ordinance 184248 (April 26, 2016).
240. For example, the ordinance does not allow lawns to be watered between 9 a.m. and 4 p.m. additionally, water cannot be used on hard surfaces like driveways, sidewalks, and parking areas. Excess water from sprinklers is not allowed to flood storm drains or gutters and leaks must not go unattended. LADWP (Ordinances and Codes- Watering Days), https://www.ladwp.com/ladwp/faces/ladwp/aboutus/a-water/a-w-conservation/a-w-c-ordinanceandcodes?_adf.ctrl-state=idvf66865_9&_afrLoop=294019537253321&_afrWindowMode=0&_afrWindowId=1cqaya0ray_26#%40%3F_afrWindowId%3D1cqaya0ray_26%26_afrLoop%3D294019537253321%26_afrWindowMode%3D0%26_adf.ctrl-state%3D1cqaya0ray_54, accessed March 8, 2022.
241. WECalc (Home-Water-Energy-Climate Calculator), www.wecalc.org, accessed December 29, 2016.
242. LADWP (Water Conservation), https://www.ladwp.com/ladwp/faces/ladwp/aboutus/a-water/a-w-conservation?_adf.ctrl-state=dyn4zic9r_50&_afrLoop=181845496192603, accessed March 4, 2022.

3.1.5.6 *Planning and Zoning Code*

Zoning codes are a valuable tool for addressing air pollution concerns because they can require new development to be located so as not to create environmental hazards. Land uses that can cause or contribute to significant air pollution include industrial plants and commercial buildings that deploy fleets of vehicles or trucks. Local planning and zoning boards can also require businesses and fleet vehicles to obtain a permit in order to operate, and this permit can be used to require them to meet criteria to reduce emissions. Included in these criteria can be restrictions on vehicle idling, traffic diversion, and operating hours.[243] Zoning codes can include provisions to expedite development in dense neighborhoods accessible to mass transit stations to reduce the need to drive and to reduce air pollution.[244] In California, cities and counties must adopt comprehensive General Plans that set long-term goals and policies for each community to use as a blueprint of how it will grow. A city adopts a zoning code to put the General Plan into action and establish the basic type and intensity of uses permitted in each land use category. Decisions related to zoning are made by locally elected officials after hearings that are open to the public.[245] The officials also receive input from the public, members of their planning staff, and developers on how to plan future development.

3.1.6 *Regulation of Utility Sector*

3.1.6.1 *Power Plant Equipment Improvement and Emission Standards*

Beginning in March 1956 with the formation of the Joint Research Council on Power Plant Air Pollution Control, the electric utility industry in LAPCD to resolve its power plant pollution problems by improving how pollution control technology, such as sulfur oxide emissions control, the development of two-stage combustion controls to reduce nitrogen oxide emissions, research on plume formation, experimental work on electrostatic precipitators and bag filter houses for particulate removal.[246] A variety of types of emission rules applicable to fuel-burning equipment was adopted by individual air pollution control districts, including the LAPCD, and the Federal Government in the early 1970s. Those emission rules relating to SO_2, NOx, and PM include maximum allowable concentrations of contaminants from smokestacks and standard

243. U.S EPA (Office of Transportation and Air Quality, Compilation of State, County, and Local Anti-idling Regulations, April 2006) pp. 46, 86, https://www.epa.gov/sites/default/files/documents/CompilationofStateIdlingRegulations.pdf, accessed November 6, 2023; Los Angeles Municipal Code Site Plan Review Ordinance Section 16.05E(4), LA, Cal, Planning and Zoning Code § 16.05(E)(4), https://codelibrary.amlegal.com/codes/los_angeles/latest/lapz/0-0-0-13 183, accessed March 9, 2022.
244. http://planning.lacity.org› zoning › new-code tps, assessed August 8, 2022.
245. *LA Department of City Planning* (Commissions & Hearings), http://planning.lacity.org, accessed March 4, 2022.
246. D.E. Bienstock et al., Formation of Oxides of Nitrogen in Pulverized Coal Combustion (1966), 16 Journal of the Air Pollution Control Association 8, 442-445 DOI: 10.1080/00022470.1966.10468498.

conditions for temperature and pressure, the maximum rate at which a contaminant may be produced from a single unit of fuel-burning equipment, and the maximum allowable[247]

3.1.6.2 *Emission Permit System*

The application of emission permit systems to stationary sources can be traced back to the late 1960s and early 1970s. At that time, the California Legislature granted power to county districts to implement permit systems, including Los Angeles County.[248] The LAPCD, that later became the SCAQMD, used its own pollution control permit system as far back as 1947.[249] The LAPCD gave authority to construct or install pollution control equipment if it approved the plans and specifications submitted by the potential emitter and then issued permits to operate the equipment after its construction or installation.[250] The permit system was applied to stationary sources of all industries, including the power plants.

The LAPCD first sought to stop violations by misdemeanor prosecutions. However, if the misdemeanor prosecution was not sufficient to deter a violator, the LAPCD did not hesitate to file injunctive proceedings against the violator and to shut it down if necessary. In August 1970, the injunctive process was used for the first time.[251] In this context, two problems arose regarding the effectiveness of the permit system. First, the emitter often would continue discharging waste into the air as long as the permit remained within the prescribed emission levels. Therefore, review and observance of the emission restrictions on a regular basis was crucial, otherwise, the permit system would be meaningless. Second, the high level of administrative discretion of enforcement was another problem; the administrative agencies have not always acted in the

247. D.E. Bienstock et al., Formation of Oxides of Nitrogen in Pulverized Coal Combustion (1966), 16 Journal of the Air Pollution Control Association 8, 442-445 DOI: 10.1080/00022470.1966.10468498.
248. E.A. Hershman, California Legislation on Air Containment Emissions from Stationary Sources (1970), 58 California Law Review 1474, 170, https://lawcat.berkeley.edu/record/1110366, accessed March 9, 2022 DOI: 10.2307/3479705.
249. R.L. Chass et al., Total Air Pollution Emissions in Los Angeles County (1960), 10 Journal of the Air Pollution Control Association 351, https://www.tandfonline.com/doi/abs/10.1080/00022470.1960.10467943, accessed November 7, 2023 DOI: 10.1080/00022470.1960.10467943.
250. E.A. Hershman, California Legislation on Air Containment Emissions from Stationary Sources (1970), 58 California Law Review 1474, 170, https://www.jstor.org/stable/3479705, accessed November 7, 2023. R.L. Chass et al., Total Air Pollution Emissions in Los Angeles County (1960), 10 Journal of the Air Pollution Control Association 351, http://www.tandfonline.com/doi/pdf/10.1080/00022470.1960.10467943, accessed March 4, 2022, at pp. 1492, 1493 DOI: 10.1080/00022470.1960.10467943.
251. E.A. Hershman, California Legislation on Air Containment Emissions from Stationary Sources (1970), 58 California Law Review 1474, 170, https://lawcat.berkeley.edu/record/1110366, accessed March 9, 2022 DOI: 10.2307/3479705.

   R.L. Chass et al., Total Air Pollution Emissions in Los Angeles County (1960), 10 Journal of the Air Pollution Control Association 351, http://www.tandfonline.com/doi/pdf/10.1080/00022470.1960.10467943, accessed March 4, 2022, at p. 1493 DOI: 10.1080/00022470.1960.10467943.

public interest due to bureaucratic inertia and industry lobbying.[252] As time passed, however, the permit system improved in practice. The SCAQMD has recorded the permit initial application and renewal processes by specifying the permit types,[253] emission standards,[254] and invitations of public participation[255] demonstrating a high degree of administrative oversight and compliance.

3.1.6.3 Cleaning the Sources of Electricity

In order to deal with the pollutants derived from fuel burning, the LAPCD adopted important Rules 62, 62.1 and 62.2 that regulated the sulfur content of fuel burned within the Los Angeles Basin.[256] Under these rules, a blanket prohibition was placed on the use of certain gaseous and liquid fuels during specified periods of the year. Fuel oils containing more than 0.5% sulfur were prohibited together with gaseous fuels containing more than 50 grains of sulfur per 100 cubic feet of gas. This regulation

252. E.A. Hershman, California Legislation on Air Containment Emissions from Stationary Sources (1970), 58 California Law Review 1474, 170. https://lawcat.berkeley.edu/record/1110366, accessed March 9, 2022 DOI: 10.2307/3479705.

    R.L. Chass et al., Total Air Pollution Emissions in Los Angeles County (1960), 10 Journal of the Air Pollution Control Association 351, https://www.tandfonline.com/doi/abs/10.1080/00022470.1960.10467943, accessed November 7, 2023 DOI: 10.1080/00022470.1960.10467943.

253. The SCAQMD has listed the following permit types: Permit to Construct (P/C), Permit to Operate (P/O), Change of Condition, Alternation/Modification, Change of Operator, Plans, Emission Reduction Credits (ERCs) among others. *See* South Coast Air Quality Management District, "Permits," http://www.aqmd.gov/home/permits, accessed June 12, 2016.

254. SCAQMD seeks to assure that the surrounding air will meet with federal and state air quality standards. Furthermore, SCAQMD has broad authority to regulate toxic and hazardous air emissions, and these regulations are enforced in the same manner as those that pertain to ambient air quality standards. These ambient air standards are health-based and apply to the following six air contaminants: sulfur dioxide, lead, ozone, nitrogen dioxide, carbon monoxide, and fine particulate matter. South Coast Air Quality Management District, "Enforcement," https://www.aqmd.gov/nav/about/authority/enforcement, accessed March 31, 2022.

255. The SCAQMD adopted 4 guiding principles and 10 initiatives seeking to assure environmental justice for all in 1997. One of the 2004/2005 Environmental Justice Enhancements was to improve public participation in the permitting decisions. To accomplish this initiative, the SCAQMD established a single location allowing public access to all public notices related to permitting activities. Public notice is required if a facility applies to permit a new or modified emission source located within 1,000 feet from the outer boundary of a school, or if the emission increase from a new or modified facility exceeds certain threshold levels, or if a facility increases the emission of toxic air contaminants that may expose a person to cancer risks above a certain threshold. Public notices are also required for new, renewed, or significantly revised Title V permits, as required by federal law. Federal law mandates the public's right to know about and comment on proposed permit actions regarding major facilities. [South Coast Air Quality Management District], "Permitting Public Notices," www.aqmd.gov/nav/about/public-notices/permitting-public-notices, accessed March 8, 2022.

    Also, an online database called FIND (Facility Information Detail) is available for the public to check facilities' public information. South Coast Air Quality Management District, "Facility Information Detail," https://www.aqmd.gov/nav/FIND/facility-information-detail, accessed March 8, 2022.

256. The Los Angeles Basin, as defined in District rules, encompasses a portion of Los Angeles County containing almost all of the county's population. *See* Los Angeles County Air Pollution Control District, Rules and Regulations, R. 2(g)(1) (1971); U.S. Dept. of Health, Education, and Welfare, Air Pollution Control Field Operations Manual, 24 (1962). Accessed March 31, 1962.

sought to require that power plants, particularly the steam-electric generating plants, reduce their pollution in an effective way.[257] In the twenty-first century, renewable energy has played a crucial role as an electricity source. The California Public Utilities Commission established the California Renewable Portfolio Standard (RPS) in 2002 through SB 1078.[258] The original RPS set a goal for each California utility to obtain 20% of its electricity sales from renewable sources by 2010, while in 2011, the law was strengthened to require all utilities to obtain 33% from renewable energy by 2020.[259]

To supplement this requirement, the electric utility, under the LADWP, matched the state's RPS in 2010[260] and ramped up its own targets to 40% by 2020, that is more stringent than required of it by the California RPS.[261] Through constructing renewable energy projects, buying energy from an existing waste digester project and generating a small amount of renewable energy from landfills, LADWP is nearing the achievement of its RPS goal.[262] Wind power has been the most important renewable energy source in the Los Angeles Department of Water & Power's (LADWP's) portfolio.[263] Re solar energy, in 2011, LADWP launched a pilot program to install small-scale solar PV in homes and businesses in its district. The utility initially capped the program at 10 megawatts (MW) but will eventually scale it up to 150 MW. LADWP also prepared an Integrated Resource Plan as a 20-year framework, to assure that LADWP provides electricity services while fulfilling its clean energy requirements, including investments in energy efficiency and renewable energy.[264]

The Los Angeles County Department of Regional Planning oversees the development of renewable energy in the county's unincorporated areas. The County's 2035 General Plan and, most importantly, its Renewable Energy Ordinance (REO) are the two important tools to guide the future development of renewable energy projects

257. The Los Angeles Basin, as defined in District rules, encompasses a portion of Los Angeles County containing almost all of the county's population. *See* Los Angeles County Air Pollution Control District, Rules and Regulations, R. 2(g)(1) (1971); U.S. Dept. of Health, Education, and Welfare, Air Pollution Control Field Operations Manual, 24 (1962). Accessed March 31, 1962.
258. UCLA, "Energy Conservation Strategies," www.energyatlas.ucla.edu/strategies/, accessed May 2, 2016.
259. Laura Wisland & Barbara Haya, "The Clean Energy Race: How Do California's Public Utilities Measure Up?" (*Union of Concerned Scientists*, July 2012), https://www.jstor.org/stable/resrep00010, accessed November 7, 2023.
260. "LA Met Its Renewable Energy Goal" (*NBC News*, January 13, 2011), www.nbclosangeles.com/news/local/la-met-its-renewable-energy-goal-113494729.html, accessed May 2, 2016.
261. "LA Met Its Renewable Energy Goal" (*NBC News*, January 13, 2011), www.nbclosangeles.com/news/local/la-met-its-renewable-energy-goal-113494729.html, accessed May 2, 2016, at p. 139.
262. A.E. Carlson, Implementing Greenhouse Gas Emissions Caps: A Case Study of the Los Angeles Department of Water and Power (2008), 55 UCLA Law Review 1479, 1493.
263. In 2012-2014, wind had taken about 12%-14% of the overall energy portfolio, that accounts about 47% of the utility's renewable energy.
264. This Plan was expanded to the Strategic Long-Term Resource Plan. *See* Los Angeles Department of Water and Power, "Strategic Long-Term Resource Plan," https://www.ladwp.com/ladwp/faces/ladwp/aboutus/a-power/a-p-integratedresourceplanning?_afrloop=461769522079226&_afrwindowmode=0&_afrwindowid=null#%40%3f_afrwindowid%3dnull%26_afrloop%3d461769522079226%26_afrwindowmode%3d0%26_adf.ctrl-state%3d275g2r6nm_29, accessed April 14, 2022.

within Los Angeles County.[265] The Los Angeles County REO is a countywide ordinance that amends Title 22 (Planning and Zoning) of the County Code to provide a set of definitions, procedures and standards for review and permitting of solar and wind energy projects. These include solar and wind projects generating energy on-site (small-scale) or off-site (utility-scale) use as well as temporary meteorological towers.[266] The REO helps the State of California accomplish its established goals for meeting energy demand using renewable resources while minimizing impacts on the environment. Furthermore, the REO is designed to encourage distributed generation by facilitating the development of solar and wind energy projects that generate energy for on-site use as well as those that are structure-mounted, such as on rooftops or over parking lots.

3.1.7 Regulation of Oil Refineries and Gas Stations

The petroleum industry in Los Angeles County accounted for over 8% of the total refining capacity of the United States and was the second-largest oil producer in the country in the 1950s.[267] The Los Angeles area contained what was to be one of the important providers and marketers of crude oil, crude refining and its products.[268] With this production capacity, the industry has contributed to the smog problem in Los Angeles because the combustion of liquid and gaseous fuels in boilers, heaters, and other process equipment from petroleum refining and chemical processing operations are a major source of aerosols, NOx, sulfur dioxide emissions and hydrocarbons.[269] In addition, fuel evaporation occurs in the oil refineries and related chemical companies, and during the utilization of fuel storage and transfer at gas stations.

In particular, the SCAQMD developed a series of rules to regulate oil refineries to reduce air pollutants throughout their operation processes, including production, storage and transportation. For example, about one-fifth of all Carbon monoxide emitted into the Los Angeles atmosphere was discharged with the flue gases from local refineries' catalytic cracking regenerators in the 1950s. In order to tackle this problem, the LAPCD developed Rule 54 that regulated the emissions generated from the process and thus got highly efficient dust control equipment installed for each of the local catalytic cracking units. During the late 1970s to early 1990s, SCAQMD adopted

265. This Plan was expanded to the Strategic Long-Term Resource Plan. *See* Los Angeles Department of Water and Power, "Strategic Long-Term Resource Plan," https://www.ladwp.com/ladwp/faces/ladwp/aboutus/a-power/a-p-integratedresourceplanning?_afrloop=461769522079226&_afrwindowmode=0&_afrwindowid=null#%40%3f_afrwindowid%3dnull%26_afrloop%3d461769522079226%26_afrwindowmode%3d0%26_adf.ctrl-state%3d275g2r6nm_29, accessed April 14, 2022.
266. Los Angeles County Department of Regional Planning, "Renewable Energy," https://case.planning.lacounty.gov/energy, accessed November 7, 2023.
267. C.V. Kanter & I.S. Deckert, Control of Air Pollution from Oil Refineries in Los Angeles County (1955), 4 Air Repair, 4, 197-212.
268. California Energy Commission, "California's Oil Refineries," www.energy.ca.gov/almanac/petroleum_data/refineries.html, accessed March 4, 2022.
269. *See*: https://spectrumnews1.com/ca/la-west/environment/2021/11/06/southern-california-enacts-new-smog-rules-on-refineries.

environmental regulations for petroleum refining activities. The rules ranged from regulating production processes to requirements for equipment in refinery plants, and some of those rules had been consistently increasing in stringency.[270] Data showed that the refinery plants on the South Coast of California, including Los Angeles, had more stringent environmental regulations than any other refinery area in the U.S., and increases in stringency of the regulations induced more investment in pollution abatement control expenditures.[271] Furthermore, stringent regulations and high investment in abatement activity on the South Coast led to increases in productivity of oil refineries in Los Angeles.[272] The LAPCD also addressed fuel evaporation in gas stations in the 1950s.[273] Nowadays, all gas station fuel nozzles must be certified to capture 95 % of fumes that would otherwise have been released into the atmosphere.[274] Furthermore, regulations were adopted that reduced by over 70 % the smog-forming emissions from portable gas cans in 1999.[275] Smog sources were further regulated by cutting smog-forming emissions and VOCs from an estimated 2,500 common household products made from petroleum, ranging from nail polish removers to glass cleaners.[276]

The oil refinery industry and the SCAQMD have had very interesting interactions in the air pollution management process. It is rare to find any strong opposition from industry when the local air quality agency proposes regulation of it. But there is a gaming aspect to environmental regulation between the industry and SCAQMD, by which refinery companies may attempt to preempt regulators from choosing a technology standard by introducing less effective and less costly new abatement technologies to the regulators for adoption.[277] This practice may be used by a company to (1) allegedly reduce the uncertainty of future regulations, or (2) impose costs on either

270. Eli Berman & Linda T.M. Bui, "Environmental Regulation and Productivity: Evidence from Oil Refineries" (May 1999), http://econweb.ucsd.edu/~elib/prod618a.pdf, accessed March 4, 2022.
271. Eli Berman & Linda T.M. Bui, "Environmental Regulation and Productivity: Evidence from Oil Refineries" (May 1999), http://econweb.ucsd.edu/~elib/prod618a.pdf, accessed March 4, 2022 at p. 300.
272. Eli Berman & Linda T.M. Bui, "Environmental Regulation and Productivity: Evidence from Oil Refineries" (May 1999), http://econweb.ucsd.edu/~elib/prod618a.pdf, accessed March 4, 2022 at p. 300.
273. Los Angeles County, "The Southland's War on Smog: Fifty Years of Progress Towards Clean Air" (May 1997), http://milesfinney.net/334/articles/la_history.htm, accessed March 8, 2022.
274. Los Angeles County, "The Southland's War on Smog: Fifty Years of Progress Towards Clean Air" (May 1997), https://searchworks.stanford.edu/view/3520731, accessed November 7, 2023.
275. California Air Resources Board, "Key Events in History of Air Quality in California" (*CA. Gov*, February 6, 2012), www.agriculturedefensecoalition.org/sites/default/files/file/new_mexico_198/198E_1_2012_CA_ARB_Key_Events_in_the_History_of_Air_Quality_in_California_Website_February_6_2012.pdf, accessed March 8, 2022.
276. California Air Resources Board, "Key Events in History of Air Quality in California" (*CA. Gov*, February 6, 2012), www.agriculturedefensecoalition.org/sites/default/files/file/new_mexico_198/198E_1_2012_CA_ARB_Key_Events_in_the_History_of_Air_Quality_in_California_Website_February_6_2012.pdf, accessed March 8, 2022.
277. California Air Resources Board, "Key Events in History of Air Quality in California" (*CA. Gov*, February 6, 2012), www.agriculturedefensecoalition.org/sites/default/files/file/new_mexico_198/198E_1_2012_CA_ARB_Key_Events_in_the_History_of_Air_Quality_in_California_Website_February_6_2012.pdf, accessed March 8, 2022, at p. 300.

existing or potential local competitors.[278] This situation also applies to regulated companies competing in a local market where all of their competitors must meet the same environmental regulations.[279]

3.1.8 Public-Private Partnerships

3.1.8.1 Joint Research Council on Power Plant Air Pollution Control

In 1956, the Joint Research Council on Power Plant Air Pollution Control was organized by the Southern California Edison Company, the LADWP, and the Air Pollution Control District. The municipal electric utilities of Glendale, Burbank, and Pasadena joined the Council immediately upon its organization, and not long after that, the Air Pollution Control Districts of the adjacent Counties of Orange, San Bernardino, and Riverside became associate members of the Council.[280] The Council's objective was "to arrive at a better understanding of the problem and to develop a program to promote progress in the development of further corrective measures of control of air pollution from fuel burning utility power plants in the Los Angeles Basin through cooperative efforts in the development and interpretation of data and free interchange of information related to air pollution control equipment; and to keep the membership advised of its activities and progress."[281]

The electric utility companies played a crucial role in this cooperation by initiating different types of research in the "relatively unstudied field of power plant air pollution control" in cooperation with the LAPCD.[282] The Southern California Edison Company, together with the Joint Research Council and the Babcock and Vilcox Company had done some experimental work called "two-stage combustion" for five years, and that eventually led to the development of burner and equipment modifications on one type of power plant boiler design that effectively reduced the average

278. California Air Resources Board, "Key Events in History of Air Quality in California" (*CA. Gov*, February 6, 2012), www.agriculturedefensecoalition.org/sites/default/files/file/new_mexico_198/198E_1_2012_CA_ARB_Key_Events_in_the_History_of_Air_Quality_in_California_Website_February_6_2012.pdf, accessed March 8, 2022, at pp. 1, 8.
279. California Air Resources Board, "Key Events in History of Air Quality in California" (*CA. Gov*, February 6, 2012), www.agriculturedefensecoalition.org/sites/default/files/file/new_mexico_198/198E_1_2012_CA_ARB_Key_Events_in_the_History_of_Air_Quality_in_California_Website_February_6_2012.pdf, accessed March 8, 2022, at p. 18.
280. California Air Resources Board, "Community Air Protection Program Framework: Concept Paper" (February 7, 2018), https://ww2.arb.ca.gov/sites/default/files/2020-05/capp_concept_paper_february_2018_acc.pdf, accessed March 4, 2022 OR California Air Resources Board (n 307), at p. 52.
281. California Air Resources Board, "Community Air Protection Program Framework: Concept Paper" (February 7, 2018), https://ww2.arb.ca.gov/sites/default/files/2020-05/capp_concept_paper_february_2018_acc.pdf, accessed March 4, 2022 OR California Air Resources Board (n 307), at p. 52.
282. R.L. Chass & R.E. George, Contaminant Emissions from the Combustion of Fuels (1960), 10 National Institutes of Health 34-43, https://www.tandfonline.com/doi/pdf/10.1080/00022470.1960.10467897, accessed November 7, 2023 DOI: 10.1080/00022470.1960.10467897.

production of nitrogen oxides by about 40% at full load operation when either oil or natural gas was used as a fuel.[283]

3.1.8.2 Urban Forestry Projects

Los Angeles has created a public-private partnership with local nonprofit organizations, community groups, residents, and businesses called "City Plants."[284] City Plants is a hybrid organization under both the LADWP and a nonprofit group called Community Partners.[285] This partnership is the consolidation of former municipal programs enacted to promote energy efficiency through tree planting.[286] Through City Plants, trees are planted in parks and public locations and free trees are available to homeowners and businesses.[287] The United States Department of Agriculture Pacific Southwest Research Station Center for Urban Forest Researchestimates that energy savings over the 35-year planting period of trees are estimated to be USD 75-USD 117 million; the air quality improvement benefit is estimated to be USD 53-USD 83 million, and the carbon dioxide reduction is expected to be USD 5.1-USD 8.5 million.[288] In addition, Cool California, a partnership between a nonprofit organization called Next10, State Agencies like the EPA, CARB, the Energy Commission, and Universities, that provides the public with information and tools to save money and reduce their environmental impact, including strategies for planting cool vegetation and building efficiency. One of the initiatives the partnership provides educates about the shading of parking areas to keep cars cool and reduce the air temperature. Planting vegetation in parking lots is promoted to lower parking lot temperatures that reduces smog-forming emissions from parked cars.[289] Decreasing the temperature of parked cars also minimizes gasoline evaporation that lessens the release of air pollutants.

283. R.L. Chass & R.E. George, Contaminant Emissions from the Combustion of Fuels (1960), 10 National Institutes of Health 34-43, at p. 312 https://www.tandfonline.com/doi/pdf/10.1080/00022470.1960.10467897, accessed November 7, 2023 DOI: 10.1080/00022470.1960.10467897.
284. *LADWP* "City Plants" (About Us), https://www.cityplants.org/our-story/, accessed March 8, 2022.
285. Community Partners, "Changes thrives here," https://communitypartners.org/, accessed November 8, 2023.
286. Community Partners, "Changes thrives here," https://communitypartners.org/, accessed November 8, 2023.
287. *LADWP*) (Our Free Tree Programs), https://www.cityplants.org/our-programs/, accessed November 7, 2023.
288. *USDA* (Los Angeles 1 Million Trees Canopy Cover Assessment, January 2008), https://www.sciencedirect.com/science/article/pii/S0169204610001982, accessed November 8, 2023.
289. The Benefits of One Million Trees (Million Tree Summary), https://www.fs.usda.gov/psw/topics/urban_forestry/products/psw_cufr666_MillionTreeSummary.pdf#:~:text=%E2%80%A2%20The%20leaves%20of%20trees%20intercept%20rainfall%2C%20reducing,leaves%2C%20branches%2C%20and%20roots%2C%20trees%20fight%20global%20warming, accessed November 8, 2023.

3.1.8.3 *Partnership Between Government and Organizations-Green Business Certification*

Los Angeleslso offers businesses the opportunity to participate in voluntary initiatives aimed at decreasing air pollution through energy efficiency. The Los Angeles Environmental Affairs Department (EAD) has partnered with Green Seal, a nonprofit organization, to stimulate the formation of green businesses.[290] Through this partnership, EAD created the LA Green Business Certification Program that gives consumers the opportunity to know which businesses have implemented "green" practices and provides businesses with an incentive to use environmentally friendly policies. A certified green business gets access to a green resource guide with instructions on how to increase efficiency. To encourage businesses to participate, the Green Seal programs allows businesses to post a "green business" certificate in their establishments and provides promotional materials, while also providing listing on the city's green businesses website.

The Green Business Certification Program also offers certificates for Green Lodging (the hospitality industry), Green Businesses (restaurants, retail stores, offices, auto-repair shops), and Green Arts (theaters, concert halls, and playhouses). To obtain certification, businesses in the program must use energy-efficient insulation, heating and cooling systems, lighting, and appliances.

3.1.8.4 *City Energy Project*

The Los Angeles City Energy Project is a collaboration between the City and two NGOs: the Natural Resources Defense Council and the Institute for Market Transformation.[291] Together, the parties or actors have developed a set of policies and programs tailored to Los Angeles that will improve the energy efficiency of buildings. The project provides information about building energy use to help owners and managers reduce waste, while also aligning financial incentives for energy efficiency. This collaborative group seeks to assure building functions optimally by encouraging leadership from major stakeholders.[292]

The City Energy Project focuses on large buildings in both the public and private sectors and provides financing building owners with capital to invest in energy efficiency. Building management in companies strongly supports the project[293] in that it allows them to be engaged in energy-saving measures. The project frees up money

290. Los Angeles Green Business Citification Program, https://www.discoverlosangeles.com/things-to-do/los-angeles-green-business-certification-program, accessed November 8, 2023.
291. The Institute for Market Transformation is a nonprofit organization that identifies challenges preventing energy markets from achieving energy efficiency and proposes research, programs and policies to increase investment in energy efficiency and sustainability, "The Institute for Market Transformation about," www.imt.org/about/, accessed March 4, 2022.
292. City Energy Project (About), accessed March 4, 2022.
293. City Energy, About the City Energy Project, https://www.cityenergyproject.org/about-the-city-energy-project/, acceced November 8, 2023.

previously spent by utilities for energy efficiency and also helps to grow building efficiency innovation and create new jobs among various skill levels.

3.1.8.5 Energy Efficiency and Solar Incentive Programs

The LADWP has several programs to help small businesses that are less likely to be able to upgrade to efficient equipment, conserve energy and minimize their contribution to air pollution because of costs. For example, the LADWP Commercial Lighting Incentive Program helps businesses replace standard lighting fixtures with high-performance lighting.[294] Small businesses receive free energy-efficient lighting assessments, equipment, rebates, and installation services. Additionally, the Small Business Direct Install Program[295] provides a free assessment of commercial buildings to identify energy-saving opportunities and then develops a plan to improve energy efficiency. Each business that participates can receive free lighting upgrades and the option to purchase efficient materials at discounted rates.

The LADWP offers residential property owners and businesses an incentive to buy and install solar power through the Commercial Solar Incentive Program.[296] This program gives customers the opportunity to install solar energy at 30% to 40% of the cost, in addition to available tax credits. Additionally, when the rooftop system generates more power than the building requires, the State provides for net metering—the owner's electricity meter runs backward, and the excess energy supplied to the utility is reflected as a bill credit.[297] This feature was recently discontinued, however because of the inequity of requiring low-income households to pay for the savings by wealthier solar installation owners, and it was replaced by incentives for solar installations by low-income households.[298]

Finally, the SCAQMD provides resources on its website to assist homeowners in making choices to minimize air pollution, such as offering information on low-VOC paints, cleaning solvents, home improvement supplies, certified residential water

294. *LADWP* "CLIP" (How to Save-Small Businesses, December 30, 2016), https://www.ladwp.com/ladwp/faces/wcnav_externalId/c-sm-lighting?_adf.ctrl-state=105k1evolb_4&_afrLoop=289188208978818&_afrWindowMode=0&_afrWindowId=duoesfmas#%40%3F_afrWindowId%3Dduoesfmas%26_afrLoop%3D289188208978818%26_afrWindowMode%3D0%26_adf.ctrl-state%3Dsipc2nb7a_79, accessed March 8, 2022.
295. *LADWP* (Rebates and Programs- Commercial Direct Install Program), www.ladwp.com/ladwp/faces/ladwp/commercial/c-savemoney/c-sm-rebatesandprograms/c-sm-rp-sbdi?_afrLoop=255929794581651&_afrWindowMode=0&_afrWindow Ibid.=null#%40%3F_afrWindow Ibid.%3Dnull%26_afrLoop%3D255929794581651%26_afrWindowMode%3D0%26_adf.ctrl-state%3Dbl9zeoh6b, accessed March 4, 2022.
296. *LADWP* (Solar Incentive Program), https://ladwp.com/ladwp/faces/ladwp/res Ibid.ential/r-gogreen/r-gg-installsolar/r-gg-sip-aboutprogram?_adf.ctrl-state=8wbacyoq1_4&_afrLoop=245855266088846, accessed March 4, 2022.
297. *LADWP* (Solar Incentive Program), https://www.ladwp.com/ladwp/faces/Search?_adf.ctrl-state=sipc2nb7a_117&_afrLoop=289525825707918, accessed March 8, 2022.
298. *LADWP* (Solar Incentive Program), https://ladwp.com/ladwp/faces/ladwp/res Ibid.ential/r-gogreen/r-gg-installsolar/r-gg-sip-aboutprogram?_adf.ctrl-state=8wbacyoq1_4&_afrLoop=245855266088846, accessed March 4, 2022.

heaters, healthy hearths,[299,300] lawn and garden equipment,[301] and wood stove and fireplace change-out incentives.[302] Additionally, SCAQMD offers discounts and, in some cases, free fireplace and woodstove updates for income-qualified residents.[303] Wood smoke is a significant source of fine particulate matter and contains toxic air contaminants. Under the program, residents can get a voucher that can be used at a participating retailer to get a discounted price on the purchase and installation of a qualified pollution control device.

3.1.9 *Market-Based Regulations and Policies*

3.1.9.1 *Pollution Trading*

In order to explore more incentive methods to reduce air pollutants, the SCAQMD approved the first pollution trading program in the United States in 1993, known as Rule 1610.[304] Rule 1610 allowed stationary source polluters (such as factories and refineries) to avoid installing expensive pollution control equipment if they purchased pollution credits generated by destroying old, high-polluting cars.[305] It was postulated that an equal or greater amount of pollution could be reduced at a much lower cost by purchasing and destroying old cars than by forcing stationary sources to install expensive pollution control equipment; thus began the market-based approach to incentivize the stationary source polluters to take action.

As the centerpiece of the SCAQMD's pollution trading strategy, the Regional Clean Air Incentives Market (RECLAIM) replaced many of SCAQMD's technology-based regulations aimed at reducing emissions of SOx and NOx. RECLAIM mandated annual emission reductions for industry but provided them the flexibility to achieve that goal with three options: (1) they could use all of their credits and pollute up to the level the credits allow; (2) they could reduce their pollution and sell the excess credits

299. South Coast AQMD Program, www.aqmd.gov/home/programs, accessed March 4, 2022.
300. South Coast AQMD (Green Painters Program), www.aqmd.gov/home/programs/community/community-detail?title = green-painter, accessed March 4, 2022.
301. South Coast AQMD (Lawn Equipment), www.aqmd.gov/home/programs/community/community-detail?title = lawn-equipment, accessed March 4, 2022.
302. South Coast AQMD "Incentives & Programs" (Wood Stove & Fireplace Change-Out Incentive Program), www.aqmd.gov/home/programs/community/community-detail?title = wood-device-incentive-program, accessed March 4, 2022.
303. South Coast AQMD "Check before You Burn" (Important Information on Buring Wood During Winter, November 2013), www.aqmd.gov/docs/default-source/planning/Wood-Burning-Device/cbybflyer_nov2013.pdf?sfvrsn = 0, accessed March 4, 2022.
304. Food & Water Watch, "Pollution Trading: Cashing Out Our Clean Air and Water" (*Food and Water Watch,* December 2012), https://foodandwaterwatch.org/wp-content/uploads/2021/03/pollution_trading_ib_dec_2012.pdf, accessed March 8, 2022.
305. R.T. Drury et al., Pollution Trading and Environmental Injustice: Los Angeles' Failed Experiment in Air Quality Policy (1999), 9 Duke Environmental Law & Policy 232-289, 246, http://scholarship.law.duke.edu/cgi/viewcontent.cgi?article = 1177&context = delpf, accessed March 4, 2022.

to other facilities; or (3) they could offset their emissions relative to their initial endowment of credits by buying credits from other facilities.[306]

The Los Angeles experiment with pollution trading became a test case for federal pollution trading policy concerning urban smog, and later EPA tried to promote Los Angeles's emission trading experience to other states.[307] Some scholars pointed out that the emissions trading program had not effectively reduced emissions and has not promoted technology innovation or public participation, although it had succeeded in saving money for industry. What's more, the emission trading program had created hotspots of air pollutants by further concentrating the area's pollution in lower-income communities and had given some industries a "free rider" from otherwise obligatory emissions reduction schedules.[308] That being said, this market-based approach was postulated to be a low-cost, innovative and flexible incentive program to invite businesses to reduce net emissions and take advantage of new technologies.

3.1.9.2 Vehicle Labeling Requirements

The CARB led the trend in mandating environmental information labels on new vehicles by developing a Smog Index Label in 1990 that allowed consumers to compare different car models based on smog emissions. The Smog Index Label was amended in 2005 by AB 1229 to include global warming emissions and was eventually largely folded into a federal labeling program, the Fuel Economy and Environment Label, developed by the U.S. EPA and the U.S. Department of Transportation. The Fuel Economy and Environment Label includes data on how many miles per gallon a vehicle can travel, as well as a smog, fuel economy, and greenhouse gas rating.[309] Furthermore, using information supplied on a manufacturer's Fuel Economy and Environment Label, the CARB has developed a very comprehensive and user-friendly website through which consumers can brow se, search, and compare vehicles based on their environmental performance.[310] Empowering consumers to make smart, less-polluting choices when purchasing a new vehicle is an important part of reducing mobile-based air pollution.

306. R.T. Drury et al., Pollution Trading and Environmental Injustice: Los Angeles' Failed Experiment in Air Quality Policy (1999), 9 Duke Environmental Law & Policy 232-289, 246, http://scholarship.law.duke.edu/cgi/viewcontent.cgi?article=1177&context=delpf, accessed March 4, 2022.
307. R.T. Drury et al., Pollution Trading and Environmental Injustice: Los Angeles' Failed Experiment in Air Quality Policy (1999), 9 Duke Environmental Law & Policy 232-289, 246, http://scholarship.law.duke.edu/cgi/viewcontent.cgi?article=1177&context=delpf, accessed March 4, 2022.
308. R.T. Drury et al., Pollution Trading and Environmental Injustice: Los Angeles' Failed Experiment in Air Quality Policy (1999), 9 Duke Environmental Law & Policy 232-289, 246, http://scholarship.law.duke.edu/cgi/viewcontent.cgi?article=1177&context=delpf, accessed March 4, 2022.
309. California Air Resources Board, "Environmental Performance Label for Medium-Duty Vehicles," https://ww2.arb.ca.gov/sites/default/files/2022-04/Final_EPL_Specs_a2021.pdf, accessed November, 2023.
310. California Air Resources Board, "Drive Clean: A Buying Guide for Clean and Efficient Vehicles," https://driveclean.ca.gov/, accessed March 8, 2022.

3.1.9.3 Rebate Program

Businesses and residents are eligible for rebates under the LADWP's Outdoor Lighting Program that provides discounted energy-efficient outdoor lighting. There are additional free rebates available for efficient refrigeration equipment such as ice machines, refrigerator doors, and vending machine controllers. The rebates offered are generous and can cover the full cost of certain replacements. The City also provides free low-flow showerheads and faucet aerators at fifteen locations in the city. Cash rebates for water-efficient appliances are also available.[311]

3.1.10 Voluntary Energy Efficiency Programs

3.1.10.1 Energy Star

Energy Star is an Energy program supervised by the EPA that was created under the authority of the CAA[312] to help citizens and businesses achieve energy efficiency.[313] It rates efficiency practices and permits satisfactory performers to display an Energy Star label. Energy Star standards have a wide range of applications, including for energy-efficient consumer products like light bulbs and appliances. Most relevant to this analysis are the standards for buildings. Energy Star standards exist for new and existing residential, commercial, and industrial buildings. The program evaluates the energy used by a building per square foot and classifies the building based on a spectrum of ratings from most to least use of energy. Buildings in the top 25 % of similar facilities nationwide are eligible to earn the Energy Star label.[314] For businesses, the ability to display the Energy Star Label is a substantial incentive for improving performance. Also, the ability to actively measure and track energy use is crucial in helping building owners set goals and create action plans for reducing energy use.[315]

3.1.10.2 Leadership in Energy and Environmental Design

The United States Green Building Council's LEED certification is a third-party verification rating system that awards a LEED label for buildings in compliance with its

311. *LADWP* (Free Water Conservation Items), www.ladwp.com/ladwp/faces/ladwp/residential/r-savemoney/r-sm-rebatesandprograms/r-sm-rp-freeconservationitems;jsessionIbid.=JMHWW5CBzZPlnFWpyxP8DfnPVpZynv0jG0ZhcCPG6mwhG2yhWWtV!-1916727289?_afrLoop=412129472752471&_afrWindowMode=0&_afrWindowIbid.=Uy0LuTn1#%40%3F_afrWindowIbid.%3DUy0LuTn1%26_afrLoop%3D412129472752471%26_afrWindowMode%3D0%26_adf.ctrl-state%3D119c3bz77n_4, accessed February 26, 2023.
312. Clean Air Act Section 103(g), 42 U.S.C. § 7403.
313. "Energy Star" (About Energy Star), https://www.energystar.gov/about, accessed November 8, 2023.
314. "Energy Star" (About Energy Star), https://www.energystar.gov/about, accessed November 8, 2023.
315. *Nat'l Institute for Standards and Technology* (What is Energy Star presentation), www.nist.gov/iaao/upload/EnergyStar.pdf, accessed March 4, 2022.

rigorous standards. The LEED program provides a method of incentivizing, standardizing and oversight for building efficiency.[316] Architects, engineers, designers, developers, and project manufacturers created LEED to measure buildings' environmental performance.[317] LEED has rating systems for new construction and existing buildings. A building can achieve certification based on a system that provides points reflecting the implementation of specified green building practices that accrue points on a checklist; projects meeting a minimum number of points are LEED Certified[318] as meeting specified standards for obtaining ratings from bronze to silver and platinum, corresponding with the number of points earned.[319]

3.1.10.3 Financial Incentives of the Clean Vehicle Rebate Program

One unique example of an interaction between regulatory authorities and nonprofit organizations is the CARB's Clean Vehicle Rebate Program. While it is a program promulgated by the state of California, it is administered by the Center for Sustainable Energy, a nonprofit organization that manages energy projects and coordinates with various stakeholders, including industry, utilities, communities, and regulators.[320] Under the Clean Vehicle Rebate Program, consumers can receive up to USD 5,000 or the purchase or lease of certain new zero-emission and plug-in hybrid vehicles. Apart from a few minor restrictions and requirements, such as that purchasers must be over 18 years of age and must retain ownership of the vehicle for at least 30 months after purchase or lease, the program's only major restriction is that rebates are available only for as long as there is funding, that is approved each year by the CARB through public input and is part of the CARB's annual appropriations in the state budget.[321] Consumers can browse qualifying vehicles on the Center for Sustainable Energy's website, and the application is very easily submitted online. Making the process easy and accessible to consumers is helpful in encouraging them to purchase less-polluting cars.[322]

316. Energy Star(*Green Buildings and Energy Star*), www.energystar.gov/buildings/about-us/how-can-we-help-you/energy-star-action/green-buildings-and-energy-star, accessed March 4, 2022.
317. *Institute for Environmental Entrepreneurship* (Sustainable Industry Sector Retrospectives at 1), https://enviroinstitute.org/wp-content/uploads/2012/09/SI-Retrospective-LEED-IEE-final.pdf, accessed November 8, 2023.
318. U.S. Green Building Council (Guide to LEED Certification), https://www.usgbc.org/tools/leed-certification/volume#introduction, accessed March 8, 2022.
319. U.S. Green Building Council "LEED Credits, Prerequisites and Points" (How are They Different?) (March 6, 2017, https://www.usgbc.org/articles/whats-difference-between-leed-credit-leed-prerequisite-and-leed-point, accessed March 4, 2022.
320. Center for Sustainable Energy, "About Us," https://energycenter.org/about-us, accessed March 4, 2022.
321. California Air Resources Board, "Implementation Manual for the FY 2014-15 Clean Vehicle Rebate Program (CVRP)" (December 2014), https://energycenter.org/sites/default/files/docs/nav/transportation/cvrp/documents/CVRP-Implementation-Manual.pdf, accessed November 8, 2023.
322. Center for Sustainable Energy, "Clean Vehicle Rebate Project," https://energycenter.org/clean-vehicle-rebate-project, accessed March 9, 2022.

3.1.10.4 *Nonfinancial Incentives of the Clean Vehicle Rebate Program*

This program grants low and zero-emitting vehicles the right to use carpool and high-occupancy vehicle lanes that can in many cases significantly reduce travel time for freeway commuters. Keeping in line with California's effort to continue reducing air pollution over time, the program no longer grants such privileges to hybrid-electric vehicles in order to encourage purchases of fully electric vehicles and cars that run on hydrogen or compressed natural gas.[323] For an area with a very large amount of daily vehicle traffic, such as Southern California and particularly Los Angeles County, such a benefit could serve as a sizable incentive to purchase qualifying vehicles. However, the program does not issue an unlimited number of decals.[324] As with financial programs, these incentives are not mandates—consumers are not required to take any particular action—but by granting consumers benefits for the purchase of specified "green" vehicles, regulators can increase the sales of such cars.[325] The manufacturers of qualifying vehicles have largely been supportive of the program. When the State came close to reaching the limit of existing decals in mid-2015, the legislature introduced a bill, that was eventually passed, to increase the number of available decals from 75,000 to 85,000.[326] Chevrolet, that manufactures the Chevy Volt, a hybrid-electric car that then qualified for the decals, supported the bill due to the strong incentive it provided for consumers to purchase hybrid and electric vehicles.[327] However, the bill was opposed by municipal authorities in the San Francisco Bay Area, where, according to the Metropolitan Transportation Commission, traffic congestion had increased substantially over the years and allowing single-occupant vehicles to drive in carpool lanes meant to decrease traffic was only exacerbating the problem.[328]

3.1.11 *Governmental Environmental Education*

In addition to the above-mentioned regulatory measures, the local governments play an important role in educating the general public about the air pollution problems. Without adequate public knowledge of the causes of any environmental problem—here the smog problem—it is difficult for the government to implement regulatory measures. Therefore, the first and foremost way to empower the public is

323. California Air Resources Board, "Current Clean Air Vehicle Decal," https://ww2.arb.ca.gov/resources/fact-sheets/current-clean-air-vehicle-decal, accessed March 8, 2022.
324. California Air Resources Board, "Current Clean Air Vehicle Decal," https://ww2.arb.ca.gov/resources/fact-sheets/current-clean-air-vehicle-decal, accessed March 8, 2022.
325. California Air Resources Board, "California Clean Vehicles Incentives," https://ww2.arb.ca.gov/our-work/topics/incentives, accessed March 8, 2022.
326. Green Car Reports, CA Carpool-Lane Stickers For Plug-In Hybrids Run Out By May—Or Sooner, https://www.greencarreports.com/news/1090580_ca-carpool-lane-stickers-for-plug-in-hybrids-run-out-by-may--or-sooner, accessed November 8, 2023.
327. Jerry Hirsch, "State Nears Carpool Lane Decal Limit for Volt, Other Plug-In Hybrids" (*Los Angeles Times*, May 19, 2015), https://www.latimes.com/business/autos/la-fi-hy-green-car-pool-lane-permit-20150518-story.html, accessed March 4, 2022.
328. Jerry Hirsch, "State Nears Carpool Lane Decal Limit for Volt, Other Plug-In Hybrids" (*Los Angeles Times*, May 19, 2015), https://www.latimes.com/business/autos/la-fi-hy-green-car-pool-lane-permit-20150518-story.html, accessed March 4, 2022.

through education. In the General Plan to address pollution, adopted by the City of Los Angeles in 1992, one of the principal goals was to increase public awareness. The city acted to make sure that the public could participate in all the decision-making processes with regard to projects that would affect air quality, including in the project planning stage. Public participation was a crucial step required in the environmental review of projects in the City of Los Angeles. The California Environmental Quality Act (CEQA) requires the analysis of projects to disclose their potential effects on the environment and to allow public participation in the environmental review process.[329] Under the CEQA, the City of Los Angeles developed a Threshold Guide, as part of the City's development reform efforts to streamline the City's permit and development processes.[330]

Both the state and local governments also require that information on air pollution control be made available to the public. For example, the state's Air Toxic "Hot Spots" Program (AB 2588) requires stationary sources to report the types and quantities of certain specified toxic substance emissions from their facilities and collect emissions data, identify localized pollution, and notify neighbors of any resulting significant risks.[331] The Act requires that facilities quantify, compile, inventory and disclose emissions in order to determine if a risk assessment must be conducted in accordance with the regulations of the Office of Environmental Health Hazard Assessment. The regulatory agency is required to compile and maintain a list of substances posing chronic health threats and make that information available to the public.[332] It also maintains toxic emissions data in the Air Toxics Emission Inventory Data System that is available to the public upon request.[333] Also, to make information more accessible to the public, the Community Health Air Pollution Information System (CHAPIS) was unveiled in 2004.[334] The development of the information used was a joint effort between the CARB and the State's 35 local air pollution control and air quality management districts.[335] CHAPIS is a free website-based tool to map various air pollution sources in California and gives an itemized account of the sources' air emissions.[336]

329. "City of Los Angeles" (*L.A. Threshold Guide*, 2006), http://ibecproject.com/PREDEIR_0013306.pdf, accessed November 8, 2023.
330. "City of Los Angeles" (*L.A. Threshold Guide*, 2006), http://ibecproject.com/PREDEIR_0013306.pdf, accessed November 8, 2023, at p. 1.
331. California Air Resources Board, AB 2588 Air Toxics "Hot Spots," https://ww2.arb.ca.gov/our-work/programs/ab-2588-air-toxics-hot-spots, accessed November 8, 2023.
332. California Air Resources Board, AB 2588 Air Toxics "Hot Spots," https://ww2.arb.ca.gov/our-work/programs/ab-2588-air-toxics-hot-spots, accessed November 8, 2023.
333. California Air Resources Board, AB 2588 Air Toxics "Hot Spots," https://ww2.arb.ca.gov/our-work/programs/ab-2588-air-toxics-hot-spots, accessed November 8, 2023.
334. California Air Resources Board, "News Release: Online Site Available to Map California Sources of Pollution" (August 11, 2004), https://ww2.arb.ca.gov/news/online-site-available-map-california-sources-pollution, accessed November 8, 2023.
335. California Air Resources Board, "News Release: Online Site Available to Map California Sources of Pollution" (August 11, 2004), https://ww2.arb.ca.gov/news/online-site-available-map-california-sources-pollution, accessed November 8, 2023.
336. California Air Resources Board, Online Site Available to Map California Sources of Pollution https://ww2.arb.ca.gov/news/online-site-available-map-california-sources-pollution, accessed November 8, 2023.

3.2 Relation of Supervision Over Regulators

3.2.1 Supervision by Federal Government

An example of the supervisory by the federal government to the state government is the "Federal enforcement" provision of Article 113 of the CAA, 1970.[337] According to this provision, the federal government has the power to enforce the CAA, while the States are principally responsible for implementation and enforcement of the law. Article 113 provides that on the basis of any information available to the administrator if the administrator of the EPA finds that any person has violated or is in violation of any requirement or prohibition of an applicable implementation plan or permit, the administrator shall notify the violator and the state in which the SIP applies. The administrator may issue an order of compliance, and an order of administrative penalty, as well as to bring a civil action to a court according to law.[338] In addition to this federal enforcement against a person, Article 113 provides that the Federal Government may take over the power of implementing the SIP from the state involved.[339]

With the improvement of pollution control technology, the emissions standards for the electric utility industry have increased accordingly for a cleaner environment. The intervention and monitoring by different NGOs were major stimulators for these measures. In March 2016, on behalf of a group of NGOs including Communities for a Better Environment, the Center of Biological Diversity and the Sierra Club, Earthjustice and the Natural Resources Defence Council brought a lawsuit against the SCAQMD in Los Angeles County Superior Court for violating California law by rejecting staff-proposed reforms to the NOx control program and supporting the approval of an oil-industry-backed measure that allowed refineries and other major polluters to delay installing equipment to reduce dangerous particulate matter and smog-forming nitrogen oxide, or NOx.[340] The groups were concerned that this measure would allow oil refineries and power plants to continue spewing massive amounts of smog-forming pollutants, threatening the health of millions of people who live in the Los Angeles areas already breathing the dirty air.[341]

3.2.2 Supervision by Nongovernmental Organizations

NGOs have played an active role in the air pollution governance process in the LA area. The CARB developed a Smog Index Label in 1998; it should be noted, however, that

337. USC, section 7413, a, (1), Federal enforcement, Clean Air Act, 1970.
338. USC, section 7413, a, (1), Federal enforcement, Clean Air Act, 1970.
339. USC, section 7413, a, (2), Federal enforcement, Clean Air Act, 1970.
340. Tony Barboza, "Southern California Air Quality Board Is Sued Over Adoption of Industry-Friendly Smog Rules" (*Los Angeles Times*, March 9, 2016), www.latimes.com/local/californi a/la-me-0310-air-board-lawsuit-20160310-story.html, accessed March 4, 2022.
341. Tony Barboza, "Southern California Air Quality Board Is Sued Over Adoption of Industry-Friendly Smog Rules" (*Los Angeles Times*, March 9, 2016), www.latimes.com/local/californi a/la-me-0310-air-board-lawsuit-20160310-story.html, accessed March 4, 2022.

labels are valuable to consumers only as long as they accurately represent smog emissions. In 2014, the International Council on Clean Transportation discovered, based on research by the University of West Virginia, that there was a significant difference between Volkswagen vehicles' on-road emissions performance and the vehicles' emissions results from laboratory tests. The discovery prompted both the CARB and the U.S. EPA to investigate the auto manufacturer, and they discovered that Volkswagen had installed "defeat devices" in some of its cars. These devices allowed vehicles to cheat emissions testing by indicating different results when a vehicle was undergoing laboratory tests versus switching on the emissions control system, but keeping the emissions controls off during actual on-road driving. Volkswagen's violations have exposed the company to criminal and civil lawsuits and billions of dollars in liability.[342] This incident represents an important example of NGOs and regulators working together to assure that auto manufacturers comply with air pollution laws. Most notably, NGOs such as the Natural Resources Defense Council (NRDC), a national organization specializing in environmental litigation, have participated as intervenors in industry lawsuits against regulators, and in this role, have supported the State's air pollution control efforts. One example of this supervision is the case of *California Dump Truck Owners Assoc. v. Nichols*, (784 F.3d 500, 503, 9th Circuit 2015).[343]

3.2.3 Supervision by Enterprises

Industry has stood both in opposition to some and in favor of other air pollution regulations. Several examples of lawsuits brought by various automobile and truck manufacturers' associations against the CARB are described below. In light of the frequent litigation against California regulators, the judiciary has also had considerable influence in shaping California's vehicle regulations.

In a challenge to the Low Emission Vehicles (LEV II) program, the International Truck and Engine Corporation (ITEC)[344] brought suit against the CARB, alleging that the new standards rendered the LEV II program technologically infeasible for light-duty diesel vehicles, that it "had the effect of eliminating the entire class of motor vehicles from the State's automobile market."[345] The California Court of Appeals affirmed the lower court's ruling in favor of the CARB and held that the rulemaking was within the CARB's authority. Specifically, the Court found that the CARB "made a finding of technological feasibility, based upon its interpretation of feasibility as requiring

342. Gilbert Gates et al., "How Volkswagen's 'Defeat Devices' Worked" (*New York Times*, March 16, 2017), https://www.nytimes.com/interactive/2015/business/international/vw-diesel-emissions-scandal-explained.html, accessed March 31, 2022.
343. *California Dump Truck Owners Assoc. v. Nichols*, 784 F.3d 500, 503 (9th Circuit 2015), further described below, in that NRDC intervened on behalf of the CARB.
344. ITEC is a truck manufacturing company founded in 1902. International Truck and Engine Corp. "About Us," www.internationaltrucks.com/trucks/aboutus, accessed March 4, 2022.
345. *International Truck & Engine Corp. v. California Air Resources Board*, 2001 WL 1297484, 3 (Cal. Court of Appeal, 4th District 2001).

achievable standards for light-duty vehicles sufficient to permit a range of similar types and models available to California consumers without regard to fuel type."[346]

The SCAQMD's expansive fleet rules have also not gone unchallenged. The Engine Manufacturer's Association, a trade association that represents heavy-duty engine manufacturers, brought suit to challenge the SCAQMD's promulgation of the "Fleet Rules" on the ground that they were "preempted" by § 209 (a) of the CAA. The Ninth Court of Appeals found that the SCAQMD's rules were not preempted and thus the Engine Manufacturer's Association was unable to thwart their implementation.[347] A number of third parties intervened in this case: for the plaintiff, the Western States Petroleum Association, also a trade group; and for the defendants, nonprofit organizations, including the Natural Resources Defense Council, the Coalition for Clean Air, the Committee for a Better Environment, Planning and Conservation League, and the Sierra Club.

In 2011, the California Dump Truck Owners Association (the Association) filed suit against the CARB, challenging the heavy-duty diesel vehicle regulations on the grounds that they were preempted by federal law. The Court ultimately dismissed on procedural grounds—for lack of subject matter jurisdiction—rather than based on the substantive arguments,[348] but this case serves as another example of the automotive industry challenging California's clean air laws. The Association subsequently changed its name to the California Construction Trucking Association in response to its expanding membership[349] and then changed it once more to the Western States Trucking Association (WSTA).[350] The WSTA is, as proclaimed on its website, "the oldest, nonaffiliated, nonprofit trucking trade association in the U.S.," and one of its explicit activities is challenging the CARB and U.S. EPA regulations of its members.[351] Indeed, as the WSTA states, "We have active lawsuits in the federal courts challenging the legality of CARB and U.S. EPA regulations that target our industry for regulation based on flawed and manipulated scientific data. Today, many regulations promoted as advancing environmental (or safety agendas) are stated to be nothing more than a 'Trojan Horse' promoted by larger entities to advance a quasi-form of economic reregulation of the industry unnecessarily burdening small-business trucker with

346. ITEC is a truck manufacturing company founded in 1902. International Truck and Engine Corp. "About Us," www.internationaltrucks.com/trucks/aboutus, accessed March 4, 2022.
International Truck & Engine Corp. v. California Air Resources Board, 2001 WL 1297484, 3 (Cal. Court of Appeal, 4th District 2001) at 12. It should be noted that the Court's opinion was not published in the court reporters and has no precedential value. However, it represents an example of the automotive industry challenging automobile regulations.

347. *Engine Manufacturer's Association and Western Petroleum Association v. South Coast Air Quality Management District*, 488 F.3d 103 (9th Circuit 2007).

348. *California Dump Truck Owners Assoc. v. Nichols*, 784 F.3d 500, 513 (9th Circuit 2015).

349. "CA Dump Truck Association Changes Name" (*Fleet Owner*, December 29, 2011), http://fleetowner.com/management/news/california-dump-truck-association-changes-name-1229, accessed March 4, 2022.

350. "About" (*Western States Trucking Association*), http://westrk.org/about/, accessed March 4, 2022.

351. "About" (*Western States Trucking Association*), http://westrk.org/about/, accessed March 4, 2022.

increased compliance costs."[352] The WSTA and other trade associations, as exemplified by the lawsuits described in this section, represent the continued effort by the automotive industry to protect industry profits even though doing so undermines clean air regulations.

3.3 Relation of Supervision Over Enterprises and Other Polluters

As the following sections show, this relation exists in different forms in the air pollution governance process of the LA area.

3.3.1 Media Disclosure and Public Responses

By the 1940s, it became clear that Los Angeles area pollution was caused by many sources, revealed significantly by two studies commissioned by and reported in the press.

In the Los Angeles Times' report, the expert, Raymond R. Tucker, made a number of recommendations for decreasing air pollution—including that diesel trucks exceeding pollution standards should receive citations—noting that existing municipal agencies didn't have sufficient power to fight air pollution and that a more robust regulatory regime was necessary.[353]

The public responded to the lack of meaningful progress on pollution control with protests. Ultimately, thanks to the combination of citizen pressure, the focus fostered by new studies on the issue, and political pressure stimulated by media coverage, a state law was proposed to enable the County Board of Supervisors to pass more effective countywide pollution control laws. The bill had support from the California League of Cities and was opposed by the oil, railroad, and agricultural industries, though when the Los Angeles Times once again stepped into the fray and publicized the oil companies' opposition—in effect, shaming them publicly—they, too, fell behind the law, and the railroad and agricultural industries also dropped their opposition.[354] As described above, press coverage of citizen discontent with, and public action against air pollution were strong drivers of the early pollution control efforts in the Los Angeles area. The media—especially print publications, such as the Los Angeles Times reporting on local and regional news studies—have played an especially important role in the development of air pollution regulations.

352. "About" (*Western States Trucking Association*), http://westrk.org/about/, accessed March 4, 2022.
353. South Coast Air Quality Management District, "The Southland's War on Smog: Fifty Years of Progress Toward Clean Air" (*Publications,* May 1997), https://www.aqmd.gov/home/research/publications/50-years-of-progress, accessed March 4, 2022. Note, however, that this study did not find automobiles to be the major source of emissions; it would take several more years for the size of the link between cars and the area's smog to become apparent. Gonzalez, at 59.
354. South Coast Air Quality Management District, "The Southland's War on Smog: Fifty Years of Progress Toward Clean Air" (*Publications,* May 1997), https://www.aqmd.gov/home/research/publications/50-years-of-progress, accessed March 4, 2022. Note, however, that this study did not find automobiles to be the major source of emissions; it would take several more years for the size of the link between cars and the area's smog to become apparent. Gonzalez, at 59.

The CARB developed a Smog Index Label in 1998; it should be noted, however, that labels are valuable to consumers only as long as they accurately represent smog emissions. In 2014, the International Council on Clean Transportation discovered, based on research by the University of West Virginia, that there was a significant difference between Volkswagen vehicles' on-road emissions performance and the vehicles' emissions results from laboratory tests. The discovery prompted both the CARB and the U.S. EPA to investigate the auto manufacturer, and they discovered that Volkswagen had installed "defeat devices" in some of its cars. These devices allowed vehicles to cheat emissions testing by indicating different results when a vehicle was undergoing laboratory tests versus switching on the emissions control system, but keeping the emissions controls off during actual on-road driving. Volkswagen's violations have exposed the company to criminal and civil lawsuits and billions of dollars in liability.[355] This incident represents an important example of NGOs and regulators working together to assure that auto manufacturers comply with air pollution laws.

3.3.2 NGOs' Participation in Litigations

Although the plants that serve some of the Los Angeles area's energy needs are located in the Interior West and don't impact the Los Angeles area's air quality, they do have a serious impact on their local air quality that poses a unique legal and environmental justice situation. A prime example is the Mohave Generating Plant, that began operations in 1971. Although the Mohave Generating Plant was operated by Southern California Edison, the LADWP, Nevada Power Company and Salt River Project also owned interests in the Plant. The Plant generated 1,500 megawatts of power to support the cities of Las Vegas, Phoenix and Los Angeles, and emitted up to 40,000 tons of sulfur dioxide (SO_2) per year, making it one of the largest sources of SO_2 in the West.[356,357] The Grand Canyon Trust, with the Sierra Club and the National Parks and Conservation Association, filed a citizen suit against the owners of Mohave Generating Plant and the LADWP in 1998 to address air pollution violations. The litigation was resolved by a consent decree, and the owners eventually closed the plant rather than pay for improvements.[358]

355. Gilbert Gates et al., "How Volkswagen's 'Defeat Devices' Worked" (*New York Times*, March 16, 2017), https://www.nytimes.com/interactive/2015/business/international/vw-diesel-emissions-scandal-explained.html, accessed March 31, 2022.
356. U.S. Environmental Protection Agency, "Final Project Mohave Report Fact Sheet" (*Federal Register*), https://www.federalregister.gov/documents/search?conditions%5Bterm%5D=EPA-R09-OAR+Nevada&order=newest, accessed March 4, 2022.
357. Bruce Polkowsky, "Robert Case Study-Mohave Generating Station" (2000), www.google.com/url?sa=t&rct=j&q=&esrc=s&source=web&cd=2&ved=0ahUKEwj_28DTwJ3VAhUDaT4KHbPQBl8QFggpMAE&url=http%3A%2F%2Fwww.westar.org%2FRA%2520BART%2FMohave%2520-%2520B.doc&usg=AFQjCNEyfoHiwH730Wie8YqlKj68xGo80Q, accessed March 8, 2022.
358. United States Environmental Protection Agency, "Final Project Mohave Report Fact Sheet" (*Air Actions, Nevada*), https://19january2017snapshot.epa.gov/www3/region9/air/mohave/mohave.html, accessed November 8, 2023.

4 ACHIEVEMENTS AND CHALLENGES

4.1 Improvement of Air Quality

California's air pollution control has been a world-renowned achievement. Innovations in industrial and energy technologies, such as the production of three-way catalytic converters and unleaded gasoline in the 1970s, and rapid advances in motor vehicle manufacturing and environmental technologies, coupled with stringent motor vehicle pollution control standards, resulted in an 85% reduction in motor vehicle pollution in California in 2010 compared to 1975.[359] In terms of stationery and area sources, California has gradually established control systems and policy measures for major air pollutants such as nitrogen oxides and sulfides, as well as toxic gases. One representative example is the South Coast Air Management District's Clean Air Incentive Market Program, launched in 1993 that, according to the US EPA, effectively reduced nitrogen oxide and sulfide emissions by 75% and 60% between 1994 and 2003. In 2015, Los Angeles $PM_{2.5}$ reached a low average of 35 micrograms per day.[360] Since 1943, Los Angeles experienced greatly improved air quality and was heralded for its multiple successes in this area. In May 2015, the American Council for an Energy-Efficient Economy rated Los Angeles as the most improved city in the United States for energy efficiency.[361] Further, the county of Los Angeles decreased its days of unhealthy ozone by 34% through the year 2000.[362] This accomplishment can largely be attributed to the strategic implementation of legislative reforms in industry, transportation, and building regulation. Pollutant reductions have provided environmental, social, and economic benefits, highlighting the urgency to apply these lessons to address current critical environmental issues such as emissions of greenhouse gases. These examples underscore the important role of data from long-term research and monitoring as part of fact-based decision-making in environmental policy.[363]

4.2 Value Change of the Society

The rather detailed introduction above on the air pollution governance process in the LA area shows that society as a whole has made a crucial value choice. In front of the

359. *See*: Hou Jiaru & Wang Qian, California Air Pollution Prevention and Control Experience, Environmental Education, 2014, p. 96.
360. *See*: Hou Jiaru & Wang Qian, California Air Pollution Prevention and Control Experience, Environmental Education, 2014, p. 96.
361. Jorge Madrid, "Energy Efficiency Grades Are In- How Did. Los Angeles Do?" (*EDF Blogs*, May 20, 2015), https://blogs.edf.org/californiadream/2015/05/20/energy-efficiency-grades-are-in-how-did-los-angeles-do/, accessed March 4, 2022.
362. *CBS Los Angeles* (Study LA-Long Beach Area Has the Worst Ozone Pollution in The Nation, April 20, 2016), http://losangeles.cbslocal.com/2016/04/20/la-long-beach-worst-ozone-pollution/, accessed March 4, 2022.
363. Timothy Sullivan, Charles Driscoll, Colin Beier, Dallas Burtraw, Ivan Fernandez, James Galloway, David Gay, Christine Goodale, Gene Likens, Gary Lovett, and Shaun Watmough, Air Pollution Success Stories in the United States: the Value of Long-Term Observations, https://www.rff.org/publications/journal-articles/air-pollution-success-stories-in-the-united-states-the-value-of-long-term-observations/, accessed November 6, *2023*.

danger to their health caused by air pollution, all people of the society of the LA area had reached a consensus on controlling air pollution. This consensus represented a value change, from a single-minded pursuit of economic growth, which was driven by the same single-minded desire for material prosperity and enjoyment, to a more balanced consideration of the value of economy and the value of environment, which was driven by a more sophisticated desire for health and economic growth. This value change is an important ethical progress. Under the newly developed ethics, a legal framework for air pollution control was established, a powerful regulation on air pollution was carried out, an effective supervision over the regulators was established, and an effective supervision over enterprises and other polluters was established. In short, a favorable governance process for air pollution control was established.

4.3 Challenges

Despite the great progress, Los Angeles ozone concentrations still exceed the US and California air quality standards by a significant margin. The national design value (i.e., the metric upon which the National Ambient Air Quality Standard (NAAQS) is based) for the monitoring stations in the SoCAB was 102 ppb in 2014, while the new ozone NAAQS requires it be reduced to 70 ppb. Significant additional emission control efforts remain to be accomplished to meet this requirement.[364] In early 2015, the area was revealed to have the highest level of ozone pollution and the fifth highest level of particle pollution of any American city in an annual, nationwide study conducted by the American Lung Association.[365]

Coal has been a dominant fuel source for the LADWP and a major source of Los Angeles air pollution. To reduce LA pollution, LADWP invested in several coal burning power plants outside of California, including the Mohave Generating Plant. These out-of-state coal-fired power plants are located in the interior West, such as Arizona, Colorado, Nevada, New Mexico, Utah, and Wyoming, to tackle the coal challenge[366] and have brought a lot of health and environmental problems to their local communities. As a main consumer of the energy generated by the coal plants in the interior West, California has been reducing its dependence on electricity supplies from existing LA coal and petroleum-coke (petcoke) plants.[367] By 2026, virtually all electricity generated by LA coal-and petcoke-fired generation resources to serve California loads is expected

364. David D. Parrish, Jin Xu3, Bart Croes & Min Shao, "Air Quality Improvement in Los Angeles—Perspectives for Developing Cities," http://daviddparrish.com/products/Parrish_et_al_2016.pdf, accessed March 1, 2023.
365. American Lung Association, "State of the Air 2015" (2015), https://www.lung.org/research/sota, accessed November 8, 2023.
366. Jana Milford et al., "Clearing California's Coal Shadow from the American West" (2005), http://ceert.org/wp-content/uploads/PDFs/reports/Coalreport.pdf, accessed March 4, 2022.
367. California Energy Commission, "paid for from a corporate tax, anticipated savings from energy savings via low-cost renewable energy, and funding of the California's Declining Reliance on Coal—Overview" (*Tracking* Progress, October 2018), https://www.energy.ca.gov/sites/default/files/2019-12/declining_reliance_coal_ada.pdf, accessed March 31, 2022.

to end;[368] that applies to the Los Angeles area as well. Statewide, California implemented regulations to promote renewable energy in the utility sector, aiming to reduce the state's air pollution from the utility sector. Power plants built outside California, however, were not required to follow these initiatives, even though these power plants' owners were from California, or their service included areas in California. This phenomenon continued, shifting the Los Angeles area's air pollution to other areas of the country, and of course, contributing to global climate change.[369]

On August 12, 2022, Congress passed The Inflation Reduction Act, "making the largest investment in combatting climate change in U.S. history, providing billions of dollars for renewable and nuclear energy, building efficiency and electrification, electric vehicles and increased efficiency standards, environmental justice, and research & development."[370] The legislation provides USD 369 billion for climate change mitigation, estimated to reduce carbon emissions by 40% by 2030. This is estimated to result in about three quarter of the reductions required to fulfill the U.S. commitments for carbon reductions, the remainder to be fulfilled by EPA and other Administration regulations.[371] The challenge is how to make those Administration regulations permanent. Another concern is that the U.S. has yielded to economic pressures from the high costs of energy and resulting inflation to temporarily encourage the production of coal, oil and gas in the U.S. and abroad, thus stalling the scientifically found necessity to promptly transition away from the use of fossil fuels in order to avoid disastrous climate change consequences. There is hope that the U.S. will be able to meet its target under the Paris Climate Conference of reducing carbon emissions by 50%-52% by 2030 and to zero by 2050, made promising with the passage of the Inflation Reduction Act, but there is a disturbing number of "ifs" as follows: if there is no adverse change in the Presidency and Congress in the 2024 elections; if the Republicans don't succeed in their promised defunding of the program in the October budged considerations; if President Biden's decision that his promotion of increased fossil fuel exploration to fend off price rises is truly temporary; if electric cars can become the nation's preference and sales are significant; if there can be built an adequate number of charging stations; if transmission can be assured from production areas to use areas; if the Supreme Court doesn't interfere with the Biden Administration energy transition plans. There is increasing pressure from energy NGOs and the press to hopefully persuade the Administration to make these ifs come true.

368. California Energy Commission, "California's Declining Reliance on Coal—Overview" (*Tracking* Progress, October 2018), https://www.energy.ca.gov/sites/default/files/2019-12/declining_reliance_coal_ada.pdf, accessed March 31, 2022.
369. California Energy Commission, "California's Declining Reliance on Coal—Overview" (*Tracking* Progress, October 2018), https://www.energy.ca.gov/sites/default/files/2019-12/declining_reliance_coal_ada.pdf, accessed March 31, 2022.
370. HR 5376-117th Congress (2021-2022), accessed August 24, 2022. The Inflation Reduction Act was so named because its cost was intended to be Internal Revenue Service to recover unpaid taxes, all anticipated to reduce inflation. It was signed into law on August 23, 2022.
371. https://earthjustice.org/brief/2022/what-the-inflation-reduction-act-means-for-climate, accessed August 24, 2022.This article contains a complete recital and evaluation of the legislation's climate mitigation provisions and its shortcomings.

CHAPTER 4
Air Pollution Governance in BTH Area of China

This chapter introduces the legal and policy experience of air pollution control in BTH area. The data and information introduced in this part are detailed and valuable for the same reasons as mentioned in Chapter 3. They help the readers to understand the broadness and in-depth of the governance processes of the two areas. Section 1 introduces the geographic and social-economic background of the air pollution control in BTH area. Section 2 introduces the legal and ethical frameworks for air pollution control governance. Section 3 explores the basic political relations in the air pollution control governance of the areas. Section 4 is about achievements and challenges in air pollution control in the areas. This part provide a strong basis for the comparative study of the next part.

1 POLITICAL PROFILE OF CHINA

China is a socialist country.[372] The leadership of the Communist Party of China (CPC) is the most essential feature of socialism with Chinese characteristics.[373] The leadership

372. Constitution of the People's Republic of China (2018), Article 1, paragraph 1 provides that "The Preamble of the Constitution provides that 'In 1949, after engaging in protracted, arduous and tortuous struggles, armed and in other forms, the Chinese people of all ethnic groups led by the Communist Party of China with Chairman Mao Zedong as its leader finally overthrew the rule of imperialism, feudalism and bureaucrat-capitalism, won a great victory in the New Democratic Revolution, and founded the People's Republic of China. The Chinese people thus secured power and became masters of their own country.'" Zhongnan University of Economics and Law, Istitutoitalo-Cinese, http://zyxy.zuel.edu.cn/2021/0323/c10984a266345/page.htm, accesseed November 28, 2021.
373. Constitution of the People's Republic of China (2018), Article 1, paragraph 2. Zhongnan University of Economics and Law, Istitutoitalo-Cinese, http://zyxy.zuel.edu.cn/2021/0323/c10984a266345/page.htm, accesseded November 28, 2021.

of the CPC is recognized as such by the Constitution of the PRC.[374] Under the leadership of the CPC, all the state power organs, including the People's Congresses and administrative governments at all levels, are organized according to the Constitution.

In terms of the form of state structure, China is a unitary and unified multi-ethnic country. There is only one organ of central political power, and all local administrative units and units of ethnic autonomy are under the unified leadership of the Central Government.

In terms of the form of organization of the state powers, China applies a system of people's congress. Article 2 of the Constitution of the PRC provides that: "All power in the People's Republic of China belongs to the people. The organs through which the people exercise state power are the National People's Congress and the local people's congresses at all levels."[375] The National People's Congress is the highest organ of state power. Local people's congresses at various levels are local organs of state power. The National People's Congress and the local people's congresses at various levels are democratically elected by the people, responsible to the people and subject to their supervision. The administrative, judicial and procuratorial organs of the state are all created by the people's congresses to which they are responsible and subject to their supervision.

In terms of the system of political party, China applies a system of multi-party cooperation and political consultation under the leadership of the CPC. In addition to the CPC, there are eight other national political parties active in the political life of China.[376] China's system of political parties is different from the two-party or multi-party competition systems in other countries.

In terms of the mechanism of economic operation, China is a country with a socialist market economy as its mechanism of economic operation. China shifted to this mechanism in 1978 when China started economic reform.

2 LEGAL AND ETHICAL FRAMEWORKS FOR AIR POLLUTION CONTROL

The air pollution control of the BTH area is under a legal framework and an ethical framework. As indicated by the EG model, those frameworks are the two circles surrounding the triangle in the model.

374. Constitution of the People's Republic of China (2018), Article 2. Zhongnan University of Economics and Law, http://zyxy.zuel.edu.cn/_upload/article/files/21/ac/d3fd5f9c427aa04d00a5a8a584aa/8b423a1a-a691-401c-aabc-6186beec55c7.pdf, accessed October 25, 2022.
375. Constitution of the People's Republic of China (2018), Article 2. Zhongnan University of Economics and Law, http://zyxy.zuel.edu.cn/_upload/article/files/21/ac/d3fd5f9c427aa04d00a5a8a584aa/8b423a1a-a691-401c-aabc-6186beec55c7.pdf, accessed October 25, 2022.
376. The eight political parties are The Revolutionary Committee of the Chinese Kuomintang, China Democratic League, China National Democratic Construction Association, China Association for Promoting Democracy, Chinese Peasants and Workers Democratic Party, China Zhi Gong Party, Jiusan Society, Taiwan Democratic Self-Government League.

2.1 Legal Frameworks

2.1.1 National Framework

The two most important national laws in the field of air pollution control are the Environmental Protection Law of the People's Republic of PRC (EPL) and the Law on Prevention and Control of Atmospheric Pollution of the PRC (LPCAP). Both were made by the Standing Committee of the National People's Congress. They are the legal framework for air pollution control in China and the BTH area.

The EPL is the basic law for environmental protection of the nation. The law has established a regulatory framework for pollution control, including air pollution control. The major elements of the framework include a pollutant discharge registration and permit system, a pollutant discharge monitoring system, an environmental impacts assessment (EIA) system, a governmental inspection system, an environmental performance rating system, and a system of law enforcement and liabilities. All of those regulatory systems apply to the BTH area.

The LPCAP is the law specialized in air pollution control. The law establishes a legal framework for air pollution control throughout the country. The major provisions of the law include emission standards for air pollutants, administrative authorities on air pollution control and their responsibilities, various administrative measures to regulate the emission of air pollutants, accountability for local government's performance on air pollution control, and legal sanctions against enterprises and other polluters which illegally discharge air pollutants. The LPCAP is primary in the field of air pollution control. Local regulations legislated by each local legislative body should not conflict with it.

In addition to the above-mentioned framework laws, the Central Government has made many plans and programs for implementing the EPL and the LPCAP, such as the National Action Plan on Prevention and Control of Air Pollution (2013),[377] the National Measures for Assessment of Implementation of the Action Plan on Prevention and Control of Air Pollution (2014),[378] the National Measures for Management of Funds for Prevention and Control Air Pollution (2018)[379] and the National Programme for Implementation of Cleaner Production Technology in Key Industrial Sectors for Prevention and Control of Air Pollution (2014),[380] the Provisions on Quantitative

377. The Central People's Government: The State Council issued the Action Plan for the Prevention and Control of Air Pollution with ten measures, http://www.gov.cn/jrzg/2013-09/12/content_2486918.htm, accessed February 2, 2023.
378. The Central People's Government: the National Measures for Assessment of Implementation of the Action Plan on Prevention and Control of Air Pollution, http://www.gov.cn/zhengce/content/2014-05/27/content_8830.htm, accessed February 2, 2023.
379. The Central People's Government: the National Measures for Management of Funds for Prevention and Control Air Pollution, http://www.gov.cn/gongbao/content/2019/content_5366490.htm?ivk_sa=1024320u, accessed February 2, 2023.
380. Ministry of Industry and Information Technology: The Ministry of Industry and Information Technology issued the Implementation Plan for Cleaner Production Technologies in Key Industries for the Prevention and Control of Air Pollution, https://www.miit.gov.cn/jgsj/jns/wjfb/art/2020/art_b869dea638654d6ea3a70049da7a245e.html, accessed February 2, 2023.

Accountability for Comprehensive Control and Crucial Actions Air Pollution Control in the Autumn and Winter in the BTH Area (2017).[381]

2.1.2 Local Framework

In addition to the national legal framework, the People's Congresses of the BTH area have made various regulations for implementing national laws and regulations in air pollution control. These legal documents mainly include the Regulations on Prevention and Control of Air Pollution in Beijing (2014),[382] the Regulations on Prevention and Control of Air Pollution in Tianjin (2015),[383] and the Regulations on Prevention and Control of Air Pollution in Hebei Province (2016).[384]

There are many legal provisions related to air pollution control in other laws, such as civil law, criminal law, administrative law and law on litigation procedures. For example, Article 338 of the Criminal Law of the People's Republic of China provides for the crime of polluting the environment, and Article 58 of the Civil Procedure Law of the People's Republic of China provides for procedures for environmental public interest litigation.

The local people's congresses of the area have incorporated air pollution control in the local outlines of the economic and social development. For example, Chapter 3 of the Outline of the 14th Five-Year Plan for National Economic and Social Development of Beijing and the Visionary Goals for 2035 of Beijing (2021) is about Green Growth and focuses on carbon emission reduction and promotion of carbon neutrality.[385] The Outline of the 14th Five-Year Plan and 2035 Vision for National Economic and Social Development of Tianjin Municipality (2021) provided to reduce the total consumption of coal, increase the use of natural gas and nonfossil energy, and raise the proportion of clean energy consumption. It required the Municipality to accelerate the process of energy clean-up, adhere to the cleaner use of fossil energy and clean energy development, promote the intensive and more efficient use of coal, expand the scale of installed renewable energy power such as wind and solar energy, and improve the

381. Ministry of Ecology and Environment: Notice on the issuance of the Provisions on Quantified Accountability for the 2017-2018 Autumn and Winter Comprehensive Control of Air Pollution in the Beijing-Tianjin-Hebei Area and its surrounding Areas, https://www.mee.gov.cn/gkml/hbb/bwj/201708/t20170831_420711.htm, accessed February 2, 2023.
382. Standing Committee of Beijing Municipal People's Congress: Regulations of Beijing on the Prevention and Control of Air Pollution, http://www.bjrd.gov.cn/rdzl/dfxfgk/dfxfg/202101/t20210106_2200190.html, accessed February 2, 2023.
    Note: This regulation was amended in 2018.
383. Tianjin People's Congress: Regulations of Tianjin on the Prevention and Control of Air Pollution, https://www.tjrd.gov.cn/flfg/system/2018/10/10/030010734.shtml, accessed February 2, 2023. Note: This Regulation has been amended three times in 2017, 2018 and 2020.
384. Hebei Provincial Department of Ecology and Environment: Regulations of Hebei Province on Air Pollution Control, http://hbepb.hebei.gov.cn/hbhjt/zwgk/zc/101633000437221.html, accessed February 2, 2023.
    Note: This regulation was amended in 2021.
385. Commission on Development and Reform, "Beijing City, Outline of the 14th Five-Year Plan for National Economic and Social Development of Beijing and the Visionary Goals for 2035" (2021), https://www.ndrc.gov.cn/fggz/fzzlgh/dffzgh/202103/t20210331_1271321.html, accessed September 4, 2021.

renewable energy power consumption guarantee mechanism. It required the municipal government to further promote Green Growth and to try to achieve peak carbon emissions and carbon neutrality, to formulate and implement an action plan to achieve peak carbon emissions ahead of schedule, to carry out action to achieve peak carbon emissions in key industries, and to promote industries such as steel and electricity while taking the lead in achieving peak reduction emissions. Furthermore, it required the municipal government to extend the construction of the carbon emission trading pilot market and to let the market mechanism play a greater role in controlling greenhouse gas emissions. It required the municipal government to establish a net-zero carbon emission zone.[386] As a legislation innovation, joint legislation of the local people's congresses has been tried for air pollution control in more than one area. During the legislation process of the Air Pollution Control Regulation of Hebei Province, the Standing Committee of Hebei People's Congress held a conference with the Standing Committees of the People's Congresses of Beijing and Tianjin. They adopted a Guideline to Strengthen the Coordination of Legislation and Relevant Legal Research Measures.[387] The Guideline requires the parties to establish a coordination mechanism, environmental impact assessment consultation, supervision cooperation and joint prevention and control. The three Standing Committees organized their members to visit and study in Beijing and Tianjin, in order to promote cooperation among them.[388]

2.2 Ethical Framework

As indicated by the EG model, principles or ideas of environmental ethics are fundamental to a health operation of environmental governance. In the air pollution control process, the traditional Chinese environmental ethic, together with stimulations from international society and some contemporary ideas or concepts proposed by the CPC and the Government of China, play crucial roles in guiding the conduct of the people and enterprises. Different from laws and regulations, those principles or ideas play their roles through people's intrinsic value judgments and voluntary actions. They provide a strong ethical framework for air pollution control in the BTH area.

2.2.1 Traditional Chinese Environmental Ethics

The traditional ethical principles or ideas of Confucianism, Buddhism, and Taoism are the main part of the traditional ethical culture of China. All of them share the theory of

386. The People's Government of Tian Jin City, "Outline of the 14th Five-Year Plan and 2035 Vision for National Economic and Social Development of Tianjin Municipality" (2021), http://www.tj.gov.cn/zwgk/szfwj/tjsrmzf/202102/t20210208_5353467.html, accessed September 4, 2021.
387. Chen Lin, "First joint legislation in atmospheric pollution control of the BTH area," http://news.xinhuanet.com/politics/2016-01/12/c_128619313.htm, accessed May 7, 2016.
388. Chen Lin, "First Joint Legislation in Atmospheric Pollution Control of the BTH Area" (January 12, 2016), http://news.xinhuanet.com/politics/2016-01/12/c_128619313.htm, accessed May 7, 2016.

harmony between Nature and all the life entities on the Earth, including the human being. The theory incorporates beliefs that there exists connection, harmony and unity between nature and humanity.[389] It believes that the human being, just as other life on the Earth, is an integral part of Nature. It believes that human being shall not violate the laws of Nature. As a philosophic idea, it has deeply influenced the Chinese people for thousands of years. Under the guidance of this theory, the Chinese people have developed environmentally sound ways of life and production in the long period of the agricultural era. Nowadays, it provides a sound ethical framework for the healthy operation of the air pollution control process in China and the BTH area.

2.2.2 Contemporary Stimulations from International Society

The contemporary ethical framework for environmental protection has been influenced deeply by the contemporary environmental ethical theories of international society. The following are the major ones that come from international society.

2.2.2.1 1972 UN Conference on Human Environment

The 1972 UN Conference on Human Environment provided the first stimulation to the environmental awareness of Chinese people. In 1972, the United Nations held the United Nations Conference on Human Environment (UNCHE) in Stockholm, Sweden. The conference called on all countries to pay attention to the environmental problems facing mankind. Although China was in the midst of the "Cultural Revolution" and the country was in chaos, The State Council (the Central Government of the PRC) sent a high level governmental delegation to the conference. By attending this conference, China was informed, for the first time, of the latest developments in the international community on the issues of environmental protection. The meeting caused the Central Government to pay attention to China's environmental problems. Soon after the UNCHE, the State Council held the first National Conference on Environmental Protection in 1973 and issued Several Provisions on Protecting and Improving the Environment (Draft for Trial Implementation). The convening of this meeting and the publication of this regulation marked the beginning of the government's environmental protection work. At that time, the general public was still in the midst of the chaos of the Cultural Revolution. They did not understand the overall environmental problems. The information on the world environmental issues taken back to China by the Chinese Governmental Delegation to the UNCHE awakened the Chinese people and raised the level of environmental ethics of the people.

2.2.2.2 1992 UN Conference on Environment and Development

The second strong stimulation to the rise of environmental awareness and environmental ethics from outside of China in the past 50 years was the 1992 UN Conference

389. Chinese Encyclopedia Dictionary, Huasha Publishing House, Beijing, 1990, p. 5.

on Environment and Development held in Rio de Janeiro. At the conference, the UN General Assembly formally recommended to all countries of the world the Strategy of Sustainable Development. China welcomed this strategy. In 1994, China formulated China's Agenda 21. In 1996, China first stipulated the "Sustainable Development" Chapter in the 9th Five-Year Planning of National Economy and Social Development. The strategy has been reflected in the local governments' economies and social development planning at various levels. All these developments are a great education for the Chinese people, greatly promoting public environmental consciousness.

2.2.3 Contemporary Chinese Environmental Ethical Ideas

When time went into the twenty-first century, the CPC and the Central Government of the PRC proposed several new ideas on the relation between human beings and the environment under the new conditions of the development of China. Those new ideas have been welcomed by Chinese people.

2.2.3.1 Scientific Outlook on Development

In August 2003, Mr. Hu Jintao, the Secretary General of the CPC, used the term of Scientific Outlook on Development for the first time when he inspected the work of the government of Jiang Xi province. He proposed "to firmly establish the coordinated development, comprehensive development, and sustainable development of the scientific outlook on development."[390] The concept of Scientific Outlook on Development was formally accepted by the CPC and the Central Government of the People's Republic of China in October 2003. By that time, the Central Committee of the CPC emphasized the need to "adhere to the people-oriented approach, establish a comprehensive, coordinated and sustainable outlook on development, and promote the all-round development of the economy, society and people."[391]

On March 10, 2004, in a symposium on environment, natural resources and development organized by the Central Committee of the CPC, Mr. Hu Jintao comprehensively elaborated the theoretical basis, profound connotation, basic requirements and guiding significance of the Scientific Outlook on Development. He said that, in the

390. *See*: The putting forward of the concept of Scientific Development, the Web of the History of the People's Republic of China, http://www.hprc.org.cn/gsgl/dsnb/zdsj/201001/t20100109_40258.html, accessed January 11, 2023. *See* further: An Explanation on the Report of the 17th National Congress of the Communist Party of China: The core is the concept of people-oriented scientific development, the Website of the Central People's Government of the People's Republic of China, http://www.gov.cn/jrzg/2007-11/12/content_802281.htm, accessed January 11, 2023.
391. *See*: The putting forward of the concept of Scientific Development, the Web of the History of the People's Republic of China, http://www.hprc.org.cn/gsgl/dsnb/zdsj/201001/t20100109_40258.html, accessed January 11, 2023. *See* further: An Explanation on the Report of the 17th National Congress of the Communist Party of China: The core is the concept of people-oriented scientific development, the Website of the Central People's Government of the People's Republic of China, http://www.gov.cn/jrzg/2007-11/12/content_802281.htm, accessed January 11, 2023.

concept of Scientific Outlook of Development, "putting people first means that we should aim to achieve all-around human development, seek and promote development in the fundamental interests of the people, continuously meet their ever-growing material and cultural needs, effectively protect their economic, political and cultural rights and interests, and ensure that the fruits of development benefit all the people. Comprehensive development means that we should take economic development as the central task, promote economic, political and cultural development in an all-round way, and realize economic development and social progress in an all-round way. Coordinated development means balanced development between urban and rural areas, between different areas, between economic and social development, between man and nature, between domestic development and opening up, between productive forces and relations of production, between the economic base and the superstructure, and between all links and aspects of economic, political and cultural development. Sustainable development is to promote the harmony between man and nature, to realize the coordination between economic development and population, resources and the environment, adhere to the civilized development path of increased production, prosperous life and sound ecology, and ensure sustainable development from generation to generation."[392]

By proposing and carrying out the concept of Scientific Outlook on Development, the Central Committee of the CPC and the Central Government of the PRC play an important role in environmental awareness and environmental education. The proposal of the concept of Scientific Outlook on Development was timely. It was a time of fast development of the economy and fast deterioration of ecological and environmental conditions in China. It was the first powerful call for changing the mode of production and lifestyle since China started economic reform in 1978. The concept of Scientific Outlook on Development is a display of the old Confucianism theory of harmony between nature and man in contemporary China. Facing serious environmental problems, the Chinese people, enterprises and governments welcomed the idea of Scientific Outlook on Development. Since that time, the idea has become the guiding principle of the national economic and social development planning of the country and influenced the people and enterprises.

2.2.3.2 Ecological Civilization

The concept of Ecological Civilization was welcomed in China, including the BTH area. In 2007, the Report of the 17th National Congress of the CPC for the first time put

392. *See*: The putting forward of the concept of Scientific Development, the Web of the History of the People's Republic of China, http://www.hprc.org.cn/gsgl/dsnb/zdsj/201001/t20100109_40258.html, accessed January 11, 2023. *See* further: An Explanation on the Report of the 17th National Congress of the Communist Party of China: The core is the concept of people-oriented scientific development, the Website of the Central People's Government of the People's Republic of China, http://www.gov.cn/jrzg/2007-11/12/content_802281.htm, accessed January 11, 2023.

forward the proposition of "building an Ecological Civilization."[393] The report said that "to promote ecological progress, we will basically form an industrial structure, growth pattern and consumption pattern that conserve energy and resources and protect the ecological environment. A circular economy has taken shape on a large scale, and the proportion of renewable energy has increased significantly. The discharge of major pollutants has been effectively controlled, and the quality of the ecological environment has significantly improved. The concept of ecological civilization is firmly established in the whole society."[394]

In 2012, the Central Committee of the CPC emphasized the idea of ecological civilization again. In his Report to the 18th CPC National Congress, Xi Jinping, the Secretary General of the Central Committee of the CPC elaborated on the connotation of Ecological Civilization. He said "Building an ecological civilization is a long-term plan for the well-being of the people and the future of the nation. Facing the severe situation of tighter resource constraints, serious environmental pollution and ecological system degradation, we must establish the concept of respecting, adapting to and protecting nature, give prominent status to ecological progress, integrate it into all aspects and the whole process of economic, political, cultural and social development, strive to build a beautiful China and realize sustainable development of the Chinese nation."[395]

In 2014, the amendment of the EPL (2014) adopted the concept of Ecological Civilization in its Article One. In 2016 and 2021, the 13th Five-Year Planning (2016) and the 14th Five-Year Planning (2021) adopted the concept, respectively. In 2018, the Constitution of the PRC adopted the concept in its Preamble, which calls for a coordinated development of "material progress, political progress, spiritual progress, social progress, ecological progress."[396] The idea of ecological civilization has not only perfectly incorporated the traditional Chinese ethical ideas on the relation between nature and humans but also reflected the reality of contemporary society. It is a perfect integration of traditional ideas and contemporary ideas.

The idea of Ecological Civilization has been welcomed in and out of China since it was proposed. For example, an International Symposium on Ecological Civilization and Global Environmental Governance was held in the Hainan University in 2019, which attracted scholars with different cultural backgrounds from many countries, and

393. *See*: The Report of Mr. Hu Jintao, in the 17th National Congress of the Communist Party of China, in the Website of the Central People's Government of the People's Republic of China, http://www.gov.cn/ldhd/2007-10/24/content_785431_4.htm, accessed January 14, 2023.

394. *See*: The Report of Mr. Hu Jintao, in the 17th National Congress of the Communist Party of China, in the Website of the Central People's Government of the People's Republic of China, http://www.gov.cn/ldhd/2007-10/24/content_785431_4.htm, accessed January 14, 2023.

395. XI Jinping, "Winning a Decisive Victory in Building a Moderately Prosperous Society in all Respects and Achieving the Great Victory of Socialism with Chinese Characteristics for a New Era—Report Delivered at the 19th National Congress of the Communist Party of China," http://www.gov.cn/zhuanti/2017-10/27/content_5234876.htm, accessed January 14, 2023.

396. Preamble, The Constitution of the PRC, https://www.gov.cn/guoqing/2018-03/22/content_5276318.htm, accessed January 14, 2023.

had an active discussion on the concept of Ecological Civilization.[397] In the symposium, Professor Paul Barrecy of Southern New Hampshire University pointed out that "the most fascinating feature of China's ecological civilization (shengtai wenming) concept is not its goals, which are essentially indistinguishable from the goals of other post-modern visions of sustainable societies, but its explicit embrace of both modern and traditional means as essential for achieving those goals."[398]

2.2.3.3 Green Growth

In 2010, the Fifth Plenary Session of the National Congress of the CPC passed "the Outline of the 12th Five-Year Plan, which for the first time put forward the idea of Green Growth" officially. The Outline calls for enhancing awareness of crisis, fostering the concept of green and low-carbon development, focusing on energy conservation and emission reduction, improving incentive and constraint mechanisms, accelerating the establishment of resource-saving and environment-friendly production and consumption patterns, enhancing the capacity for sustainable development, and improving the level of ecological civilization.[399] The idea of Green Growth was elaborated and called for by the National Committee of the CPC and the Central Government again in 2012, 2015, 2017 and 2022. A later report of the Central Committee of the CPC (2022) calls for building of a beautiful China, upholding integrated protection and systematic management of mountains, rivers, forests, farmland, lakes, grass, and sand, coordinating industrial restructuring, pollution control, ecological protection, and climate change, and working together to reduce carbon, reduce pollution, promote green growth, and giving priority to ecological, economical, intensive, green and low-carbon development.[400] Nowadays, the idea of Green Growth is popular in China. It has been

---

397. Articles contributed to the symposium had been collected and published by the fourth issue of the Chinese Journal of Environmental Law (2020) (in English). For more details, *see* International Symposium on Ecological Civilization and Global Environmental Governance, co-sponsored by the Institute of Environmental Law of Wuhan University, the International Environmental Law Committee of the China Society of Environmental and Resources Law, the Southern Base of Institute of Environmental Law of Wuhan University, the Research Center for Ecological Civilization Rule of Law of Hainan University, the International Council of Environmental Law (ICEL), the Chinese Journal of Environmental Law, the 2019 Annual Conference of International Environmental Law of the China Society of Environmental and Resources Law and the 22nd Luojia Environmental Law Forum, and the School of Law, Hannan University, Haikou, Hainan Province, October 22-24, 2019, http://www.riel.whu.edu.cn/view/1712.html, accessed February 1, 2023.
398. B. Boer, R. Cantley-Smith & Q. Tianbao eds., (2020), 4 Chinese Journal of Environmental Law, p. 235.
399. *See*: Outline of the 12th Five-Year Plan for Economic and Social Development, in the Website of the Central People's Government of the People's Republic of China, http://www.gov.cn/2011lh/content_1825838_7.htm, accessed January 14, 2023. *See also*: Communique of the Fifth Plenary Session of the 17th CPC Central Committee in the Website of the Central People's Government of the People's Republic of China, http://www.gov.cn/ldhd/2010-10/18/content_1723271.htm, accessed January 14, 2023.
400. *See*: Xi Jinping, "Holding High the Great Banner of socialism with Chinese Characteristics and Striving together to build a modern socialist country in an all-round way—Report delivered to the 20th National Congress of the Communist Party of China holding high the great banner of socialism with Chinese characteristics and striving together to build a modern socialist country

implemented through the various situations of national and local economic and social developments. Together with the ideas of Sustainable Development, Scientific Outlook of Development, and Ecological Civilization and the idea of Green Growth helped to raise the level of environmental ethic of Chinese society to a new height.

2.2.4 Development of Environmental Ethics Since the 1950s

The following graph shows how the environmental ethic of the Chinese people developed since the early 1950s.[401] It shows that while there was moderate growth before the year 2000, the serious environmental problems accumulated since the 1980s and the proposals of the ideas of Sustainable Development, Scientific Outlook of Development, Ecological Civilization and Green Growth have stimulated a dramatic rise of the environmental awareness and environmental ethic of the population in 2020:

Curve of the development of public Environmental Awareness in China (1950–2022)

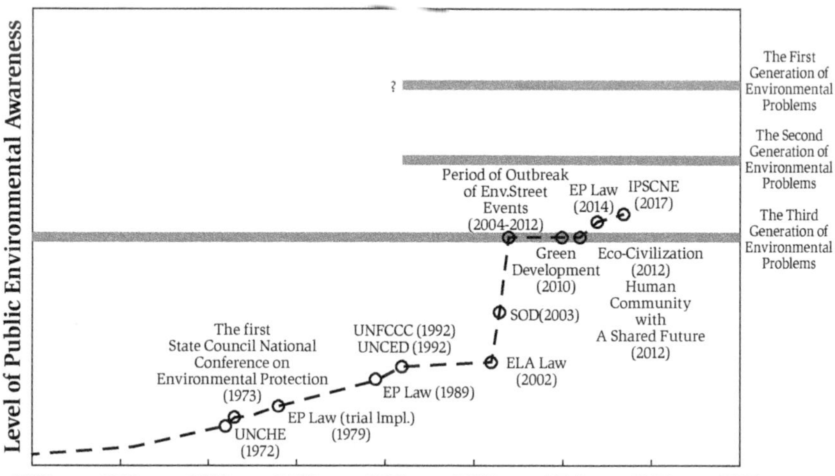

Note:
1. The "IPSCNE" means "Identification of the Principal Social Contradiction in the New Era".
2. The "SOD" means "the Scientific Outlool on Development".

---

in an all-round way—Report delivered to the 20th National Congress of the Communist Party of China," http://www.gov.cn/xinwen/2022-10/25/content_5721685.htm, accessed January 14, 2023.

401. The graph was published in Chinese for the first time in W. Xi, A Comparison of the Political and Cultural Background of Environmental Legislation between China and the United States: From the Perspective of the Evolution of Public Environmental Consciousness, in Environmental Impact Assessment (July 2022) 44, pp. 30-37, at p. 33.

3 POLITICAL RELATIONS IN AIR POLLUTION GOVERNANCE

Since 2003, haze has become a focus of national attention in China. Targeting air pollution control, national and local legislative bodies (People's Congresses), national and local administrative bodies, (governments), enterprises, and all the "third parties" (including grassroots organizations, courts, media and residents) actively participate in the discussion and gradually reached an agreement on measures for air pollution control. Similar to what the LA area has done, the BTH area has the same three political relations in its air pollution governance process. They are a relation of regulation, a relation of supervision of regulators, and a relation of supervision over enterprises and other polluters.

3.1 Relation of Regulation

3.1.1 National Regulatory Measures

The Central Government issued, for the first time, a Plan for Air Pollution Control in Key Cities in October 2012, which provided strict objectives and measures on air pollution control in 13 national key cities and areas, including the BHT area.[402]

In order to carry out national air pollution control law, regulations and plans, the Ministry of Environmental Protection, joined by the National Development and Reform Commission, the Ministry of Industry and Information, and the Ministry of Finance, issued Implementation Rules of Air Pollution Control Action Plan for the BTH area in September 2013.

3.1.1.1 Goals and Targets

Mr. Li Keqiang, the Premier of the State Council, declared that "we will resolutely declare war against pollution." He proposed to carry out joint prevention and control measures for controlling haze in the key cities. He required that nitrogen emissions must be lowered by 2%, the emissions of sulfur dioxide and nitric oxide must be lowered by 3% respectively, and the fine particles ($PM_{2.5}$) concentration in key must be continuously lowered.[403]

On September 3, 2020, Premier Li Keqiang held a meeting on strengthening scientific prevention and control of air pollution and promoting Green Growth. He required, based on the results already achieved, according to the causes of pollution in the BTH area, the strengthening of the precise resolution of individual problems. He put forward three priorities: to replace loose coal with clean energies, to prevent and

402. Ministry of Ecology and Environment: Notice on the issuance of the 12th Five-Year Plan for the Prevention and Control of Air Pollution in Key Regions, https://www.mee.gov.cn/gkml/hbb/bwj/201212/t20121205_243271.htm, accessed February 2, 2023.
403. The Central Government of the People's Republic of China, "Report on Government Work" (March 5, 2016), http://www.gov.cn/guowuyuan/2016zfgzbg.htm, accessed October 29, 2021.

control pollution of diesel vehicles, and to strengthen the control of ammonia emissions in agricultural and animal husbandry production. He also called for coordinated control of fine particulate matter ($PM_{2.5}$) and ozone, as well as strengthening joint prevention and control in the key areas.[404]

3.1.1.2 *Funding*

The Central Government set up funds for air pollution prevention and control. In 2018, a total of RMB 20 billion was arranged for national air pollution prevention and control funds, an increase of 25 % over 2017; RMB 25 billion was arranged for 2019, continuing to maintain a high growth ratio of 25 %.[405]

3.1.1.3 *Action Plans*

On October 28, 2020, the Ministry of Ecology and Environment (MEE), together with the National Development and Reform Commission, the Ministry of Industry and Information Technology, the People's Government of Beijing Municipality, the People's Government of Tianjin Municipality and the People's Government of Hebei Province, released the Action Plan for Comprehensive Control of Air Pollution in Autumn and Winter in Beijing, Tianjin, Hebei and Surrounding Areas and Fenwei Plain, proposed to be effective from 2020 to 2021.[406]

3.1.1.4 *Emission Trading*

In order to further regulate the national registration, trading and settlement of carbon emission rights and protecting the legitimate rights and interests of all participants in the national carbon emission trading market, the MEE issued three documents on May 17, 2021, namely the Management Rules on Carbon Emission Rights Registration (for trial implementation), Management Rules on Carbon Emission Rights Trading (for trial implementation), and Management Rules on Carbon Emission Rights Settlement (for trial implementation). On July 16, 2021, the China Carbon Emissions Trading Market was officially launched, with the trading center located in Shanghai. On the first day of the market, the trading volume was 4.104 million tons, with a turnover of over RMB 210 million and an average transaction price of RMB 51.23 per ton.[407]

404. The Central Government of the People's Republic of China, "Li Keqiang Deploy to Strengthen Scientific Air Pollution Prevention and Control and to Promote Green Development" (September 3, 2020) accessed July 17, 2021.
405. Ministry of Ecology and Environment, "Reply to the Recommendation No.5181 of the Second Session of the 13th National People's Congress" (October 29, 2019), http://www.mee.gov.cn/xxgk2018/xxgk/xxgk13/201910/t20191029_739604.html, accessed July 20, 2021.
406. Ministry of Ecology and Environment, "Announcement on Print and Issue the Action Plan for Comprehensive Control of Air Pollution in Autumn and Winter in Beijing, Tianjin, Hebei and Surrounding Areas and Fenwei Plain from 2020 to 2021" (October 30, 2020), http://www.mee.gov.cn/xxgk2018/xxgk/xxgk03/202011/t20201103_806152.html, accessed July 17, 2021.
407. Xi Hanren, "After the Opening of the National Carbon Emission Trading Market, the Price of the First Transaction Close to the Trading Limit!" (July 16, 2021), https://mp.weixin.qq.com/s/KEj8Rk8xxNtcfsbDULbMuA, accessed July 19, 2021.

3.1.1.5 *Assessment*

On May 27, 2014, the General Office of the State Council issued the Measures on the Assessment of the Implementation of the Action Plan for the Prevention and Control of Air Pollution (For trial Implementation). The Measures apply to the annual and final assessment of the implementation of the Action Plan for the Prevention and Control of Air Pollution (hereinafter referred to as the "Ten Articles of the Atmosphere") by the people's governments of all provinces, autonomous and municipal governments covered by the Measures. The Measures make it clear that the BTH area must make a percentage reduction in the annual average concentration of $PM_{2.5}$ as an indicator of this assessment.[408]

3.1.2 *Local Regulatory Measures*

3.1.2.1 *Local Regulations, Plans and Targets*

In order to make a breakthrough in air pollution control in the BTH area, from 2016 to 2017, Beijing formulated and implemented the Implementation Plan for Enhanced Air Pollution Prevention and Control Measures in the BTH area (2016-2017) and the Detailed Implementation Plan for Comprehensive Air Pollution Control in Autumn and Winter (2017-2018). In 2018, Beijing issued a Three-year Action Plan for Beijing to Win the Battle for a Blue Sky, a roadmap for future air pollution prevention and control.[409] Since 2014, Beijing revised the Beijing Air Pollution Emergency Plan five times. This resulted in improvements in the warning classification, emergency measures, emergency response and organizational safeguards.[410] In 2015, under the organization and coordination of the Coordination Group for Air Pollution Control in the BTH area, Beijing had signed cooperative agreements with Baoding and Langfang, respectively. Tianjin had signed cooperative agreements with Tangshan and Cangzhou respectively and then established a forewarning consultation platform for heavy air pollution.[411]

3.1.2.2 *Emission Permit*

Based upon Article 45 of the EPL and Article 19 of the LPCAP, a permit was required for any major emission of air pollutants in the area. For example, as to the emission

408. General Office of the State Council, "Notice on the Measures on the Assessment of the Implementation of the Action Plan for the Prevention and Control of Air Pollution (For trial Implementation)" (May 27, 2014), http://www.gov.cn/zhengce/content/2014-05/27/content_8830.htm, accessed July 17, 2021.
409. City Government of Beijing (fn 9).
410. General Office of the State Council, "Notice on the Measures on the Assessment of the Implementation of the Action Plan for the Prevention and Control of Air Pollution (For trial Implementation)" (May 27, 2014), http://www.gov.cn/zhengce/content/2014-05/27/content_8830.htm, accessed July 17, 2021. City Government of Beijing (fn 9).
411. People's Government of Hebei Province: The Beijing-Tianjin-Hebei air cooperation has launched regional joint law enforcement, http://www.hebei.gov.cn/hebei/11937442/10765642/12737612/12737652/13326705/index.html, accessed February 2, 2023.

reduction of VOCs in key industries, a total of 51 enterprises in thermal power, paper making, cement, iron and steel and petrochemical industries have completed the issuance of emission permits.[412]

3.1.2.3 *Improving Industrial Structure*

The governments in the BTH area had made great efforts to improve the industrial structure of the area. The industrial structure of the BTH area as a whole was not balanced. The imbalance contributed to the air pollution problem considerably. For example, the tertiary industry ratio in Beijing was 70%-80% of the total industrial activity, with a high concentration of science, technology and finance industries. Both the secondary and service industries were close to 50% in Tianjin. The secondary industries amounted to 50% of the industrial structure of Hebei Province.[413]

Beijing adopted a three-pronged approach of "prohibition, phasing out and treating" to optimize its industrial structure. Firstly, polluting industries were prohibited from being established in Beijing. The Catalogue of Production Process Adjustment and Withdrawal and Equipment Elimination in Industrial Polluting Industries in Beijing (2017 edition) and The Catalogue of Prohibitions and Restrictions on New Industries in Beijing (2018 edition) were revised and published for this purpose. Secondly, polluting industries already were required to be phased out. Since 2013, more than 2,600 polluting enterprises in the printing, casting and furniture industries have been shutdown. The classified disposal of 11,000 "scattered pollution" enterprises was completed. From 2013 to 2017, industrial restructuring measures contributed 17% to the reduction of $PM_{2.5}$ concentrations, 10% to the reduction of NOx and 49% to the reduction of VOCs.[414]

3.1.2.4 *Technology Innovation*

Polluting industries were required to update their production processes and technologies so as to reduce the discharge of pollutants. This includes a general updating of the burning technologies of boilers. More than 400 environmental protection technology renovation projects were completed.[415] The governments in the area promoted technologies such as technologies of de-sulfurization, dust removal, and emission reduction. For example, the Iron and Steel Group of Hebei Province had achieved significant

412. Ministry of Ecology and Environment, "*See* The History of Air Pollution Control, 2013-2018" (September 24, 2019), http://www.mee.gov.cn/xxgk2018/xxgk/xxgk15/201909/t20190924_735251.html, accessed July 20, 2021.
413. Beijing Morning Post, "Beijing will invest RMB 16.54 billion to control atmospheric pollution" (January 23, 2016), http://money.163.com/16/0123/03/BE01HUGH00253B0H.html, accessed May 7, 2016.
414. Ministry of Ecology and Environment, "*See* The History of Air Pollution Control, 2013-2018" (September 24, 2019), http://www.mee.gov.cn/xxgk2018/xxgk/xxgk15/201909/t20190924_735251.html, accessed July 20, 2021.
415. Ministry of Ecology and Environment, "*See* The History of Air Pollution Control, 2013-2018" (September 24, 2019), http://www.mee.gov.cn/xxgk2018/xxgk/xxgk15/201909/t20190924_735251.html, accessed July 20, 2021.

progress in this regard by application of energy conservation and advanced technology such as technologies for recycling combustible gases such as gases from blast furnaces and converters.[416]

3.1.2.5 Optimizing Energy Structure

An unreasonable energy structure was one of the main causes of the air pollution problem in China.[417] According to statistical data, the national total coal consumption was 3.61 billion tons in 2015, which occupied 65.7% of the total energy consumption. In the winter heating period of Northern China, the seasonal decline of air quality was particularly apparent.[418] In 2014, the amount of annual average coal burning in Beijing was 21 million tons, while in Tianjin, it was about 70 million tons and in Hebei Province, it was close to 300 million tons.[419]

On February 25, 2021, Liu Bingjiang, Director of the Department of Atmospheric Environment of the MEE, said at a regular press conference that China's share of coal in primary energy consumption continued to decrease. Between 2017 and 2020, the national share of coal consumption in primary energy consumption dropped from 60.4% to about 57%, and the share of nonfossil energy consumption increased from 13.8% to 15.8%. About 100,000 small coal-fired boilers with no hope of treatment were to be eliminated, and coal-fired boilers of less than 35 steam tons per hour in keys were to be basically zeroed out. The central financial support for clean heating pilot projects in northern areas achieved full coverage in Beijing, Tianjin, plus 26 surrounding cities and the Fenwei Plain, and a total of 25 million households that burning loose coal were replaced with natural gas.[420]

The governments in the BTH area took the adjustment of energy structure seriously. For example, the 2013-2017 Beijing Clean Air Action Plan stipulated that by 2017, the total amount of coal burning of the whole city should be 13 million tons lower than in 2012 and be limited to 10 million tons; the ratio of coal in energy consumption should be lowered to less than 10% and the energy consumption ratio of high-quality

416. The General Net on Information of Building Materials, "Energy conservation and emission reduction efforts of iron and steel enterprises in Hebei province have been intensified" (March 4, 2016), http://www.tanpaifang.com/jienenjianpai/2016/0303/51091.html, accessed October 29, 2021.
417. Net of the National People's Congress of the People's Republic of China, "Report on the Inspection of the Implementation of the Law on Prevention and Control of Air Pollution issued by the Law Enforcement Inspection Team of the Standing Committee of National People's Congress" (October 29, 2014), http://www.npc.gov.cn/zgrdw/npc/xinwen/2014-10/29/content_1883581.htm, accessed May 7, 2016.
418. Ma Hui, "Atmospheric pollution control: how to reduce the total annual coal consumption of 3.6 billion tons?" (October 31, 2014), https://huanbao.bjx.com.cn/news/20141031/559522.shtml, accessed October 29, 2021.
419. People's Net, "The situation of atmospheric pollution control is severe and the problem of air pollution caused by coal-burning is serious" (November 2, 2014), http://energy.people.com.cn/n/2014/1102/c71661-25954746.html, accessed October 29, 2021.
420. Ministry of Ecology and Environment, "The proportion of coal consumption in China Decreased from 60.4 Percent to 57 Percent in 2017-2020" (2020) accessed July 19, 2021.

energy had to be increased to more than 90%.[421] In addition, the Action Plan required vigorous development of renewable energy such as wind power, hydropower, solar power and nuclear power.[422]

In March 2015, the provincial government proposed to build a cleaner coal distribution center and a supply network and increase the use of clean energy.[423] One year later, in March 2016, the Provincial Government reported that the provincial government had invested RMB 24 billion in energy structure adjustment and air pollution control and had shut down 505 surface mines.[424] In January 2020, the Provincial Government reported that a total of 7.59 million households were renovated for clean heating, and a new breakthrough was made in the treatment of loose coal.[425] In February 2021, the Provincial Government reported that 11.25 million households had changed their energy from coal burning to natural gas or electricity.[426] In March 2022, the Provincial Government reported that it had issued guidelines on carbon peak and carbon neutrality and proposed to reduce energy consumption per unit of GDP by more than 5% and carbon dioxide emissions by 5.8%. In order to achieve the goal of carbon neutrality, the Provincial Government proposed that it would accelerate the adjustment of the structure of industries, energy, and transportation, curb the blind development of projects that consume energy and promote the shift to controlling both the total amount and intensity of carbon emissions. In addition, the Provincial Government proposed to strengthen the cleaner and more efficient use of coal, to actively develop wind power, photovoltaics, and hydrogen energy, to increase the installed capacity of renewable energy by 8 million kW, to develop new types of energy storage technologies and devices, to transform key industries into green and low-carbon consumption ones, to create a number of green factories, to advance trading of energy use rights and pollution discharge rights, to enhance the capacity of carbon sink of ecosystems, and to alter the production mode and lifestyle into a green one.[427]

421. Bureau of Ecology and Environment, Beijing City, "2013-2017 Action Plan for Clean Air of Beijing" (April 1, 2017), https://www.beijing.gov.cn/zhengce/zhengcefagui/201905/t20190522_59933.html, accessed October 29, 2021.
422. Bureau of Ecology and Environment, Beijing City, "2013-2017 Action Plan for Clean Air of Beijing" (April 1, 2017), https://www.beijing.gov.cn/zhengce/zhengcefagui/201905/t20190522_59933.html, accessed October 29, 2021.
423. People's Daily of Hebei Province, "2015 Work Report of the Hebei Provincial Government" (February 26, 2015), http://www.71.cn/2015/0226/803356.shtml, accessed October 29, 2021.
424. People's Daily of Hebei Province, "2016 Work Report of the Hebei Provincial Government" (January 25, 2016), http://www.ce.cn/culture/whcyk/136795/qywhdt/201601/25/t20160125_8546341.shtml, accessed October 29, 2021.
425. Hebei Provincial People's Government: Report on the Work of Hebei Provincial Government in 2020, http://www.hebei.gov.cn/hebei/14462058/14471802/14471805/14867283/index.html, accessed February 3, 2023.
426. Hebei Provincial People's Government: Report on the Work of Hebei Provincial Government in 2021, http://www.hebei.gov.cn/hebei/14462058/14471802/14471805/14867283/index.html, accessed February 3, 2023.
427. Hebei Provincial People's Government: Report on the work of the Hebei Provincial Government in 2022, http://www.hebei.gov.cn/hebei/14462058/14471802/14471805/15310129/index.html, accessed April 27, 2022.

3.1.2.6 *Regulating of Major Polluting Sources*

3.1.2.6.1 Automobiles

The large quantity of vehicles and high frequency of car use contribute considerably to the air pollution of the area. According to the data from the Beijing Municipal Statistical Bureau, up to the end of 2014, the total number of automobiles in Beijing was 5.591 million; that is 523.5 thousand tons, which is 31 % of the total NOx emissions from all kinds of NOx emission sources of the city.[428] The contribution rate of automobile exhaust to the pollution of $PM_{2.5}$ in Beijing, Tianjin and Shijiazhuang is 31% 20% and 15%, respectively.[429]

In order to put automobile pollution into control, the governments of the area applied the following measures: First, registration. All of the marketable motor vehicles and non-road-based motor vehicles were required to be registered with the local governmental authority and meet the emission standards stipulated by national and local law. Beijing has applied for a lottery for car registrations since January 2011.[430] Second, inspection. All automobiles were required to be regularly inspected, and only qualified automobiles could receive technical inspection approval for vehicle safety and be granted the qualified label for environmental protection and safety required for their use. Third, traffic restrictions. Traffic restrictions were adopted in given areas according to the need to protect the atmospheric environment. Fourth, compulsory end-of-life for automobiles. When a vehicle has reached the service life stipulated by the state or can't meet the national emission standards, it will be forced to be abandoned and scrapped. To speed up the elimination of old vehicles, Beijing has implemented a plan to further promote the elimination and replacement of old high-emission vehicles (2020-2021). By the end of September 2021, the city had retired a total of 95,000 vehicles.[431]

In 2020, in response to the pollution caused by automobiles, the governments of the BTH area collaborated in drafting the Regulations on the Prevention and Control of Emissions from Motor Vehicles and Non-Road Mobile Machinery.[432] The governments of Beijing City, Tianjin City and Hebei Province voted and passed the Regulations

428. Hebei Provincial People's Government: Report on the work of the Hebei Provincial Government in 2022, http://www.hebei.gov.cn/hebei/14462058/14471802/14471805/15310129/index.html, accessed April 27, 2022.
429. Hebei Provincial People's Government: Report on the work of the Hebei Provincial Government in 2022, http://www.hebei.gov.cn/hebei/14462058/14471802/14471805/15310129/index.html, accessed April 27, 2022.
430. Hebei Provincial People's Government: Report on the work of the Hebei Provincial Government in 2022, http://www.hebei.gov.cn/hebei/14462058/14471802/14471805/15310129/index.html, accessed April 27, 2022.
431. Beijing Bureau of Ecology and Environment: Beijing Mobile Source Pollution Prevention and Control Press Conference in 2021, http://sthjj.beijing.gov.cn/bjhrb/index/xxgk69/sthjlyzwg/fthg/11143035/index.html, accessed April 27, 2022.
432. Ministry of Ecology and Environment of the People's Republic of China, "Year Report of Ministry of Ecology and Environment on Environmental Management of Mobile Polluting Sources" (2021), https://www.mee.gov.cn/hjzl/sthjzk/ydyhjgl/202109/t20210910_920787.shtml, accessed September 12, 2021.

separately. The Port Regulations were implemented simultaneously in the BTH area on May 1, 2020. The main innovations of the regulations included the inclusion of non-road mobile machinery in the scope of emission regulation, the strengthening of coordination and realization of joint prevention and control through information sharing, cooperative supervision in vehicle emission and joint enforcement.[433]

3.1.2.6.2 Port

Beijing does not have any ports. It uses the port in the city of Tianjin. In 2015, the Ministry of Transport issued the Implementation Plan for Emission Control Zones for Ships in the Pearl River Delta, Yangtze River Delta and Bohai Sea Rim (BTH area) Waters. The plan aims to control the emissions of sulfur oxides, nitrogen oxides and particulate matter from Chinese ships, to improve the ambient air quality in coastal and riverine areas, especially in port cities, and to lay a foundation for the comprehensive control of air pollution from ships by establishing emission control zones for ships (hereinafter referred to as "emission control zones"). One of the Emission Control Zones is the Bohai Sea Rim (BTH area) Emission Control Zone for Ships.[434]

On August 2, 2017, the Tianjin Municipal People's Government issued the Implementation Plan for the Tianjin Emission Control Zone for Ships. The Plan required that ships sailing, berthing and operating in the emission control zone shall strictly implement the emission control requirements on sulfur oxides, nitrogen oxides and particulate matters under the existing international conventions and domestic laws, regulations, codes and standards; ships shall use fuel oil with sulfur content ≤ 0.5% m/m (mass ratio) during the period of berthing alongside (except for one hour after berthing and one hour before leaving port, the same below); ships are encouraged to use fuel oil with sulfur content ≤ 0.1% m/m during berthing ashore and are encouraged to use fuel oil with sulfur content ≤ 0.5%m/m when entering the emission control zone; and that any modification to the fuel oil system by ships is required to be inspected and approved by the corresponding ship inspection agency.[435]

In December 2019, the Ministry of Transport issued the Provisions on the Administration of Shore Power for Ports and Ships (hereinafter referred to as "the Provisions"). The Provisions clarified the division of responsibilities for the construction and use of shore power; specified the scope of application for the construction and

433. Ministry of Ecology and Environment of the People's Republic of China, "Year Report of Ministry of Ecology and Environment on Environmental Management of Mobile Polluting Sources" (2021), https://www.mee.gov.cn/hjzl/sthjzk/ydyhjgl/202109/t20210910_920787.shtml, accessed September 12, 2021.
434. The Portal of the Central Government, "Ministry of Transportation issued the Implementation Plan for Emission Control Zones for Ships in the Pearl River Delta, Yangtze River Delta and Bohai Sea Rim (BTH) Waters" (December 4, 2015), http://www.gov.cn/xinwen/2015-12/04/content_5019932.htm, accessed October 15, 2021.
435. The People's Government of Tian Jin City, "The Tianjin Municipal People's Government issued the Implementation Plan for the Tianjin Emission Control Zone for Ships" (May 19, 2020), https://www.tj.gov.cn/zwgk/szfwj/tjsrmzfbgt/202005/t20200519_2370392.html, accessed October 15, 2021.

use of shore power; set out the requirements for the installation of receiving facilities for ships; and also set out the requirements for the priority use of shore power.[436]

3.1.2.6.3 Dusts

Dust pollution is a by-product of urban development. Tianjin is an example of dust control. In order to effectively solve its dust pollution problem, Tianjin adopted the following measures: first, a requirement that requires that all the construction projects adopt measures to control dust, including building enclosures, tarpaulin covers, and hardening, spraying and washing roads according to relevant regulations; second, a requirement that requires all the bulk material yards of coal, coal cinder, gravel and dust to be closed and sealed for those that cannot be closed and sealed, effective cover measures should be adopted to prevent dust blowing; third, a requirement to use special vehicles for closed and sealed transportation.

3.1.2.7 Phasing out Polluting Industries and Replacement of Employees

The local governments in the BTH area worked hard to phase out enterprises with poor economic performance, high energy consumption and serious pollution. In China, this task is called "cutting off excess production capacity." Taking Hebei Province as an example, in 2015, there were 42 profitable enterprises and 27 unprofitable ones in the iron and steel industry in which the amount of their deficits was bigger than the amount of profit.[437] It was hard for the unprofitable ones to meet the environmental protection standards. The best choice was to compel them to shut down. The Work Report of Hebei Provincial Government mentioned that the whole province was going to reduce production capacity by 10 million tons for iron-making, 8 million tons for steel-making, 1.5 million tons for cement-making and 6 million gross weights for boxes of plate glass-making.[438]

In the process of energy consumption reduction, some enterprises had to dismiss employees due to the reduction in capacity of production. For example, Hebei Province was facing the tough task of cutting excess production capacity and had to relocate 547 thousand employees. Among those employees, 426 thousand were in the industries of iron and steel.[439] How to relocate those people was a big problem. The relocation measures adopted by Hebei Province included the following: first, internal placement.

436. Lianyungang Maritime Bureau, "Provisions on the Administration of Shore Power for Ports and Ships" (January 1, 2020), Fujian Provincial Department of Transportation: http://jtyst.fujian.gov.cn/zwgk/zcfg/flfg/201912/t20191225_5168987.htm, accessed October 15, 2021.
437. Xie Wei, "Hebei Part of the Rust Belt: Under the haze, but Difficult to Cut the Capacity of Steel Production" (May 9, 2016), https://www.sohu.com/a/74423760_123753, accessed October 29, 2021.
438. Hebei Daily, "2016 Work Report of the Hebei Provincial Government" (January 25, 2016), http://www.ce.cn/culture/whcyk/136795/qywhdt/201601/25/t20160125_8546341.shtml, accessed October 29, 2021.
439. Net of Hebei News, "Where Should Employees Go in the Process of Cutting Off Production Capacity" (March 4, 2016), http://world.hebnews.cn/2016-03/04/content_5373833.htm, accessed May 7, 2016.

The local governments encouraged enterprises to adjust and restructure their product structures to keep and place displaced employees internally. Up to the end of October 2015, the quantity of employees involved in industrial structure adjustment was 518 thousand and the quantity of internal placement and continue-to-employ was 248.7 thousand. Nearly half of the employees who needed to be relocated were relocated internally.[440] Second, external placement. departments of local governments such as social security departments and labor unions actively organized special job fairs to help the unemployed people get a new job in other entities. Third, encouraging self-employment. The relevant departments of local governments were actively organizing work skill training programs for unemployed people. Local governments arranged for small loans and subsidies to encourage them to self-employ. For example, Tianjin invested RMB 1 billion to compensate 80% to 100% of training expenses for the employees attending job training programs.[441] Fourthly, internal retirement and volunteers for public interest work. The local governments provided internal retirement arrangements and work as volunteers of public interest workers for those unemployed people nearing retirement age. Sixthly, financial compensation. The State Council (the Central Government) dedicated RMB 100 billion to compensate the people who lost their jobs in the iron and steel industry.[442] This fund was applicable to Hebei Province.

3.1.2.8 Ban of Open Burning

The governments of the area issued orders to ban the open burning of leaves, trash, electronic waste, rubber, plastic, leather and so on.

3.1.2.9 Law Enforcement

Enforcement of law by the local administrative authorities was resolute in the BTH area. For example, it was reported that in 2015, 16.8 thousand cases had been filed for investigation or enforcement. Administrative fines reached RMB 1.41 billion, and over 5700 illegal companies had been shut down in the area.[443]

The three governments in the BTH area formulated a Joint Law Enforcement Action Plan to jointly enforce the related laws on air pollution control.[444] In October

440. Sohu News, "Overcapacity Cuts Will Prevent the Creation of Zero-Employment Household, They Divert Workers by This Way" (May 10, 2016), https://www.sohu.com/a/74495777_13 1990, accessed October 29, 2021.
441. Sohu News, "Overcapacity Cuts Will Prevent The Creation of Zero-Employment Household, They Divert Workers by This Way" (May 10, 2016), https://www.sohu.com/a/74495777_13 1990, accessed October 29, 2021.
442. Long Mingjie, "The Central Government Arranges Payment of RMB 100 Billion for Relocating the Employees in the Industries of Coal, Iron and Steel" (March 5, 2016), http://china.huanq iu.com/hot/2016-03/8656026.html, accessed May 7, 2016.
443. NDRC talks about the atmospheric pollution control in BTH area: 16.8 thousand illegal cases have been investigated and fined in last year (March 14, 2016), http://finance.sina.com.cn/ roll/2016-03-14/doc-ifxqhfvp0956881.shtml, accessed May 7, 2016.
444. Jia Nan, "BTH Was to Carry Out Joint Enforcement Actions in Five Areas from 2021 to 2022," http://cn.chinagate.cn/environment/2021-06/28/content_77592047.htm, visited on July 19, 2021.

2013, the Collaborative Group of BTH area Air Pollution Prevention and Control was established. In 2016, Beijing, Tianjin and Hebei unified the implementation of the National Fifth Class emission standards for motor vehicles and oil quality standards; in 2017, the "2 + 26" cities fully supplied automotive oil products in line with the National VI standard, and Beijing, Tianjin and Hebei jointly issued a "Standard of Volatile Organic Compounds for Construction Paints and Adhesives."[445] In June 2021, the ecological and environmental departments of Beijing City, Tianjin City, and Hebei (2021-2022) adopted a plan specifying five key areas for enforcement actions, including air, water, solid wastes (including hazardous wastes), mobile polluting sources and violations happening in administrative boundary areas. As to air pollution, the enforcement actions focused on boiler-using units, industrial dust and VOC emission units, straw burning, construction sites, etc., as well as industrial enterprises that ceased or limited production during the period of emergency response to heavily polluted weather.[446]

3.2 The Relation of Supervision on Regulators

3.2.1 The Supervision of the National Peoples' Congresses

The National People's Congress (NPC) and the Central Government attached great importance to the enforcement of laws and regulations. The NPC Standing Committee inspected the enforcement of the Air Pollution Prevention and Control Law on many occasions.[447] Article16 of the LPCAP stipulated that local governments should annually report to the local People's Congress on the atmospheric environmental quality and the implementation of their air pollution control plans and that they should accept the supervision of the local People's Congress on this matter.

3.2.2 Supervision by the Local Peoples' Congresses

The local People's Congresses and their Standing Committees in the BTH area actively exercise the power of supervision to assure that the target of air pollution control is finally achieved. For example, in September 2014, law enforcement inspection teams of the Standing Committee of National People's Congress were dispatched to 10 cities and inspected the implementation of LPCAP in those localities.[448] The task of the

445. Ministry of Ecology and Environment, "The History of Air Pollution Control, 2013-2018" (2018), http://www.mee.gov.cn/xxgk2018/xxgk/xxgk15/201909/t20190924_735251.html, accessed July 20, 2021.
446. Jia Nan, "BTH Will Carry Out Joint Enforcement Actions in Five Areas from 2021 to 2022" (June 28, 2021) accessed July 19, 2021.
447. Net of National People's Congress, Report on the inspection of the implementation of the Law on Prevention and Control of Air issued by the Law Enforcement Inspection Team of the Standing Committee of National People's Congress, http://www.npc.gov.cn/zgrdw/npc/xinwen/2014-10/29/content_1883581.htm, accessed May 7, 2016.
448. Net of National People's Congress, "Report on the Inspection of the Implementation of the Law on Prevention and Control of Air Issued by the Law Enforcement Inspection Team of the

inspections was to investigate any problems in implementation of the air pollution control measures and to fully listen to opinions about the problems in implementation of LPCAP from local governments, deputies to the People's Congresses at all levels, experts and scholars, and environmental law enforcement officers at the local level and owners of enterprises, so as to promote and strengthen air pollution control for the localities.[449] The Standing Committee of Tianjin Municipal People's Congress conducted an inspection on the implementation of Tianjin Air Pollution Control Regulations from November to December 2015.[450] While affirming the achievements of the Tianjin Municipal Government on air pollution control, the inspection team put forward advice about dust pollution control. The team suggested that all of the enterprises, local governments and residents of the city should make further efforts to make sure that they are carrying out, respectively, their duties on air pollution control.

3.2.3 Ecological and Environmental Inspection

One unique and powerful way for supervision of the environmental performance of the local governments is the Central Ecological and Environmental Inspection (hereinafter referred to as "CEEI") organized and conducted by the Central Government that is headed by a leader of the Ecological Ministry and joined by various related ministries or commissions of the Central Government. The CEEI usually gets information on suspected illegal activities of the enterprises or other polluters,[451] as well as the local governments from either governmental sources or residents' complaints. Once the Inspection has identified and confirmed the existence of illegal activities, it will notify the local provincial government and the local government must investigate the case. Once the suspected illegal activities are confirmed, the local government will go through either an internal discipline procedure or a legal procedure to punish those who have violated relevant laws in these cases. It is reported that from the beginning of 2017 to September 28 of that year, Hebei Province found a total of 37,321 defects in implementation of law and policies in air pollution control. Among those defects, 36,894 have been corrected, involving investigation and punishment of 11,341

Standing Committee of National People's Congress" (October 29, 2014), http://www.npc.gov.cn/zgrdw/npc/xinwen/2014-10/29/content_1883581.htm, accessed May 7, 2016.

449. Net of National People's Congress, "Report on the Inspection of the Implementation of the Law on Prevention and Control of Air Issued by the Law Enforcement Inspection Team of the Standing Committee of National People's Congress" (October 29, 2014), http://www.npc.gov.cn/zgrdw/npc/xinwen/2014-10/29/content_1883581.htm, accessed May 7, 2016.
450. Net of the People's Congress of Tianjin City, "The Standing Committee of Tianjin Municipal People's Congress Inspected the Implementation of the Tianjin Air Pollution Control Regulations" (December 24, 2015), http://www.npc.gov.cn/zgrdw/npc/xinwen/2015-12/24/content_1956014.htm, accessed October 29, 2021.
451. Ministry of Ecology and Environment, "All the Information about Air Pollution Control and CEEI in Wen'an County in this study comes from the following source: Inspection and rectification indicates the results (3): Strive to transformation and upgrading to safeguard green mountains and clear waters—Achieving green development of man-made wooden board industry regulation in Wen'an County, Hebei Province" (January 8, 2021), http://www.mee.gov.cn/ywgz/zysthjbhdc/dczg/202101/t20210108_816687.shtml, accessed October 27, 2021.

people.[452] The punishments include organizational discipline, including suspension of work, removal from position, demotion, dismissal, change of post, disciplinary sanctions, and transfer to public prosecutors. There were 220 governmental officials, including 42 cadres who came from the Communist Party, that were held accountable.[453]

A good example of the supervision of CEEI is the CEEI inspection in the Wen'an County of Langfang City, Hebei Province, in 2017.[454]

Wen'an County is about 55 km south of Beijing. For a long time, Wen'an had developed a strong industry of man-made wooden boards. Wen'an is one of the four man-made wooden board production bases in China. By 2017, for every seven pieces of such wooden board produced in China, one was produced in Wen'an. At its peak, there were more than 2,000 wooden board enterprises in Wen'an. Those enterprises employed nearly 100,000 employees.

Because of backward production technology and poor environmental management, the wooden board production in Wen'an used to cause serious air pollution. In 2016, Wen'an's air quality ranked last in Langfang City. The serious air pollution caught the attention of the Ministry of Environmental Protection by that time. A CEEI group was sent and conducted a detailed investigation of the air pollution problem in April 2017.

Under the strong supervision of the CEEI group, the county government took strong law enforcement actions against the polluting enterprises. It was reported that of the more than 2,000 wooden board manufacturers in the county, only 415 had been retained, 1,529 coal-fired boilers had been dismantled, and more than 5,000 leather pickling, powder and board-splitting factories had been closed down. Meanwhile, under great pressure from the local government, enterprises had taken measures to upgrade production technology. In cooperation with the State Forestry Administration, the Chinese Academy of Forestry and Beijing Forestry University, a Wood Industry Technology Research and Development Center and a state-of-the-art wooden board industry demonstration park had been successfully established in Wen'an.

The Central Ecological Environmental Inspection (CEEI) action caused a quick improvement in the air quality. Under the supervision of CEEI, the county government took regulatory measures against polluting industries, such as closing down and

452. China Environment News: Hebei issued quantified regulations on accountability for the fall and winter gas crackdown, https://m.huanqiu.com/article/9CaKrnK5x1H, accessed April 24, 2022.

453. Xinhua Net, "Hebei Province investigated over 10 thousands people for ineffective solutions in haze Control, and held 22 0 leading cadres accountable" (September 29, 2017), http://finance.sina.com.cn/roll/2017-09-29/doc-ifymkxmh7939565.shtml, accessed July 19, 2021.

454. Ministry of Ecology and Environment, "All the Information about Air Pollution Control and CEEI in Wen'an County in this study comes from the following source: Inspection and rectification indicates the results (3): Strive to transformation and upgrading to safeguard green mountains and clear waters—Achieving green development of man-made wooden board industry regulation in Wen'an County, Hebei Province" (January 8, 2021), http://www.mee.gov.cn/ywgz/zysthjbhdc/dczg/202101/t20210108_816687.shtml, accessed October 27, 2021.

suspending production, dismantling of boilers, banning, and prosecuting illegal enterprises. The following photos[455] show the closing down and the phase-out of boilers, respectively:

By the end of 2017, the air composite index in Wen'an was 6.45, down 22.29% year on year. The $PM_{2.5}$ concentration was 63µg/m3, down 33.26% year on year. In

455. Ministry of Ecology and Environment, "All the Information about Air Pollution Control and CEEI in Wen'an County in this study comes from the following source: Inspection and rectification indicates the results (3): Strive to transformation and upgrading to safeguard green mountains and clear waters—Achieving green development of man-made wooden board industry regulation in Wen'an County, Hebei Province" (January 8, 2021), http://www.mee.gov.cn/ywgz/zysthjbhdc/dczg/202101/t20210108_816687.shtml, accessed October 27, 2021.

2018, the air composite index was 5.73, down 11.16% year on year. $PM_{2.5}$ concentration was 55μg/m3, down 12.7% year on year. In 2019, the air composite index was 5.69, down 4% year on year. $PM_{2.5}$ concentration was 52μg/m3, down 3.7% year on year. In the first half of 2020, the air composite index was 5.46, down 10.64% year on year. $PM_{2.5}$ concentration was 53μg/m3, down 8.62% year on year.

While air pollution was successfully under control, the economy of Wen'an kept growing. The total output value of the wooden board industry before 2017 was RMB 18.6 billion, accounting for 18.9% of the county's total output value; after rectification, the total output value of the industry reached RMB 23.09 billion, accounting for 20.3% of the total output value of the county. Tax revenue increased year by year from 2016 to 2019, reaching RMB 117 million and RMB 160 million, RMB 300 million and RMB 416 million respectively, accounting for 8.55%, 9.33%, 14.81% and 18.76% of the total fiscal revenue of the county.

In order to prevent blindly pursuing local GDP growth and avoiding environmental regulation by the local governments, the discipline inspection and supervision departments of Hebei Province strengthened their administrative accountability system. Forty discipline-violating cases related to air pollution were investigated, and 201 officials were disciplined in 2013.[456] This means that the local administrators were placed under double pressure to achieve both environmental protection and economic development.

3.3 Relation on Supervision Over Enterprises and Other Polluters

There was a relation of supervision over enterprises and other polluters in the governance process of the air pollution control in the BTH area. Environmental NGOs, news media, and courts are all active in the relation.

3.3.1 Supervision by NGOs

National and local environmental NGOs are active in supervising the environmental performance of enterprises and other polluters in the BTH area.

3.3.1.1 Participating in Governmental Decision-Making Processes

Environmental organizations are authorized to access governmental information on the environment by the EPL (2014). The law devoted a new chapter to information disclosure and public participation. Article 53 of the chapter provided that citizens, legal persons and other organizations have the right to obtain environmental information, and participate in and supervise environmental protection in accordance with the

456. National Development and Reform Commission, "The Medium-Term and Long-Term Atmospheric Pollution Control Planning in BTH | Is on the Way, Atmospheric Pollution" (March 14, 2016), http://finance.sina.com.cn/china/bwdt/2016-03-14/doc-ifxqhmve9153503.shtml, accessed May 7, 2016.

law. The LPCAP (2018) also has provisions for governmental information disclosure. Paragraph 2 of Article 14 of the law provided that opinions of relevant trade associations, enterprises and institutions, experts and the public shall be solicited when drawing up a plan for meeting the standard of urban atmospheric environment quality within a time limit. It was reported that 18 environmental NGOs jointly sent a letter about the air pollution source information disclosure policy to the Ministry of Environmental Protection and asked for full disclosure of the information in 2015.[457]

3.3.1.2 Reporting

Each local government in the BTH area had an improved air pollution reporting system and released the numbers of hotline telephones and websites on air pollution control to the public. For example, Article 21 of the Beijing Air Pollution Control Regulation provides that "the municipal people's government shall improve the system for reporting air pollution, make public the telephone number and website of reporting to the public, and clarify the scope of acceptance and responsibilities of the relevant government departments. After receiving a report, the relevant government department had to deal with it in a timely manner according to law and report the result to the informant."[458]

3.3.1.3 Public Interest Litigation

China has seen a rapid growth in environmental public interest legal challenges since January 2015, when the revised version of the EPL authorizing it came into effect. It was reported in 2018 that "Nearly 100 lawsuits have been filed by both NGOs and public prosecutors (or 'people's procurators'), and while many of these cases are still in process, of the ones that have been resolved almost all have been won or mediated."[459] The following is the case of *China Biodiversity Conservation and Green Growth Foundation v. Qinhuangdao Fangyuan Packaging Glass Co.* (2016), which was filed by environmental NGOs in the BTH area. It reflects the supervision of enterprises by environmental NGOs.

In 2016, the Qinhuangdao Intermediate People's Court in Hebei Province heard the case of *China Biodiversity Conservation and Green Growth Foundation (hereinafter referred to as "China Green Growth Foundation") v. Qinhuangdao Fangyuan Packaging Glass Co. (hereinafter referred to as "Fangyuan")*. The case was the first public interest

457. Zhou Chen, "There Are Many Errors and Omissions in the Disclosure of Information on Air Pollution Sources; Environmental Groups Say They Should Be Linked to the Assessments of Local Government" (February 5, 2015), https://www.thepaper.cn/newsDetail_forward_1301139, accessed October 29, 2021.

458. Standing Committee of Beijing Municipal People's Congress: Regulations of Beijing on Prevention and Control of Air Pollution, http://www.bjrd.gov.cn/rdzl/dfxfgk/dfxfg/202101/t20210106_2200190.html, accessed April 24, 2022.

459. China Biodiversity Conservation and Green Development Foundation, "China File: The Future of Public Interest Litigation in China" (January 4, 2018), http://www.cbcgdf.org/English/NewsShow/5010/4154.html, accessed October 29, 2021.

litigation on air pollution in the BTH area. Fangyuan is an enterprise mainly engaged in the manufacturing and processing of various glass packaging bottles, and it has four glass kilns. The company was repeatedly subject to administrative penalties by the Environmental Protection Bureau of the Seaport District of Qinhuangdao (hereinafter referred to as "the Seaport District Environmental Protection Bureau") for excessive emissions. Fangyuan paid an administrative fine of RMB 80,000 on March 18, 2015. From April 13, 2016, to November 23, 2016, the administrative fine was paid in 24 installments totaling RMB 12.81 million. In 2016, the China Green Growth Foundation filed an environmental public interest lawsuit against Fangyuan. On April 10, 2018, the Intermediate People's Court of Qinhuangdao City, Hebei Province, handed down its judgment which ordered Fangyuan to pay compensation of RMB 1,549,600 for the damage caused by the excessive emission of air pollutants, to publish an apology statement for polluting the air environment in the national media, to pay RMB 30,000 to the China Green Growth Foundation for the reasonable expenses incurred in this case, and to cover the costs of the litigation[460]

3.3.2 Supervision by News Media

The exposure of atmospheric environmental violations by news media effectively deterred illegal enterprises and individuals, creating a good atmosphere of public opinion for the implementation of laws and regulations.[461] For example, China Central TV reported the violations of three plastic factories in Wen'an County, Langfang City, Hebei Province, on January 23, 2018. The factories violated the requirement for off-peak production in the heating season. The MEE immediately dispatched an investigation group to the factories when it heard the TV report. On January 24, 2018, the Wen'an County government took firm measures such as cutting off water, power, and raw materials supply to force the factories to stop operation. Moreover, The People's Government of Hebei Province held the leaders of the Party Committee, government and relevant departments of Wen'an County accountable. The managers of the three factories were held accountable too.[462]

460. Supreme People's Court: *China Biodiversity, Conservation and Green Development Foundation v. Qinhuangdao Fangyuan Packaging Glass Co.*, http://www.court.gov.cn/shenpan-xiangqing-216941.html, accessed July 21, 2021.
461. Standing Committee of Beijing Municipal People's Congress: Report of the Law Enforcement Inspection Group of the Standing Committee of the Beijing Municipal People's Congress on the Inspection of the Implementation of the Law of the People's Republic of China on the Prevention and Control of Air Pollution and the Regulations of Beijing Municipality on the Prevention and Control of Air Pollution, http://www.bjrd.gov.cn/zyfb/bg/202012/t20201222_2180163.html, accessed April 27, 2022.
462. The Central People's Government: the first quantitative accountability case of the atmospheric pollution control action of the BTH areas released, http://www.gov.cn/xinwen/2018-02/25/content_5268709.htm, accessed February 3, 2023.

3.3.3 *The "Supervision" by Courts*

According to the EPL and the LPCAP, an entity that causes an air pollution hazard will be liable for eliminating the hazard and compensating the entities or individuals that suffered from the hazard. According to the law in China, disputes about liability and compensation can be mediated and solved by the environmental protection department of the local government based on the request of the parties involved. If mediation is not successful, the parties involved can file a lawsuit in the People's Court, or the parties involved can directly file a lawsuit to the People's Court without going through the mediation process.

By adjudicating public environmental litigations, including litigation against enterprises and competent governmental administrations, the courts can play a special role of "supervision" in the process of pollution control. The above-mentioned case of *China Biodiversity Conservation and Green Growth Foundation v. Qinhuangdao Fangyuan Packaging Glass Co.* is an example of the case in this regard.

4 ACHIEVEMENTS AND CHALLENGES

4.1 Achievements

China and the BTH area have made great progress in air pollution control.

4.1.1 *Optimization of Energy Structure and Energy Consumption*

4.1.1.1 *Nationally Optimization*

Nationally, coal consumption decreased a lot and the structure of energy was improved remarkably from 1978 to 2020. The following table shows the total energy consumption and the proportion in total energy consumption of China during this period:[463]

Total and Composition of Energy Consumption (China)

Years	*Total Energy Consumption (Ten Thousand Tons of Standard Coal)*	*Proportion in Total Energy Consumption (%)*			
		Coal	*Oil*	*Natural Gas*	*Primary Power and Other Energy Sources*
1978	57,144	70.7	22.7	3.2	3.4
1980	60,275	72.2	20.7	3.1	4.0
1985	76,682	75.8	11.7	2.2	4.9
1990	98,703	76.2	16.6	2.1	5.1
1991	103,783	76.1	17.1	2.0	4.8

463. The data in the chart is available from the National Bureau of Statistics, https://data.stats.gov.cn/easyquery.htm?cn=C01, accessed February 27, 2023.

Total and Composition of Energy Consumption (China)					
Years	*Total Energy Consumption (Ten Thousand Tons of Standard Coal)*	*Proportion in Total Energy Consumption (%)*			
		Coal	*Oil*	*Natural Gas*	*Primary Power and Other Energy Sources*
1992	109,170	75.7	17.5	1.9	4.9
1993	115,993	74.7	18.2	1.9	5.2
1994	122,737	75.0	17.4	1.9	5.7
1995	131,176	74.6	17.5	1.8	6.1
1996	135,192	73.5	18.7	1.8	6.0
1997	135,909	71.4	20.4	1.8	6.4
1998	136,184	70.9	20.8	1.8	6.5
1999	140,569	70.6	21.5	2.0	5.9
2000	146,964	68.5	22.0	2.2	7.3
2001	155,547	68.0	21.2	2.4	8.4
2002	169,577	68.5	21.2	2.4	8.4
2003	197,083	70.2	20.1	2.3	7.4
2004	230,281	70.2	19.9	2.3	7.6
2005	261,369	72.4	17.8	2.4	7.4
2006	286,467	72.4	17.5	2.7	7.4
2007	311,442	72.5	17.0	3.0	7.5
2008	320,611	71.5	16.7	3.4	8.4
2009	336,126	71.6	16.4	3.5	8.5
2010	360,648	69.2	17.4	4.0	9.4
2011	387,043	70.2	16.8	4.6	8.4
2012	402,138	68.5	17.0	4.8	9.7
2013	416,913	67.4	17.1	5.3	10.2
2014	428,334	65.8	17.3	5.6	11.3
2015	434,113	63.8	18.4	5.8	12.0
2016	441,492	62.2	18.7	6.1	13.0
2017	455,827	60.6	18.9	6.9	13.6
2018	471,925	59.0	18.9	7.6	14.5
2019	487,488	57.7	19.0	8.0	15.3
2020	498,000	56.8	18.9	8.4	15.9

Based on the above table, the following two graphs are made by the authors to show the changes more visually. One of them is about the total energy consumption (ten thousand tons of standard coal), that is the following:

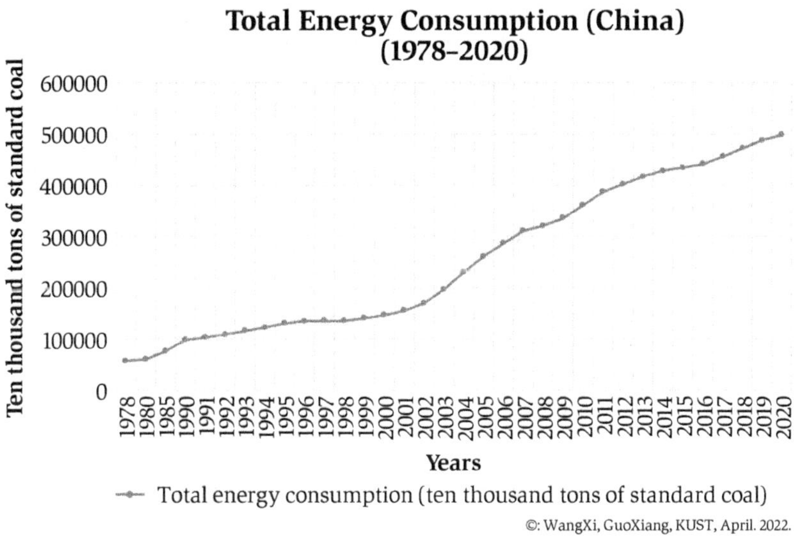

The graph shows that the total energy consumption had increased a lot. This increase reflects that more Chinese people had gotten rid of poverty and had an essential and regular energy supply through 2020.

The other graph is about the proportion or the different shares of energy in the total energy consumption in China, that is as the following:

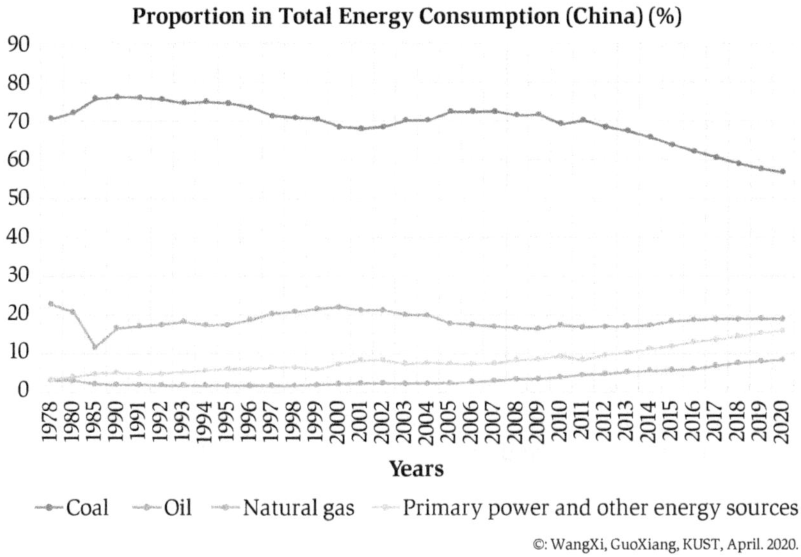

This graph shows that in the total increased energy consumed from 1978 to 2020, the trend of coal consumption had been consistently decreasing, except for a few years of increase in the 1980s. By the year 2019, the consumption of coal had decreased about 20% and the consumption of oil had decreased about 3%. It is noted that in the same period, the consumption of other cleaner primary energy, such as natural gas, nuclear energy, solar power, hydronic power and wind power had increased respectively, with natural gas increased to about 7% and all the others (solar power, hydronic power and wind power) increased to about 14%. In general, the curves were encouraging.

4.1.1.2 Optimization in the BTH Area

The BTH area had made great achievements in optimization of energy structure and energy consumption in the past two decades.

Based on the data of the Beijing Municipal Bureau of Statistics, the authors made the following chart, which shows the total consumption of energy in Beijing from 2010 to 2020:[464]

Total and Composition of Energy Consumption, Beijing (2010-2020)

Years	*Total Energy Consumption (Tons of Standard Coal)*	*Proportion in Total Energy Consumption (%)*					
		(Coal)	*(Oil)*	*(Natural Gas)*	*(Primary Power)*	*(Net Electric Power Input (+), Output (−))*	*(Other Energy)*
2010	6,359.49	29.59	30.94	14.58	0.45	24.35	0.09
2011	6,397.30	26.66	32.92	14.02	0.45	25.62	0.33
2012	6,564.10	25.22	31.61	17.11	0.42	25.38	0.26
2013	6,723.90	23.31	32.19	18.20	0.35	24.99	0.96
2014	6,831.23	20.37	32.56	21.09	0.41	24.03	1.54
2015	6,802.79	13.05	33.79	29.18	0.40	21.71	1.88
2016	6,916.72	9.22	33.14	31.88	0.66	23.37	1.73
2017	7,088.33	5.06	34.00	32.00	0.65	26.15	2.14
2018	7,269.76	2.77	34.14	34.17	0.61	25.68	2.63
2019	7,360.32	1.81	34.55	34.01	0.67	25.79	3.17
2020	6,762.1	1.50	29.27	37.16	0.84	26.96	4.26

Based on the above chart, the authors made the following graph, which shows the trend of the energy consumption (tons of standard coal) of Beijing from 2010 to 2020:

464. The data in the chart is available from the Beijing Municipal Bureau of Statistics, https://nj.tj.beijing.gov.cn/nj/main/2020-tjnj/zk/indexch.htm, accessed February 27, 2023.

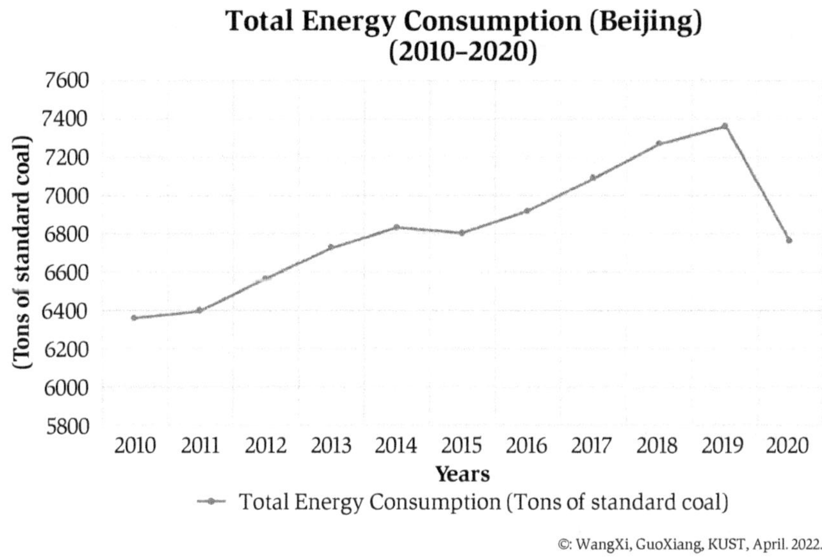

Also based on the above chart, the authors made the following graph, which shows the ratio of different energy consumed in the total energy structure from 2010-2020 in Beijing. It shows that coal consumption had decreased a lot, while natural gas consumption had increased a lot. This change was one of the major reasons for the improvement of the air quality of the BTH area.

4.1.2 Improvement of Air Quality

Air quality of the BTH area was improved. Since 2013, through the great efforts of each of the major players at the national and local levels, air pollution control in the BTH area was achieved as a preliminary success. The following chart shows the changes in concentration of major pollutants in the BTH area from 2013 to 2020.[465] A recent study by the University of Birmingham, UK, confirmed the improvements:[466]

465. Ministry of Ecology and Environment, https://www.mee.gov.cn/, accessed October 24, 2021. It is noted that the data and the from 2013 to 2017 reflects the changes of Beijing, Tianjin and Hebei Province only, while the data from 2018 to 2020 shows the changes in not only Beijing, Tianjin and Hebei Province, but also other surrounding cities, i.e., the "2 plus 26 cities." The "2" means Beijing and Tianjin. The "26" means Shijiazhuang, Tangshan, Handan, Xingtai, Baoding, Cangzhou, Langfang, Hengshui and Xiongan New District in Hebei Province; Taiyuan, Yangquan, Changzhi and Jincheng in Shanxi Province; Jinan, Zibo, Jining, Dezhou, Liaocheng, Bingzhou and Heze in Shandong Province; Zhengzou, Kaifeng, Anyang, Hebi, Xinxiang, Jiaozuo and Puyang in Henan Province.
466. University of Birmingham, China's stricter clean heating policies may have saved thousands of lives—study, News Release February 1, 2023, https://www.eurekalert.org/news-releases/977940?, accessed February 2, 2023.

Changes in Concentrations of Major Pollutants in the BTH Region (2013-2020)

	Pollutant ($\mu g/m^3$)			
Years	SO_2	NO_2	$PM_{2.5}$	PM_{10}
2013	69	51	106	181
2014	52	49	93	158
2015	38	46	77	132
2016	31	49	71	119
2017	25	47	64	113
2018	20	42	60	109
2019	15	40	57	100
2020	12	35	51	87

Based on the above chart, we made the following graph that shows the changes more visually:

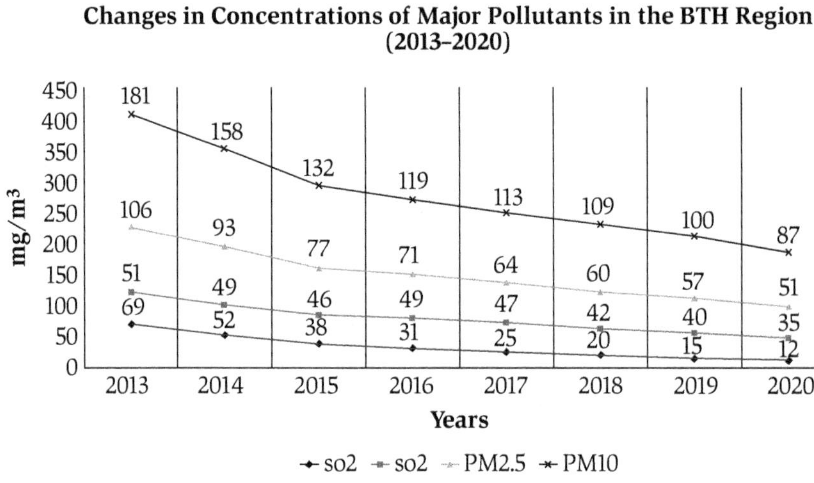

©: WangXi,GuoXiang, KUST,Oct.2021.

Particulate (PM_{10}) was 56 μg/m3, a decrease of 17.6% compared to the data of the same time the previous year, meeting the national secondary standard (70 μg/m3). Compared to 2015, the city's annual average concentrations of fine particulate matter, sulfur, nitrogen dioxide and respirable particulate matter decreased by 52.9%, 70.4%, 42.0% and 44.8% respectively in the four subsequent years.[467] In 2020, the proportion of days with good air quality in Beijing was 75.4%, an increase of 9.6% compared to 2019. Compared to 2015, the city's annual average concentrations of fine particulate

467. Bureau of Ecology and Environment, "Beijing City" (Bulletin of the Bureau of Ecology and Environment, Beijing, 2020), http://sthjj.beijing.gov.cn/bjhrb/resource/cms/article/1718882/10985106/2021051214515686015.pdf, accessed July 16, 2021.

matter, sulfur dioxide, nitrogen dioxide and respirable particulate matter decreased by 52.9%, 70.4%, 42.0% and 44.8% respectively.[468] The following tables[469] show the total energy consumption and its composition in Beijing from 2010 to 2019. As shown in the table, the share of coal in Beijing's total energy consumption had been decreasing year by year since 2010, and as of 2019, coal consumption in Beijing only accounted for 1.81% of the total annual energy consumption.[470]

The above-mentioned progress was confirmed, to a large extent, by data from Greenpeace in 2017. Greenpeace released the Ranking of $PM_{2.5}$ concentration in 365 Chinese Cities in 2017 on January 10, 2018. The data shows that the Phase I targets of the National Action Plan for the Prevention and Control of Air Pollution were basically met in 2017, but the national air pollution situation remained grim, with remarkable ozone pollution and air pollution in the BTH area. In 2017, the average $PM_{2.5}$ concentration in 74 key cities across the country was 48 $\mu g/m^3$, down 33.3%, compared to 72 $\mu g/m^3$ in 2013. In 2017, the average $PM_{2.5}$ concentrations in the BTH, Yangtze River Delta and Pearl River Delta were 64.6 $\mu g/m^3$, 44.7 $\mu g/m^3$ and 34.8 $\mu g/m^3$ respectively, a decrease of 39.2%, 33.3% and 26.0% respectively compared to the data of 2013, meeting the specific targets set out in Article 10 of the Action Plan. In 2017, the average $PM_{2.5}$ concentration in Beijing was 57 $\mu g/m^3$, the annual average concentration decreased by 36.0% compared to 2013, fulfilling the target of 60 $\mu g/m^3$ as stipulated by the Action Plan.[471]

The efforts to combat air pollution in the BTH area yielded significant results. According to data released by the MEE in 2020, the proportion of excellent days in the BTH area ranged from 49.5% to 75.4%, with an average of 63.5%, 10.4% higher than that of 2019.[472] The number of days with $PM_{2.5}$, O3, PM_{10} and NO_2 as the primary pollutants exceeding the standard accounted for 48.0%, 46.6% and 0.2% of the total number of days exceeding the standard, respectively, and there was no day with SO_2 and CO as the primary pollutants exceeding the standard.[473] The annual average concentration of $PM_{2.5}$ in the BTH area in 2020 was 51 micrograms per cubic meter, a

468. Bureau of Ecology and Environment, "Beijing City" (The Bureau of Ecology and Environment of Beijing City Issues Bulletin on Ecology and Environment of Beijing City 2020), http://sthjj.beijing.gov.cn/bjhrb/resource/cms/article/1718882/10985106/2021051214515686015.pdf, accessed July 16, 2021.
469. Bureau of Statistics, "Beijing City" (Beijing Statistical Year study 2021), http://nj.tjj.beijing.gov.cn/nj/main/2020-tjnj/zk/indexch.htm, accessed September 2, 2021.
470. Bureau of Statistics, "Beijing City" (Beijing Statistical Year study 2021), http://nj.tjj.beijing.gov.cn/nj/main/2020-tjnj/zk/indexch.htm, accessed September 2, 2021.
471. Green Peace: (Green Peace issued the Ranking of $PM_{2.5}$ for 365 Cities of China in 2017: the Targets set by "Ten Provisions on Atmosphere" were met and were needed to strengthen ozone pollution and air pollution control in non-BTH areas, January 10, 2018), https://www.greenpeace.org.cn/air-pollution-2017-city-ranking, accessed July 22, 2021.
472. Ministry of Ecology and Environment, "Bulletin on the Ecology and Environment of China" (2020) accessed July 16, 2021.
473. Ministry of Ecology and Environment, "Bulletin on the Ecology and Environment of China" (2020) accessed July 16, 2021.

decrease of 10.5% compared with 2019.[474] The annual average $PM_{2.5}$ concentration was 87 micrograms per cubic meter, a 13.0% decrease from 2019.[475] The annual average SO_2 concentration was 12 micrograms per cubic meter, a 20.2% decrease from 2019.[476]

The following graph shows that concentrations of $PM_{2.5}$, PM_{10} and SO_2 in the air of the BTH area dropped a lot from 2014 to 2020.[477] The annual average concentration in the BTH area in 2020 dropped by 42 micrograms per cubic meter or about 45.2%; the annual average PM 10 concentration dropped by 71 micrograms per cubic meter, or about 45.4%; and the annual average SO_2 concentration dropped by 40 micrograms per cubic meter, or about 23.1%.[478] It indicates that the air quality situation had improved significantly from 2014 to 2020:

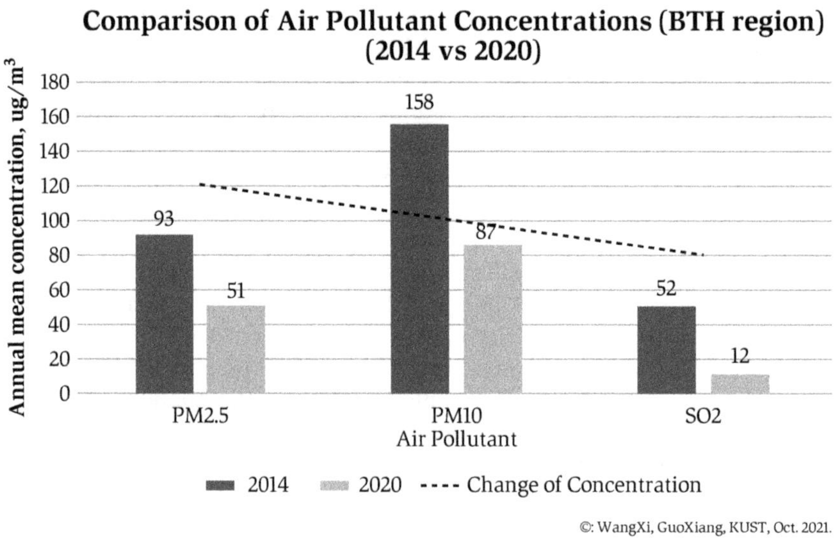

474. Ministry of Ecology and Environment, "Bulletin on the Ecology and Environment of China" (2020) accessed July 16, 2021.
475. Ministry of Ecology and Environment, "Bulletin on the Ecology and Environment of China" (2020) accessed July 16, 2021.
476. Ministry of Ecology and Environment, "Bulletin on the Ecology and Environment of China" (2020) accessed July 16, 2021.
477. Ministry of Ecology and Environment: Bulletin of the State of China's Environment in 2014, https://www.mee.gov.cn/gkml/sthjbgw/qt/201506/W020150605383406308836.pdf; Bulletin of the State of China's Environment in 2020, https://www.mee.gov.cn/hjzl/sthjzk/zghjzkgb/202105/P020210526572756184785.pdf, accessed February 28, 2023.
478. The Ministry of Ecology and Environment, "Bulletin on the Ecology and Environment of China" (2020), https://www.mee.gov.cn/hjzl/sthjzk/zghjzkgb/202105/P020210526572756184785.pdf, accessed March 24, 2022.

4.1.3 Air Pollution Governance

As introduced by the above sections, the air pollution control in the BTH area made great progress in terms of environmental governance since 2013.

4.1.3.1 Regulatory Relation

An effective regulatory relation between the regulators and the regulated communities was established. As indicated by the above-mentioned facts and statistics, all the local governments in the BTH area strengthened environmental regulation of air pollution. All the national and local laws and relations related to air pollution control had been implemented and enforced at a strength and strictness that they never had before. Evaluated by the EG Model, a good regulatory relation (i.e., the bottom side of the triangle of the model) was established. Achievements in air quality in the area are largely due to the health improvements of the relationship.

4.1.3.2 Relation of Supervision Over Regulators

The relation of supervision over regulators was effective. The regulation as shown in the above-mentioned example of Wen'an Country, a strong Central Ecological Environmental Inspection (CEEI) system was established and played an effective role in the BTH area. In addition to the CEEI system, both the local people's congresses and the provincial governments strengthened their supervision over the environmental performance of local governments in the area.

4.1.3.3 Relation of Supervision Over Enterprises and Other Polluters

The relation of supervision over enterprises and other polluters was effective. As indicated by the above-mentioned facts, environmental NGOs participated in the process of air pollution control by means of environmental education, environmental propaganda and filing environmental public interest litigation. The courts "supervised" the environmental performance of enterprises and local governments through adjudicating environmental cases. The news media awakened public environmental consciousness by discovering and reporting on environmental problems. They put the enterprises' illegal emissions and discharges and governmental failure in environmental protection under the magnifying glass of public supervision.

4.2 Value Change in the Society

The most important and far-reaching achievement in the BTH area is the dramatic change of mainstream societal values on environment. Just as what happened in the LA area, when faced with a serious challenge to people's health, the people of the BTH area realized that they had to change their traditional mode of economic growth and adopt an environmentally friendly approach. Once they reached this consensus, they acted through the legislature to establish a legal framework for air pollution control. They requested the local governments to regulate air pollution. They acted to supervise the air pollution regulation of the local government. They acted to supervise polluters through media and courts. The numerous data, stories, and judicial cases introduced above are practical results of such a dramatic change in values.

4.3 Challenges

Although air pollution control in the BTH area has achieved considerable success, there is still a long way to go to realize the objective of fundamental improvement of atmospheric environmental quality. For a more positive interaction among the various major actors in the process of environmental governance, many problems remain to be solved.

First, polluting enterprises have a problem adapting to the tough policy on air pollution control. On the one hand, they are facing increasingly heavier pressure from local environmental administrations and local communities. On the other hand, they are facing difficulties in upgrading their production technologies or transforming their products as well as replacing their employees. For example, Hebei Province changed its previous industrial development policy from one encouraging polluting industries such as the iron, steel and cement industries, into one that encourages environmentally friendly and higher-added value manufacturing industries. This change made it difficult for enterprises to adapt in a short time.

Second, further measures are needed for further improvement of air quality. Although the emission of air pollutants such as particular matter and SO_2 had been reduced a lot, some other air pollutants had not been under adequate control.[479] Therefore, there was still a long way to go for the BTH area to achieve a better air environment.

Third, as to the regulators in air pollution control, the three governments in the area were facing a problem in balancing and fairly sharing the costs of air pollution control. For example, in terms of economic development, Beijing had the highest level of economic development and Hebei Province had the lowest one. But in terms of air pollution from industries, Hebei Province was the major contributor. Thus, Hebei province had to bear a major part of the economic burden of air pollution control, while the improvement of the air quality was equally shared by all three places. The issue of sharing the costs of air pollution control has not been completely resolved.

Fourth, there is a large room for the different Third Parties such as local people's congresses, environmental NGOs, media and courts to play in air pollution control. In recent years, the local people's congresses need to strengthen their supervision over

479. It is reported that "from the perspective of time change, although the emissions of major pollutants have declined overall since the 12th Five-Year Plan, NOx and VOCs have not dropped as significantly as SO_2 and primary particulate matter, and especially VOCs emissions had been basically flat. Pollutant discharge was still at a high levlel, and it was easy to form a al pollution process in the event of adverse meteorological conditions.

the local governments. The joint legislation for air pollution control in the BTH area is still in an experimental stage. There is still a long way to go for implementation of the joint air pollution control agreements assigned by the authorities of the area. There is room for local governments in the area to improve environmental information disclosure. As to the role of NGOs, there is a need to enhance their professional capacity for better participation in the environmental governance process. Their standing to file environmental lawsuits against local governments has not been recognized by law.

Fifth, the energy structure should be further adjusted. There is a need to use more renewable and clean energies in the area.

Sixth, the recent increase in coal consumption brought about concerns about its impact on the national climate policy. It is noteworthy that on September 22, 2020, President Xi Jinping announced at the 75th General Debate of the United Nations General Assembly that China will increase its autonomous national contribution and adopt stronger policies and measures to strive to achieve its commitment to achieve a peak of CO_2 emissions by 2030 and work towards achieving carbon neutrality by 2060.[480] However, it is noted that from the second half of 2021 to August 2022, China increased its consumption of coal. China produced 4.13 billion tons of coal in 2021.[481] An additional 300 million tons of coal capacity is expected to be added in 2022,[482] which means that China's coal capacity is expected to increase by about 7.3% in 2022 compared to 2021. There are two main reasons for this increase in coal capacity. On the international front, due to the COVID-19 pandemic and the impact of international situations such as the war between Russia and Ukraine, the global energy supply is tight, so China had to increase its capacity of coal.[483] On the domestic front, development is the foundation and key to solving all its problems in China.[484] The per capita carbon emission of China is still low. Therefore, in order to develop domestic production, improve people's lives, and meet the needs of the international market, China had to increase its coal consumption.[485]

480. Xi Jingping, (Build on Past Achievements and Forge Ahead to Embark on a New Global Journey to Tackle Climate Change): Remarks at the Climate Ambition Summit, People's Daily, December 13, 2020, p. 1.
481. National Energy Administration: China's energy independent guarantee capacity remains above 80%, http://www.nea.gov.cn/2022-07/29/c_1310647946.htm, accessed August 16, 2022.
482. National Energy Administration: Interpretation of The State Council Executive Meeting: Play the role of coal as the main energy source; this year's Increasing coal production capacity by 300 million tons this year, http://www.nea.gov.cn/2022-04/22/c_1310569203.htm, accessed August 16, 2022.
483. National Energy Administration: China's energy independent guarantee capacity remains above 80%, http://www.nea.gov.cn/2022-07/29/c_1310647946.htm, accessed August 16, 2022.
484. Ministry of Ecology and Environment: Li Keqiang presided over a meeting of the National Energy Commission, stressing the importance of ensuring stable energy supply and security and enhancing the ability to support green development, https://www.mee.gov.cn/ywdt/szyw/202110/t20211011_956109.shtml, accessed August 16, 2022.
485. National Energy Administration: Interpretation of The State Council Executive Meeting: Play the role of coal as the main energy source; this year's Increasing coal production capacity by 300 million tons this year, http://www.nea.gov.cn/2022-04/22/c_1310569203.htm, accessed August 16, 2022.

However, this increase in coal consumption as stated by the CP will not delay the country's goal of "reaching carbon peak and becoming carbon neutral." This is said to be because China's coal capacity increase is tightly constrained by the following "dual carbon target." On the one hand, new coal power plants must meet the latest emissions standards for carbon and other air pollutants; on the other hand, these plants will have to take their share of the growing renewable energy generation quota. Moreover, the increased use of coal in China could be offset by progress towards "carbon neutrality" described as follows: China has introduced a variety of "carbon neutral" measures, such as vigorously developing renewable energy; vigorously promoting the reforms in linkage of coal and electricity; the requirement that all new coal power units shall be built in accordance with ultra-low emission standards; the requirement that coal consumption standards of industries shall reach the international advanced standards; construction of a modern coal market system, etc.[486] The latest increase in coal consumption is only a blip in the long process of lowering the coal consumption in the area in the recent decade. It said that it will not change the general trend that coal consumption will continue to decline. Therefore, the trend of improvement of the air quality in the BTH area may not be intercepted by the blip.

486. National Development and Reform Commission and National Energy Administration: Notice on the Printing and Distribution of the "14th Five-Year Plan for Modern Energy System," https://www.ndrc.gov.cn/xxgk/zcfb/ghwb/202203/t20220322_1320016.html?code=&state=123, accessed August 16, 2022. Note: The "the three combined reforms" are referred to the combined reforms in energy saving and carbon reduction transformation, flexibility transformation and heating transformation.

CHAPTER 5
Comparison and Findings

In Chapter 3 and Chapter 4, backgrounds and the fundamental elements of the air pollution governance processes in the LA area and the BTH area are identified and analyzed. The rich facts, stories, cases and statistics introduced in those parts demonstrate that great efforts were made by all the major actors for combating air pollution during the period studied.[487] The rich information indicates that the two areas had abundant means, strong regulations, strong supervision, and effective legal and ethical frameworks for control of air pollution. Most importantly, the air quality in the two areas were remarkably improved. Therefore, we are confident in stating that there is a strong correlation between the processes of air pollution governance and the improvement of air quality.

Bearing in mind the success of the air pollution governance in the two areas, here are some questions for the comparison: how the two areas, which are so different in their political profiles, have accomplished the same great achievements in air pollution control? What are the major factors determining the success or failure of the air pollution governance in the two areas? This part tries to answer these questions by identifying the various correlations between the improvement of air quality and the major relevant elements of the governance processes of air pollution control in the two areas and tries to reveal the practical and theoretical significances of the correlations.

In order to answer the above-mentioned questions, we are trying to conduct a macro comparison and a micro comparison. The macro comparison targets the background for air pollution governance such as political profiles and the demographic and economic structures. The micro comparison aims at the major elements of the air pollution governance process such as legal and ethical frameworks and the basic political relations.

487. The information in this study ends roughly in December 2022.

1 MACRO COMPARISON

Political profile and demographic and economic structure are the profound social backgrounds for any air pollution governance process. The macro comparison tries to identify two correlations from the experience of the air pollution governance processes of the two areas. One is the correlation between the political profile of the country and the improvement of air quality. The other is the correlation between the demographic and economic structures of the countries, on the one side, and the air quality improvement, on the other side.

1.1 Correlation Between Political Profiles and Air Quality Improvement

As mentioned in Chapter 3 and Chapter 4, there is a huge difference in the political profiles between the United States and China. However, air pollution does not necessarily recognize any political profile, just as it does not recognize any administrative boundary. The huge difference in political profiles such as the nature of state, the form of state structure, the form of organization of state powers, and the system of political party, did not prevent the two areas from making great achievements in improving air quality. The success or failure of air pollution control was not decisively dependent upon those factors. Therefore, here is a finding that the correlation between political profile and air quality improvement is pale and weak. The basic reason for the pale or weak correlation lies in the fact that the ecosystem and the environment, including the air environment, is a global public domain which does not recognize political profiles of the states. This finding reveals that countries with different political profiles can exchange their experience in air pollution governance and learn from each other, no matter how different their political profiles are from each other.

1.2 Correlation Between Economic Structure and Air Quality Improvement

Contrasting to the pale or weak correlation between political file and air quality improvement, the study finds that there has been a remarkable positive correlation between the demographic and economic structures and the air quality improvement in the two areas. Chapters 3 and 4 clearly demonstrate that the higher a society's level of economic development and the larger its middle class, the greater the potential for the success of air pollution governance in the society. The success of air pollution control would not have been possible without the accumulated economic strength and the growth of the middle classes in the two countries and the two areas. This finding reveals that successful air pollution control in a country or area has to be based upon a strong economic foundation. It shows that environmental protection, including air pollution control, and economic development are integrated and are not separated and contradictory to each other. This finding consists of and proves the Principle of the UN Rio Declaration of Environment and Development, which says that "[I]n order to achieve sustainable development, environmental protection shall constitute an integral part of the development process and cannot be considered in isolation from it."[488]

2 MICRO COMPARISON

The experience of air pollution control in the two areas indicated that an environmental governance process consists of legal and ethical frameworks and three major political relations of the major actors in the processes. In this section, the comparison targets of the frameworks and the major political relations.

2.1 Comparison of Legal and Ethical Frameworks

2.1.1 Comparison of Legal Frameworks

Both areas developed relatively complete legal frameworks for air pollution control. The frameworks consisted of national and local laws and regulations, as well as other norms such as technical standards. As described in Chapter 3 and Chapter 4, the coverage of the legal frameworks was broad, covering all the major sources of air pollution and major political relations.

The rich data, stories and judicial cases of air pollution control in the two areas revealed that there was a remarkable positive correlation between the completeness of the legal and ethical framework and the improvement of air quality. The more completed the legal and ethical frameworks were, the more improvements in the air quality were likely to be. In both areas, the legal frameworks consist of national and local laws and regulations on air pollution control. The national law sets national goals, standards and regulatory systems for air pollution control. The state law or provincial law must be consistent with the national law and standards. In some circumstances, the state law or provincial law can set air pollution control standards which are stricter than their national counterparts. There are usually supervisory or checking provisions in national law, which look after the performance of the state or provincial or lower levels of government in carrying out their environmental duties. There are provisions in national law which authorize and guarantee the participation of all the stakeholders, especially the general public, in the state environmental affairs, such as environmental public interest litigation. The legal framework is the baseline and last protection of the political relations in the air pollution governance processes of the areas. In both areas, the air quality improvements started with the enactment of laws and regulations. Therefore, no effort is spared to establish and strengthen the legal frameworks in both areas.

488. United Nations General Assembly, Report of the United Nations Conference on Environment and Development* (Rio de Janeiro, June 3-14, 1992), Annex I Rio Declaration on Environment and Development, https://www.un.org/en/development/desa/population/migration/general assembly/docs/globalcompact/A_CONF.151_26_Vol.I_Declaration.pdf, accessed August 4, 2023.

2.1.2 *Comparison of Ethical Frameworks*

2.1.2.1 *Comparison of Historical Developments of Environmental Ethics in the United States and China*

The graph below imitates and compares the development processes of environmental ethics in China and the United States in the past 70 years. The graph comes from a comparative study of Chinese and American environmental impact assessment systems completed by a joint team of Chinese and American scholars in September 2020.[489] The graph provides a broad historical context for understanding the ethical frameworks for air pollution control in the two areas. It is an overlay of the curves of the development of environmental ethics in the United States and China (1950-2020). The overlay is indeed a comparison. The following comparison is based on three aspects of the process of the ethical development of the two areas. They are the aspects of peak times, evolutionary trends, and driving forces:

Comparison of public environmental awareness levels in China and the United States (1950–2022)

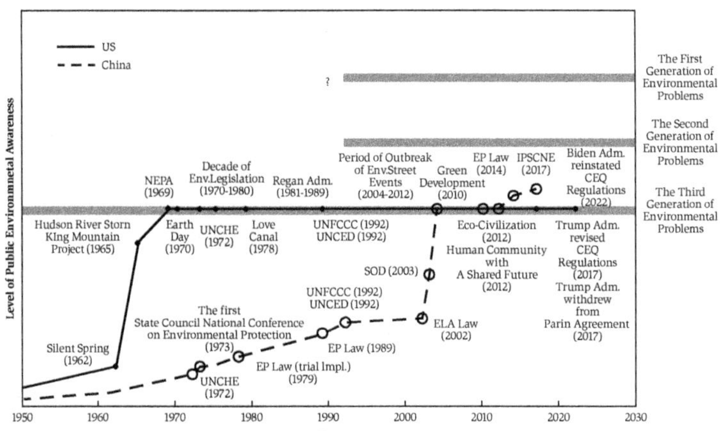

Note:
1. The "IPSCNE" means "Identification of the Principal Social Contradicition in the New Era".
2. The "SOD" means "the Scientific Outlool on Development".

489. It is the Research Project on Comparative Study of the EIA Laws in China and the USA, which was granted by the Ministry of Ecology and Environment of the P.R.C. in July 2019. Professor Wang Xi is the project leader. The members of the project include a group of Chinese environmental law scholars from all over China, including Luo Wenjun, Zhou Wei, Zhou Yanfang, Yang Huaguo, Wang Xiaojun, Tang Tang, Xie Haibo, Lu Kun, Zhang Yan, Yuan Xiaofei, and Gao Qianwen, and a group of American scholars from various law schools and other institutes, including Nicholas Robinson, Dan Tarlock, Sam Kalen, Lawrence Watters, Paul Barressi, Robert Lifset, Ellen Spitalnik, and Shiyan Jiang. A report of this study was submitted to the Ministry in September 2020. The graph was published in Chinese for the first time in W. Xi, A Comparison of the Political and Cultural Background of Environmental Legislation between China and the United States: From the Perspective of the Evolution of Public Environmental Consciousness, in Environmental Impact Assessment (July 2022), 44, pp. 30-37, at p. 34.

2.1.2.1.1 Peak Times

The graph shows that there was a point in time when the level of environmental ethics rose suddenly and substantially both in the United States and China. In the United States, this time point was in the 1970s, marked by the national Earth Day event in April 1970. In China, the time point was in the first decade of the twenty-first century, marked by the breaking out of many environmental mass events during that period.

The difference in the peak times is mainly due to the difference in the stage of economic development of the two countries. The United States experienced environmental crises earlier than China because of its earlier industrialization. As a result of this earlier experience, the peak time of the U.S. came earlier than China. As to China, it only accelerated its industrialization after it adopted reforms and opened up policy in 1978. The problems of serious environmental pollution, ecological damage and significant depletion of natural resources mostly came out after 1978. By the first decade of the twenty-first century, the environmental problems had accumulated and reached a level that critically affected people's vital interests in survival (access to clean air, fresh water, clean land, a quiet environment, and problems of storms, floods, wildfires, and draughts, etc.) and sustainable economic and social development. The severe smog that broke out in the BTH area around 2013 is one of the results of accumulated environmental pollution. As a result, people awakened and the level of environmental ethics had a sudden and sharp rise in the first decade of the twenty-first century.

The fact that sooner or later people will be environmentally awakened and their environmental ethics rise suddenly and sharply tells us that there is a correlation between the environmental crises and the environmental political action of the people. In the LA area, people started that action in the 1940s, while in the BTH area, people started that action in the 2010s. Those actions led to successful air pollution governance processes in the two areas and finally resulted in the improvement of air quality. In this sense, there is a positive correlation between the rise of environmental ethics and the improvement of air quality.

2.1.2.1.2 Evolutionary Trends

As the graph above shows, the evolutionary curve of the American people had an early sharp rise in the late 1960s and early 1970s. The curve reached a peak point in 1970 when the National Environmental Policy Act (NEPA) was enacted and has kept that height so far until now. Due to the serious haze problem in the late 1940s, the rise of environmental ethics in the LA area was earlier than in other parts of the country. As to China, as the graph shows, the evolutionary curves of the environmental ethic had been a long, slow, upward-sloping line for many years and then a sharp rise to the first peak point, which was about the same height as the American curve of the environmental ethic by 2004.

However, it is interesting to see that the Chinese curve of environmental ethics had a gentle rise again in 2012 when the Chinese Communist Party and the Central Government proposed the concept of a Scientific Outlook of Development and that the curve kept rising after that because the Chinese Communist Party and the Central Government promoted the environmental ethic by proposing and carrying out a number of new ideas and concepts such as Ecological Civilization and Green Growth. The gentle rise of the curve in 2012 indicates that the trend of the development of the environmental ethic in China had a second rise and started to move to a new and higher level.

By contrast, in 2012, the American curve of the environmental ethic was at a standstill at the level of 1970. By the time of 2017, things went sour. Preside Trump revised the NEPA Regulation, relaxing EIA requirements and withdrew from the Paris Agreement on Climate Change. There was a deep divide between the Republican party followers of President Trump and the Democrats for what President Trump did. The different direction of the trend, as indicated by the above graph, shows that when the Chinese Government made a new effort to carry out its duty in environmental education, the U.S. Government was at a standstill in this regard. The standstill meant less leading and educational role played by the U.S. Government.

2.1.2.1.3 Driving Forces

As indicated in Chapter 3 and Chapter 4, the driving forces take the forms of from bottom to up and from up to bottom. As to the driving force of from-up-to-bottom, there were some examples in which the governments play an important role in educating the public on environmental matters. As reported in Chapter 3, numerous governmental programs such as the General Plan to address pollution adopted by the City of Los Angeles in 1992, the CEQA, the Air Toxics Emission Inventory Data System, the Air Toxics Emission Inventory Data System, and the CHAPIS have the function of environmental education. As to the driving force of from-bottom-to-up, there were innumerable examples. The protests of the public for air pollution in the LA area in the later 1940s and 1950s, prompted by the media, had a strong push from the local legislatures to establish and strengthen laws and regulations on air pollution control, especially, controlling the pollution from the major industries. The first Earth Day commemoration in 1972 is another excellent example of this driving force in the early 1970s.

In China and the BTH area, both the from-up-to-bottom and the from-bottom-to-up driving forces exist. As to the from-up-to-bottom driving force, as reported by Chapter 4, both the Central Government and all the provincial and local governments have played an important role in environmental enlightenment and environmental education even since the early 1970s. Both the key messages from the 1972 UNCHE (Stockholm) and the 1992 UNCED (Johannesburg) were transmitted to China through the Chinese Governmental Delegations to the conferences and had a profound and long-term influence in China. This is an endogenous driving force throughout the whole process of the air pollution control in China and the BTH area. As to the from-bottom-to-up driving force, the story of air pollution control in the BHT region is a good example. By the time of 2004 to 2012, haze was so serious in the BTH area that people had a very strong desire to eliminate the air pollution. Finally, the two driving forces joined together and generated a tremendous impetus that quickly pushed the environmental ethic to a high level and pushed the government to take firm action to control air pollution in the first decade of the twenty-first century.

In both areas, while the driving force of from-bottom-to-up, represented by the efforts of governmental environmental education, was based on the leading and educational duties of the government, the driving force of from-bottom-to-up, represented by public environmental actions, was based on the longing for survival of the people from serious pollution and the need for sustainable development.

One of the basic similarities in the driving forces is the desire for survival. Facing severe pollution (albeit at different times and degrees in the two countries), the people in both areas felt a great threat to their health, safety and even survival. Therefore, many of them recognized the need to change human behavior towards nature. The perceived threat to survival is the basic internal reason for the environmental awareness and willingness to take environmental political action by the people in both areas. This perception is largely a driving force of from-bottom-to-up for the rise of environmental ethics. The stronger the desire is, the sooner the establishment of the legal and ethical framework for environmental governance is made possible. Therefore, there is a correlation between the driving force of from-bottom-to-up and the improvement of air quality.

2.1.3 Comparison of Value Change of Society

As indicated by Chapter 3 and Chapter 4, in front of the serious air pollution, the mainstream social values of both the LA and the BTH area had been changed dramatically toward human health and environmental protection. As mentioned above, although the changes took place at different times, they indeed happened and were basically the same. The social value had changed from neglecting the environmental externality, which includes harmful effects on human health, to paying great attention to it and putting great efforts into internalizing it. This change is a key intrinsic driving force for fighting air pollution. The change was powerful. It caused the actions of all entities in the two areas. The legal framework, numerous measures responding to air pollution, three political relations, and governance processes in the two areas all come into existence due to the changes in social values. The change of the mainstream social value on environment is actually the change of ethics on the relation between human beings and nature. The laws of ecology were for the first time popularized and became an integrated part of the mainstream social ethic in both two areas. As indicated in Chapter 3, this value change in the United States and the LA area was represented by the Earth Day Celebration in 1972 and many other activities of environmental awakening, while in the BTH area, this value change was represented by the acceptance and popularization of new concepts, such as "sustainable development" and "ecological civilization" in the 1990s and 2000s as indicated by Chapter 4.

Professor Francis Fukuyama suggested that in order to understand changes in political systems, people should comprehend economic growth, social mobilization, and ideas regarding justice and legitimacy.[490] According to him, "social mobilization" means "different groups in society realize that their members have common interests and identity, so as to organize and take collective action."[491] The stories of air pollution control in the two areas, especially the establishment and smooth operation of the air pollution governance processes, demonstrate that the societies of the two places had been successfully organized and mobilized to fight against air pollution. All the entities in the governance processes believe that controlling air pollution is in their common interest. Professor Francis Fukuyama pointed out that "legitimacy represents a broad consensus that certain social arrangements are just."[492] The stories of air pollution control in the two areas demonstrate that all entities involved in the governance process have reached a consensus that fighting against air pollution is a legitimate course of action, and as such, they have taken numerous measures to eliminate the pollution. In short, the stories of air pollution control in both areas not only demonstrate successful social mobilization for controlling air pollution but also reflect a broad and strong social consensus on the issue. It is worth noting that both the social mobilization and social consensus are based on the same values changes in the societies of the two areas. Only by reaching a consensus can the framework of environmental governance and the three political relationships within that framework be formed, and such a variety of regulatory and supervisory measures be adopted.

It is obvious that there is a positive correlation between the development of environmental ethics and the improvement of air quality in the two areas. The new environmental ethics provided strong support to the health operation of the air pollution governance processes in the two areas. The governance processes supported by the new environmental ethics, in turn, led to the improvement of the air quality. The experience of value change approves that value choice or value change is the core of the air pollution governance processes of the two areas.

2.2 Comparison of Regulatory and Other Measures

As indicated in Part Three and Chapter 4, numerous regulatory and other measures were applied in the air pollution governance processes of the two areas. They were applied through the three major political relations in the governance processes. They are the results of specific environmental games and decision-making, which were represented by the symbol of value choice in the center of the EG Model.

490. Written by Francis Fukuyama, translated by Mao Junjie, Political Order and Political Decay, in Chinese, published by Guangxi Normal University, 2015, p. 40. Francis Fukuyama is a political scientist at Harvard University of the United States.
491. Written by Francis Fukuyama, translated by Mao Junjie, Political Order and Political Decay, in Chinese, published by Guangxi Normal University, 2015, p. 40.
492. Written by Francis Fukuyama, translated by Mao Junjie, Political Order and Political Decay, in Chinese, published by Guangxi Normal University, 2015, p. 36.

2.2.1 Measures Categorized by Political Relations

We are trying to determine the political relations that the various measures serve in air pollution governance in the two areas. As the following "Chart of Measures Categorized by Political Relations" shows, all those measures can be categorized into three political relations:

Chart of Measures Categorized by Political Relation

©: WangXi,GuoXiang, KUST, February.2023.

In other words, the three political relations—the relation of regulation, the relation of supervision over the regulators, and the relation of supervision over enterprises and other polluters—jointly constitute an internal structure of the governance processes. Therefore, with the help of the EG Model, we are able to identify the major political relations from the mess of the application of those various measures. After this identification and analysis, an air pollution governance process is not a big mess or an irregular combination of the implementation of various measures anymore. Instead, it becomes a thing that can be examined according to some normative standards. This is perhaps one of the major achievements of this comparative case study.

By the following Pie Chart of Measures categorized by political relation, we try to demonstrate the comparative importance of each of the three political relations in the air pollution governance of the two areas. It shows that, of the total 67 measures, 55% were applied in regulatory relations; 31% were applied in relation to supervision over governments; 14% were applied in relation to supervision over enterprises and other polluters.

It is noted that the distribution of those measures in the three relations was not even. The pie chart demonstrates that, first, the relation of regulation was the overwhelming and fundamental relation of the air pollution governance. This figure coincides with the general suggestion of economists that "for almost all pollution, as well as other health and safety externalities, governments rely on direct regulatory controls; these are often called *social regulations*. ... For example, the 1970 Clean Air Act reduced allowable emissions of three major pollutants by 90 percent. In 1977, utilities were told to reduce sulfur emissions at new plants by 90 percent. In a series of regulations over the last decades, firms were told they must phase out ozone-depleting chemicals. And so it goes with regulation."[493]

Second, it shows that while regulation was essential, supervision over the regulators was indispensable. The pie chart shows that this relation occupied 31% of the whole pie chart. Without this supervision, the regulation, in many circumstances, would be a failure. Professor James M. Buchannan and Professor Geoffrey Brennan pointed out the reasons for supervising government in the 1980s.[494] They said "Our purpose is to develop the intertemporal theme with the aid of distinct and familiar examples drawn from economic problems of the 1970s and 1980s in the United States and other Western nations. We shall discuss the 'high-tax trap', the 'inflation trap,' and the 'public-debt trap', all of which demonstrate the general problem of imprudence in modern democratic polities, different countries having experienced these separate problems in differing degrees of relative importance. The inferences to be drawn for our larger and more comprehensive theme become clear as the analysis is developed; governments can be induced to take the long view only if they are appropriately constrained by constitutional rules that do not now exist. These reasons for rules emerge from an understanding of the workings of modern political economies."[495] Professor James Salzman and Professor Barton Thompson further pointed out that "Given the risk of state enforcement agencies catering to local industry interests, EPA reserves the right to step in and interfere with state enforcement actions, even if the state has imposed sanctions. If the state fails to take 'timely' and 'appropriate' enforcement action, the EPA can impose additional penalties on violators. In simple terms, if EPA officials believe that state enforcement agencies are too slow to respond to a violation (i.e., fail to take action for 90 to 120 days from the date of discovery of the violation) or are too lenient (i.e., the punishment for the violation does not match its severity), EPA can increase fines or take other measures, as long as those measures are consistent with state law in the state where the environmental violation is located because the EPA approved state enforcement in lieu of federal enforcement."[496] Therefore, both economists and jurists approve of the necessity of this relation. The

493. Paul A. Samuelson & William D. Nordhaus eds., Chen Xiao, etc. translated and illustrated, Economics (Eighteenth Edition) (Version for Bilingual teaching), Posts & Telecom Press, 2021, p. 374. Professor Paul A. Samuelson (1915-2009) is an American economist who was awarded the Nobel Prize in Economic Sciences in 1970.
494. Professor James M. Buchannan (1919-2013) is an American economist who was awarded the Nobel Prize in Economic Sciences in 1986. Professor Geoffrey M. Brennan (1944-2022) is an Australian economist who worked and co-authored articles and books with Professor James M. Buchannan.
495. Geoffrey M. Brennan & James M. Buchannan, The Reasons of Rules: Constitutional Political Economy, Cambridge University Press, 1985; Foreword and coauthor note, 2000, Liberty Fund, Inc., 2000, p. 93.
496. James Salzman & Barton Thompson eds., Xu Zuoran, Hu Muyun translated, Environmental Law and Policy (Fourth Edition), In Chinese, Beijing University Press, 2016, p. 67.

necessity of this relation was approved by the legislation of the PRC too. The Standing Committee of the National People's Congress issued the Decision on Authorizing the Supreme People's Procuratorate to Carry Out Pilot Work of Public Interest Litigation in Some Regions in 2015. The Decision provides that the purpose of public interest litigation is "to safeguard national and public interests."[497]

Thirdly, it shows that the relation of supervision over the polluters was necessary. The measures applied in this kind of relation occupied 14% of the whole pie chart. This figure demonstrates that entities such as residents, media professionals, NGOs, and even the courts played important roles in the air pollution governance processes:

Pie Chart of Measures Categorized by Political Relation

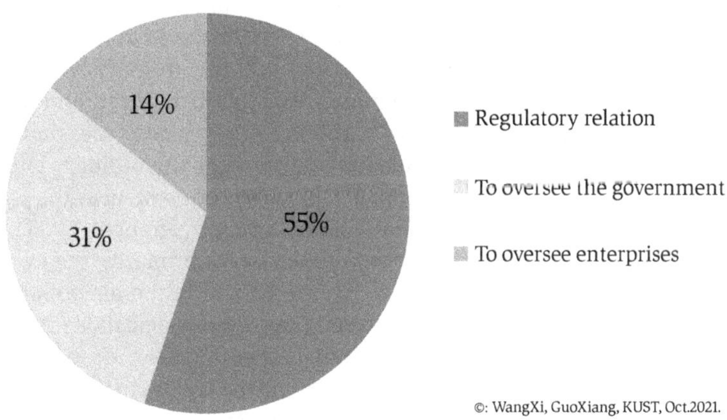

2.2.2 *Measures Categorized by Actors*

By the following "Chart on Measures Categorized by Actor" and "Pie Chart on Measures Categorized by Actor," we are trying to identify and distinguish the status and roles of the major actors or parties in the air pollution governance of the areas. The two charts show that the 66 measures applied for air pollution control had been distributed among the three groups of actors, i.e., government, enterprises and other polluters, and the third parties.[498]

---

497. The Standing Committee of the National People's Congress, The Decision on Authorizing the Supreme People's Procuratorate to Carry Out Pilot Work of Public Interest Litigation in Some Regions, 2015, https://www.gov.cn/xinwen/2015-07/01/content_2888125.htm#: ~ :text, accessed July 26, 2022.

498. For a brief English introduction of the political and legal structure of the People's Republic of China, *see* Wang Xi & Lu Kun, Environmental Law in China, Second Edition, Kluwer Law International BV, 2017, section 2 of Chapter One, General Introduction, pp. 17-23, and Chapter Three, pp. 35-41, as well as Chapter Four, pp. 41-54.

They show three commonalities: First, as the regulators, governments (administrative authorities both at the central (federal) and local levels (state and city)) were the main actors in implementation of air pollution control measures. Of the 66 air pollution control measures, 36 were implemented by administrative authorities, accounting for 58% of the total. Second, all third-party actors were indispensable actors and played an essential role in air pollution control. There were 24 measures implemented by the third-party actors, accounting for 33% of the total. Particularly, it shows that courts played an important role in supervision of both the regulators and the polluters. In both the LA and the BTH areas, there were many environmental public interest litigations (in the United States, those cases are called "citizen suits"). They are either cases on supervision of regulators or cases on supervision of polluters. Citizens or environmental NGOs put great pressure on both the regulatory administrations of the government and the polluting enterprises through those public interest litigations. This is just as what Professor Joseph L. Sax[499] said "... the availability of a judicial forum is a measure of the willingness of government to subject itself to challenge on the merits of decisions made by public officials; to accept the possibility that the ordinary citizen may have useful ideas to contribute to the effectuation of the public interest; and to submit to them if—in the rigorous process of act gathering—those ideas are shown to have substantial merit. Litigation is thus a means of access for the ordinary citizen to the process of governmental decision-making. It is in many circumstances the only tool for genuine citizen participation in the operative process of government."[500] Third, as the regulated polluters, enterprises and other polluters were primarily the bearers of air pollution control obligations and responsible for achieving the air pollution control measures imposed on them by law and policy. They were responsible for carrying out six measures, mostly reactive to the regulation, accounting for 9% of the total. The three commonalities reflect reasonably the roles played by the major three groups of actors in the air pollution governance of the two areas:

499. Joseph L. Sax is an American Law Professor Who Proposed the Idea of Environmental Citizen Suit and the Public Trust Doctrine in 1970s.
500. Joseph L. Sax, Defending the Environment: A Strategy for Citizen Actions, Published by Alfred A. Knopf, 1971, p. 57.

Chart of Measures Categorized by Actor

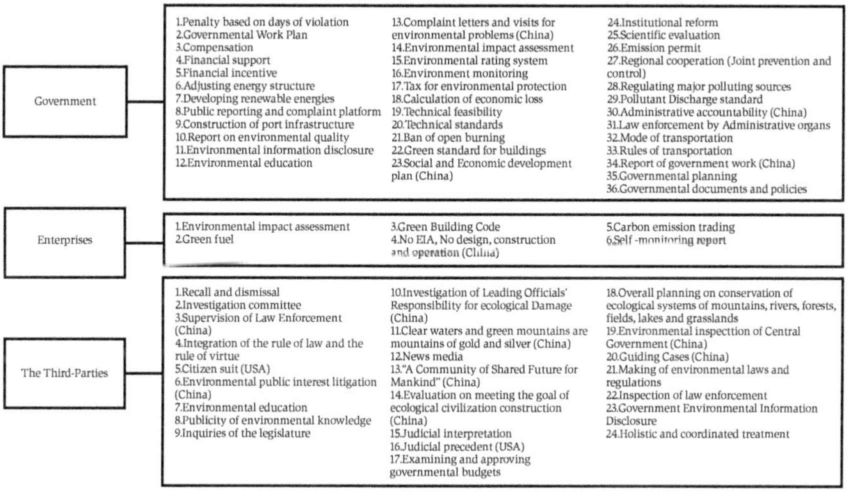

©: WangXi,GuoXiang, KUST, February.2023.

Pie Chart of Measures Categorized by Actor

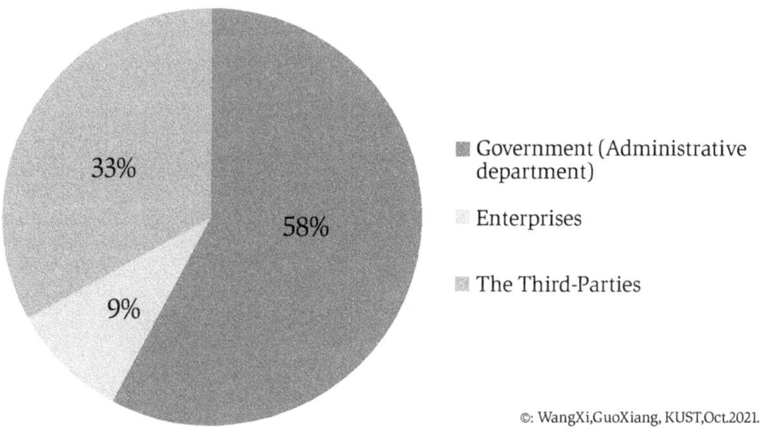

2.2.3 Measures Categorized by Nature

We are trying to identify the different natures of the various measures applied in air pollution governance in the two areas, in order to determine which instruments are being used to establish the legal and ethical frameworks for air pollution control in the two areas. The following "Chart of Measures Categorized by Nature" and "Pie Chart on Measures Categorized by Nature" show that, of the total 67 measures, 67% were laws and regulations; 17% were disciplines of CPC and the Chinese government; 16% were ethical rules. It is noted that because the disciplines of CPC and the Chinese government are generally not comparable with those of the USA, they should be removed from the comparison. But even with their removal, the pie chart still shows that 67% of the measures were laws and regulations. Those charts demonstrate that, in both the areas, legally binding rules or norms of conduct, such as laws and regulations, were the primary instruments for controlling air pollution. Additionally, ethical norms played an indispensable role in air pollution control:

Chart of Measures Categorized by Nature

©: WangXi,GuoXiang, KUST, February.2023.

Pie Chart of Measures Categorized by Nature

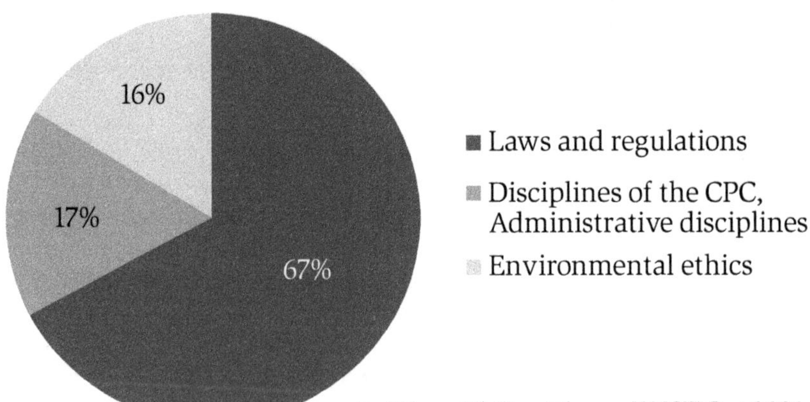

©: WangXi,GuoXiang, KUST,Oct.2021.

2.2.4 *Measures Categorized by Function*

We are trying to determine the main functions of the different measures applied in air pollution control in both areas. The following "Pie Chart of Measure Categorized by Function" shows that they mainly played eight functions such as to regulate, to oversee the government, to oversee the enterprises and other polluters, to provide financial reports, to make use of market force, to provide information, to construct infrastructure, and to reform industrial structure.

The pie chart shows, firstly, that the first three of the functions, i.e., to regulate, to oversee the government, to oversee the enterprises and other polluters, occupy 77% of the pie. This overwhelming occupation of the pie shows that the measures with the three functions were essential to the air pollution governance of the two areas. Without them, the governance processes of air pollution control would be empty talk. They were the empirical evidences for the existence of the three major political relations in the governance processes. Secondly, the pie chart demonstrates that measures with regulatory functions were dominant in the air pollution governance of the two areas. They occupy 39% of the pie. That means that their success or failure determined the success or failure of the governance processes. Thirdly, the pie chart demonstrates that measures with function of supervision over regulators were an indispensable part of air pollution governance. They occupy 26% of the pie. They were the empirical evidences for the "governmental failure" theory proposed by the Public Choice Theory of the neo-political economy, which insists on the necessity of supervision of governments. Without supervision, the relationship of regulation will not be good because the regulators tend to evade their regulatory duties. Fourthly, the pie chart demonstrates that the measures with function of supervision over enterprises or other polluters were indispensable too. It occupies 12% of the pie, a substantial part. They were the empirical evidence of the necessity of supervision over enterprises and other polluters. Lastly, the pie chart demonstrates that there are some other measures with various other functions in the air pollution governance processes, such as market measures, information measures, etc. Their functions were significant but complementary to the first three groups of the measures:

Pie Chart of Measures Categorized by Function

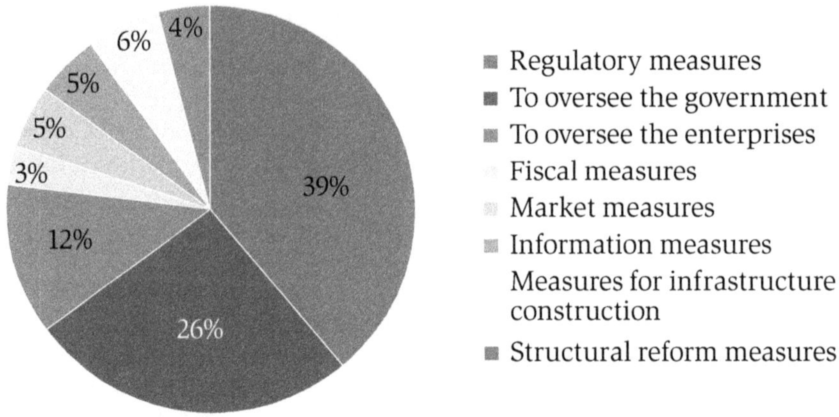

©: WangXi,GuoXiang, KUST, February.2023.

2.2.5 A Summary

The numerous measures analyzed here are strong evidences of the great efforts made by all the actors in air pollution control of the two areas. They are the evidence of the dramatic change in mainstream values of the societies. They demonstrate, firstly, that the regulation of air pollution in the two areas is comprehensive and powerful; secondly, that the supervision over regulators and polluters is rigorous. They are not only the evidence of the existence of the three political relations in the governance processes of air pollution control but also the evidence of strong substantive capacity of a state in air pollution control.

2.3 Comparison of Governance Processes

The air pollution governance processes in the LA and BTH areas have many things similar to each other, although there are many things different at the same time. The major things that are similar to each other in general include the existence of a legal framework, an ethical framework, three major groups of actors or players, three political relations as well as a decision-making process for value choice.

2.3.1 Comparison of Relation of Regulation

As indicated by Chapter 3 and Chapter 4, strong regulatory relations existed and operated well in the air pollution governance processes of the two areas. In both the areas, generally speaking, the national, state (provincial) and local administrations were the regulators of air pollution. All the related laws and regulations were implemented and enforced by them. The enterprises and other polluters were mainly regulated entities. They had the duty to strictly abide by the law and regulations and to cooperate with the regulators.

The regulation of air pollution in the two areas covers a large number of industries. In the LA area, the industries under the regulation include transportation (including fuels), ports, buildings, utilities, oil refineries, gas stations, and coal-fired power plants. In the BTH area, those under the regulation, include transportation (including transport fuels), boiler, oil refinery, cement, iron and steel, and nonferrous metals and coal-fired power plants and reform of energy structure.

There are numerous similarities in terms of regulated industries between the two areas, such as transportation (including fuels), ports, oil refineries, and coal, oil, and gas-fired power plants. The reason for this similarity is that all of those industries are essential to both the LA and the BTH areas.

There are differences in the categories of the regulated industries. For example, in the Los Angeles area, great efforts were made to improve the efficiency of buildings, while in the BTH area, building efficiency seems not to have been a priority for air pollution control. Great efforts were made to reduce the air pollution caused by households' coal burning, cement plants, iron and steel plants and nonferrous metals smelting plants in the BTH area. But those industries or practices seem not to be a problem in the LA area. This difference is due to the different stages of industrialization and the different industrial structures of the two areas. The remarkable differences in industrial structures of the two areas did not prevent them from the successes of air pollution control. That means that industrial structure is not a determinative factor for such a comparative legal study.

2.3.2 Comparison of Relation of Supervision Over Regulators

A dynamic relation of supervision over the regulators in the air pollution governance processes exists in both areas too. As reported in Chapter 3, in the LA area, as to the relation between the federal government and the State government, the relation was reflected by the "federal enforcement" provision of Article 113 of the CAA (1970). As to the supervision over environmental performance of the local governments, this relation was reflected by the revelations of the air pollution sources and the deficiency of the local regulatory powers by the Pasadena Star-News and the Los Angeles Times in 1940s, and the litigation related to the NOx control program of the SCAQMD filed by a group of environmental NGOs in Los Angeles County Superior Court in 2016. As to the support given to the State Government by the environmental NGOs, this relation was reflected by the case of *California Dump Truck Owners Assoc. v. Nichols* in 2015, the case of *International Truck & Engine Corp. v. California Air Resources Board* in 2001, the case of *Engine Manufacturer's Association and Western Petroleum Association v. South Coast Air Quality Management District* in 2007, and the case of *California Dump Truck Owners Assoc. v. Nichols* in 2015.

As reported in Chapter 4, a strong relation of supervision over the regulators in the air pollution governance processes existed in the BTH area. It is reflected by the regular inspections conducted by the Standing Committee of the National Peoples'

Congress and the local Standing Committee of the Peoples' Congresses in the BTH area and the CEEI inspection in the cities and counties of the BTH area, such as the CEEI inspection in the Wen'an County of the BTH area in 2017.

It is noted that while there was a strong relation of supervision over local regulators such as environmental authorities of local governments, notable differences exist. Firstly, while the environmental NGOs and enterprises were active in supervising the environmental performance of the local governments in the LA area, the same kind of supervision in the BTH area was comparatively weak. For example, the Chinese law has not recognized the standing to sue against environmental administrations of the government.[501] Secondly, while the supervision was largely conducted through channels of the Communist Party and the national and local legislatures in China, the supervision over local regulators was largely conducted through the channels of news media, public protests and litigations in the courts. Thirdly, while NGOs were not conveyed the right to sue the governments for their malfunction in environmental regulation in China by law, litigation (such as citizen suits) has been a regular way for the NGOs to supervise the environmental performance of the governments in the LA area.

There was a positive correlation between the relation of supervision over regulators and the improvement of air quality in the two areas. In general, the relation of supervision over regulators operated well in the two areas. Under the supervision of the third-party actors, the local administrations did well in carrying out their regulatory duties in air pollution control. The regulation led to the improvement of air quality.

2.3.3 Comparison of Relation of Supervision Over Enterprises and Other Polluters

A relation of supervision over enterprises and other polluters existed in the air pollution governance processes of both areas. In the LA area, as reported briefly in Chapter 3, this relation was reflected by the news reports of the media, the public protests, and the citizen suits against polluting enterprises. As to the BTH area, as reported in Chapter 4, pressures were put on enterprises and other polluters, and it "forced" them to take care of their image in the society and to take measures to eliminate their pollution. The courts played a special role of supervision by correcting the violations of the polluters, on the one hand, and by correcting the malfunctions of governmental regulators on the other hand, through adjudication of environmental litigations. All of those supervisions led to the improvement of air quality eventually.

It is noted that information disclosure is a key to the success of this supervision in both areas. The law on environmental impact assessment played an important role in this supervision. By requiring disclosure of environmental information from both the

501. The author Wang Xi of this book had suggested the National People's Congress to make up this drawback by revising the relevant law. For detail of this drawback and suggestion, *see* Xi Wang, Chapter 17 Drawbacks in the System Design of the Environmental Public Interest Litigation and Ways for Improvement, in Xi Wang, Xiaobo Zhao and Noeleen McNamara, edited, Environmental Public Interest Litigation in China, Springer Nature, Switzerland, AG 2023, pp. 383-397.

governments and the polluting enterprises and other polluters, the law authorizes all the stakeholders the right to environmental information. With such a legal right, all stakeholders, particularly pollution victims, are able to express their concerns in court and obtain remedies.

2.3.4 A General Pattern of Air Pollution Governance

From the above categorization and analysis, a general pattern of air pollution governance emerged, regardless of the huge difference in political profiles. The pattern can be described as "three political relations normalized and legitimized by legal and ethical frameworks for combating air pollution." The EG model is a plane geometry expression of the pattern. The formation of the legal and ethical framework and the three main political relationships, which are the main components of this general air pollution control pattern, all depend on the progress of the mainstream social ethics of society.

The numerous measures introduced in Chapter 3 and Chapter 4 are the empirical evidences of the existence and operation of this general pattern. One of the authors of this book, Professor Wang Xi had said that "China's environmental process is a process involving multiple actors; a process influenced by political, economic, social, and technological conditions, a process driven downward by the top levels of government, a process full of difficulties and obstacles, a process in the right direction, and a process that we should vigorously promote and strive for."[502] This summary applies to the air pollution governance process of the BTH area. It may apply to the LA area with some major modifications such as the role the government played in the governance processes.

The existence and operation of the general pattern show that the environmental law and policy in the two areas are in convergence, rather than in divergence. The convergence provides a good basis and condition for the cooperation and mutual learning in policy and law on air pollution control in the two areas and the two countries.

502. Wang Xi, Efforts to Improve the Legal Guarantee of Environmental Governance: Review of the Revision of the Environmental Protection Law, in Qin Tianbao, Chief Editor, Ke Jian, Executive Chief Editor, Wuhan University Environmental Law Review, 1, 2018, p. 91.

CHAPTER 6

Conclusions

A health operation of a general pattern of air pollution governance has brought about in the improvement of air quality in the two areas. The remarkable improvement in air quality in the LA and BTH areas has proved that the air pollution governance in the two areas is the so-called "good governance" in terms of political science. Their legal and policy experience demonstrates that when mainstream social values shift towards favoring control of air pollution, and workable legal and ethical frameworks are established, along with the establishment and operation of the three basic political relations related to air pollution control, a good and effective governance process of air pollution control will start to work.

We are trying to use the following "Chart of Air Quality Improvement and Correlated Factors" to conclude this comparative study. We are trying to use the chart to show the factors directly correlated to the improvement of air quality and the factors not directly correlated to the improvement of the air quality in the two areas:

Chart of Air Quality Improvement and the Correlated Factors

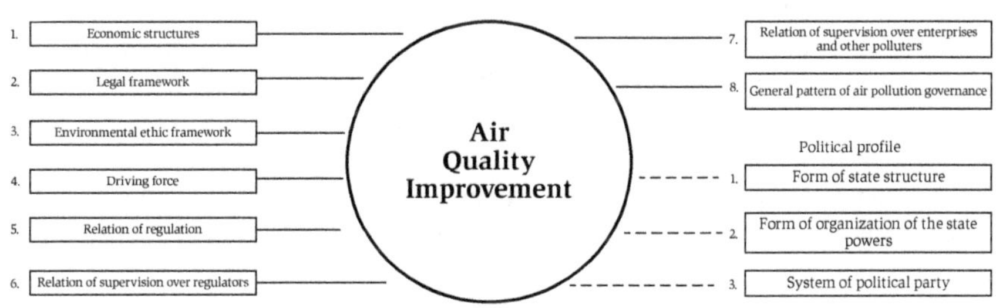

Note:

The solid line indicates a strong correlation. Dotted line indicates little or no correlation.

©: WangXi,GuoXiang, KUST, February.2023.

As the chart shows, there are eight factors directly contributing to the improvement of air quality in the two areas. Those positive factors are:

(1) economic structure;
(2) legal framework;
(3) environmental ethic framework;
(4) driving forces;
(5) relation of regulation;
(6) relation of supervision over regulators;
(7) relation of supervision over enterprises and other polluters;
(8) general pattern of air pollution governance.

The eight factors are represented by the rectangles in the following chart. The solid lines between the rectangles and the circle in the center of the chart mean the factors in the rectangle contribute to or have a positive correlation with the improvement of air polity. The stronger or better those factors are, the larger the contributions they make to the improvement of air quality. Therefore, the "tale" of the "two cities (the LA and the BTH area)" told us that, in order to put down air pollution and protect human health, all the entities (governments, enterprises and other polluters, citizens, social organizations, media and courts, etc.) should put great efforts to strengthen those positive factors.

The chart shows that there are three factors not directly contributing to the improvement of the air quality of the two areas. They are the following:

(1) Form of state structure.
(2) Form of the organization of the state powers.
(3) System of political parties.

They are represented by three rectangles under the subheading of "political profile" in the chart. The dotted lines between them and the circle in the center of the chart mean a pale or weak correlation between the political profiles and the improvement of air quality. In other words, the dotted lines mean that the success or failure of an air pollution governance does not depend on those factors. However, it is worth noting that the pale or weak correlation of those factors to the improvement of air quality does not mean they are not valuable in this comparative legal study. They are actually valuable because the noncorrelation between them and the improvement of air quality proves that the air pollution governance in different countries can be comparatively studied. In other words, those noncorrelations prove the possibility of learning from each other about the legal and policy experience of air pollution control in different countries.

The conclusions conveyed by the chart are consistent with the argument of "effective states,"[503] an interesting and convincing point proposed by Professor Francis

503. Written by Francis Fukuyama, translated by Mao Junjie, Political Order and Political Decay, in Chinese, published by Guangxi Normal University, 2015, p. 33.

Fukuyama. He had argued that "[w]hat is more important than the size of government is the quality of government ... Yet there is a very clear correlation between the quality of government and good socio-economic outcomes."[504] The eight rectangles in the chart are not only the factors correlating to the improvement of the air quality but also factors correlating to the quality of government or the effectiveness of a state. We believe that they are actually the key indicators of a state's substantive capability, while the three rectangles under the subheading of "political profile" are more or less superficial or formal. It is not the political profile of a state, but the substantive capability of a state that determines the success or failure of an air pollution governance process.

We are trying to summarize, in addition to capacity in technology, engineering and science,[505] the substantive capabilities correlating to the improvement of the air quality of the two areas, as the following ones:

(1) capability of environmental ethical support;
(2) capability of legal framework building;
(3) capability of good governance.

Capability of environmental ethical support is based on mainstream value change in society. Environmental ethics or the changed social value on environment is the inherent driving force for the mobilization of the society to fight against air pollution. It is important to remember that it is the dramatic change of social value on environmental matters in the LA and the BTH areas that triggered new social processes on air pollution control.

Capability of legal framework building is based on, in addition to the environmental ethical support, many other factors, such as economic capacity, science and technology capacity, technological capacity, capacity of legislation, and capacity of law implementation and enforcement. The experience of air pollution governance in the two areas indicates that both the countries and the areas have this capability.

Capability of good governance is a more comprehensive term. It refers to the capability to create a good governance pattern and to keep a healthy operation of the governance process. This study finds that a good pattern of governance has been established for air pollution control in both areas. By national and local legislations, which are supported by high levels of environmental ethics in the societies, the two areas have been able to establish the three essential political relations for compacting air pollution. Those relations have been operated considerably well, i.e., the regulators have been able to regulate the enterprises and other polluters under the legal framework, and the third parties have been able to supervise both the regulators and the enterprises and other polluters through the various legal channels. As a result of the

504. Written by Francis Fukuyama, translated by Mao Junjie, Political Order and Political Decay, in Chinese, published by Guangxi Normal University, 2015, pp. 33-34.
505. Technology is an essential substantive capability for air pollution control. Because this study focuses on policy and law, so technology is not covered.

good operation of the governance processes, air quality has improved remarkably in the two areas.

The stories of air pollution control in the LA area and the BTH area tell us, among other things, that both countries are "effective states." It is because both the countries and the areas have the substantive capability to establish and smoothly operate a decent pattern of air pollution governance. If there is anything that other countries or areas may learn from the experience of the two areas, it is the eight factors that correlate with improved air quality in the chart and the three substantive capability buildings summarized above. They are the most commonalities discovered by this study.

Finally, we must point out that although both the LA and the BTH areas have made remarkable achievements in air pollution control in the past, they are facing serious challenges in this campaign today. The first challenge is about how to maintain the achievements in air quality improvement in the time of climate change. Recent economic necessities for the U.S. and China caused both countries to resume a temporary return to the support of exploration and use of fossil fuels. Would these increases offset the established achievements in air quality improvements in the two areas? It is a matter that remains to be seen in the future. The second challenge comes from climate change. Climate change has been called the second generation of environmental problems in the world. It is a more critical and fundamental environmental problem. It is not only a problem of human survival but also a problem of the survival of the ecological system of the Earth. It is related but different from the air pollution experienced by the LA and the BTH areas in the past. It is more difficult to deal with. The United States and China are the two largest greenhouse gas emitters in the world. It is a tossup to judge the relative possibilities of the eventual success of the two areas in timely meeting their climate mitigation goals at this moment. Both the LA and the BTH areas have to be able to meet highly difficult domestic and international challenges not exclusively within their control. Therefore, the experiences and lessons from these stories have limited value because they do not address struggles against new or second-generation environmental problems like climate change and loss of biodiversity. Both the LA and BTH areas are facing serious challenges in integrating conventional and tactical air pollution control with long-term, broad, and comprehensive climate change strategies in order to maintain the achievements gained from the fighting against air pollution. Both areas will try. It would be helpful to both, and to the cause of climate mitigation, if they could tackle these challenges together.

In order to tackle the second generation of environmental problems, such as climate change and the loss of biodiversity, societies both in the United States and China, including the LA area and the BTH area, need to further change their mainstream social values. Just as Professor Richard N.L. Andrew had said "the most revolutionary element of this new public consciousness was powerful new awareness of the environment as living system—a 'web of life' or ecosystem—rather than just a storehouse of commodities to be extracted or a physical or chemical machine to be manipulated."[506] We need a new and higher mainstream social value which respects not only human survival but also the survival of all the species and their habitats on the Earth. Therefore, for maintaining and continuously increasing the substantive capability as mentioned above, both the countries and the areas have to make great efforts now and in the future.

506. Richard N.L. Andrews, Managing the Environment, Managing Ourselves: A History of American Environmental Policy 223-226 (1999). Quoted from A.D. Tarlock, New Direction in Environmental Law: Then and Now (2010), 32, Washington University Journal of Law & Policy 4.

Bibliography

Environmental Law in the United States

Wang Xi, Introduction to American Environmental Law, Wuhan University Press, Wuhan, China, 1992, in Chinese.

Richard L. Revesz, Environmental Law and Policy, Thomson Reuters/Foundation, New York, 2009.

Steven Ferrey, Environmental Law (Seventh Edition), Wolters Kluwer, New York, 2016.

Zygmunt J.B. Plater, Robert H. Abrams, Robert L. Graham, Lisa Heinzerling, David A. Wirth, Noah D. Hall, Environmental Law and Policy: Nature, Law, and Society, (Fifth Edition), Wolters Kluwer, New York, 2016.

Daniel. A. Farber, Roger W. Findley eds., Tian Qiyun, Huang Biao translated, Environmental Law in Nutshell, the Eighth Edition, in Chinese, Nankai University Press, Tianjin, China, 2016.

James Salzman, Barton Thompson eds., translated by Xu Zuoran, Hu Muyun, Environmental Law and Policy, the Fourth Edition, Peking University Press, Beijing, 2016.

Richard J. Lazarus, The Making of Environmental Law, The University of Chicago Press, Chicago, 2004.

Frank P. Grad and Joel A. Mintz, Environmental Law (Fourth Edition), LEXIS, Danvers, 2000.

Geoffrey Brennan, James M. Buchanan, The Reason of Rules: Constitutional Political Economy, Liberty Fund, Indianapolis, 2000.

Mark S. Squillace and David R. Wooley, Air Pollution (Third Edition), Anderson, Cincinnati, 1999.

J. Clarence Davies and Jan Mazurek, Pollution Control in the United States: Evaluating the System, Resources for the Future, Washington, 1998.

Richard L. Revesz, Foundations of Environmental Law and Policy, Foundation Press, New York, 1997.

Bruce Pardy, Environmental Law: A Guide to Concepts, Butterworths, Toronto and Vancouver, 1996.

William H. Rodgers, Jr., Environmental Law (Second Edition), West Publishing Company, Saint Paul, 1994.

The Council on Environmental Quality, 23rd Annual Report on Environmental Quality, United States Government Printing Office, Washington, 1993.

John E. Bonine and Thomas O. McGarity, The Law of Environmental Protection: Cases-Legislation-Policies (Second Edition), West Publishing Company, Saint Paul, 1992.

Roger W. Findley and Daniel A. Farber, Environmental Law, West Publishing Company, Saint Paul, 1991.

Joseph L. Sax ed., translated by Wang Xiaogang, Defending the Environment: A Strategy for Citizen Action, the Press of China University of Political Science and Law, Beijing, 2011.

Roger W. Findley and Daniel A. Farber, Environmental Law: Cases and Materials (Second Edition), West Publishing Company, Saint Paul, 1985.

Frederick R. Anderson, Daniel R. Mandelker, A. Dan Tarlock, Environmental Protection: Law and Policy, Little, Brown and Company, Boston and Toronto, 1984.

William H. Rodgers, Jr., Environmental Law, West Publishing Company, Saint Paul, 1977.

Xi, W., "The Standing to Sue in Environmental Cases Adjudicated by the U.S. Supreme Court, (in Chinese)," (2021) 15 Tsinghua University Law Journal.

Environmental Law in China

Wang Xi and Lu Kung, Environmental Law in China, (Third Edition), Kluwer Law International BV, The Netherlands, 2022.

Charles R. McElwee, Environmental Law in China: Mitigating Risk and Ensuring Compliance, Oxford University Press, Oxford and New York, 2011.

Xi Wang, Xiaobo Zhao and Noeleen McNamara, eds., Environmental Public Interest Litigation in China, Springer Nature, Switzerland, AG 2023.

Comparative Environmental Law

Emma Lees and Jorge E. Vinuales, The Oxford Handbook of Comparative Environmental Law, Oxford University Press, London, 2019.

Capacity Building for Environmental Law in the Asian and Pacific Region: Approaches and Resources (Volume 1) (Second Edition), Asian Development Bank, Manila, 2003.

E. Burleson, L.H. Lye, Nicholas Robinson (eds.), Comparative Environmental Law and Regulation (West Law, 2011-2017), vols. I-III.

Boer, B., "The Rise of Environmental Law in the Asia Region" (1999) 32 University of Richmond Law Review 1503.

Tarlock, D. and P. Tarak, "Overview of Comparative Environmental Law" (1983) 13 Denver Journal of International Law and Policy 85.

Wang Xi, Chapter 20, Comparative Environmental Law and the Legal System of Environmental Protection, in Guiding Committee of Television Educational Program of China Environmental Law System: China Environmental Law System, the Defense industry Press, Beijing, 1994, in Chinese.

Economics and Political Economics

James M. Buchanan and Gordon Tullock, The Calculus of Consent: Logical Foundations of Constitutional Democracy, Liberty Fund, Indianapolis, 2014.

Paul A. Samuelson, William D. Nordhaus eds., translated and noted by Chen Xiao, Jiang Jingyuan, etc., Economics, Eighteenth Editions, Bilingual Edition, Posts & Telecom Press, Beijing, 2011.

James M. Buchanan, Liberty, Market and State Political Economy in the 1980s, New York University Press, New York, 1985.

Geoffrey Brennan and James M. Buchanan, The Reasons of Rules: Constitutional Political Economy, Cambridge University Press, 1985.

Francis Fukuyama, translated by Mao Junjie, The Origins of Political Order: From Prehuman Times to the French Revolution, in Chinese, Guangxi Normal University Press, Guilin, China, 2014.

Francis Fukuyama, translated by Mao Junjie, Political Order and Political Decay: From the Industrial Revolution to the Globalization of Democracy, in Chinese, Guangxi Normal University Press, Guilin, China, 2014.

Francis Fukuyama, translated by Huang Shengqiang, Xu mingyuan, State-Building: Governance and World Order in the 21st Century, in Chinese, China Social Science Press, Beijing, China, 2007.

Other Books

Glen A. Love and Rhoda M. Love, Ecological Crisis: Readings for Survival, Harcourt, Brace, Jovanovich, 1970.

James R. Pfafflin and Edward N. Ziegler, Encyclopedia of Environmental Science and Engineering (Second Edition), Gordon & Breach Science, New York, 1983.

The Encyclopedia Britannica: The Annals of America, Volume 11, Grolier Incorporated, 1981.

Rice Odell, Environmental Awakening: A New Revolution to Protect the Earth, The Conservation Foundation, 1980.

Index

1972 UN Conference on Human Environment, 84
1992 UN Conference on Environment and Development, 21, 84-85
2 plus 26 cities, 6

A

Achievable standards, 73
Achievements, 10, 19, 23, 58, 76-78, 79, 101, 107-120, 127, 142
Acid rain, 20
Action, 43-47, 91
Action plan, 43-48, 67, 81, 83, 90-92, 94, 95, 99, 113
Action Plan for the Prevention and Control of Air Pollution ("Ten Articles of the Atmosphere"), 24, 92, 113
Adjudicating, 107, 115
Administrative accountability system, 104
Administrative boundary, 100, 120
Administrative discretion of enforcement, 56
Administrative proceeding, 20
Agricultural era, 84
Air pollutant emission standard, 25
Air pollution, 8-10, 23-118, 137
Air pollution governance processes, 2, 23, 25, 71, 74, 76, 90, 119-121, 123, 126, 127, 129, 133-137, 141
Air pollution reporting system, 105
Air pollution sources, 10, 29, 70, 105, 135
Air quality, 10-11, 30-31, 33-34, 76, 111-114, 120-121
Air Quality Management Plan (AQMP), 30, 43
Air Quality Monitoring Network, 30
Air quality monitoring station, 30
Air quality surveillance system, 30
Air Toxic "Hot Spots" Program (AB 2588), 70
Alternative emissions reduction plan, 40
Alternative fuel, 35, 38
Alternative fuel vehicles, 38
Alternative Marine Power (AMP) program, 44
Ambient Air Quality Standard, 25, 26, 30, 42, 77
American Council for an Energy-Efficient Economy, 76
American Lung Association, 77
American Trucking Association Inc. (ATA), 48
Annual inspection, 41
Annual meeting, 41
Annually report, 100
Arie Haagen-Smit, 33, 35
Assessment, 30, 41, 51, 64, 70, 81, 83, 92, 122, 136
Atmospheric environmental quality, 100, 116

Automatic Idling Reduction Devices (AIR devices), 40
Automobile industry, 7
Automobiles, 7, 33-36, 43, 72, 96-97
Automotive market, 8

B

Backyard incinerator, 31-33
Bay wide standards, 44
Beijing Municipal Bureau of Statistics, 110
Beijing-Tianjin-Hebei Area (BTH area), 1, 79-118
Biden Administration, 78
Bill credit, 51, 64
Blanket prohibition, 57
Boilers, 59, 61, 93, 94, 100, 102, 103, 135
Bubble policy, 26
Buddhism, 83
Building code, 48, 50, 52
Building energy efficiency standards, 48, 49
Building industry, 7, 29, 48-55
Bureaucratic inertia, 57

C

California Air Resources Board (CARB), 30, 31, 33-41, 45-47, 49, 50, 62, 66, 68, 70-73, 75, 135
California Energy Code, 49-50
California Energy Commission, 45, 49, 50
California Environmental Quality Act (CEQA), 70, 124
California Green Building Standards Code (CAL Green), 50
California Motor Vehicle Pollution Control Board, 36
California Renewable Portfolio Standard (RPS), 58
Capability of environmental ethical support, 141
Capability of good governance, 141
Capability of legal framework building, 141
Car registration, 96
Carbon dioxide, 38, 42, 62, 95
Carbon emission trading, 83, 91
Carbon neutrality, 82, 83, 95, 117, 118
Carbon peak, 95, 118
Center for Sustainable Energy, 68
Central Ecological and Environmental Inspection (CEEI), 101, 102, 115, 136
Central political power, 80
China Biodiversity Conservation and Green Growth Foundation, 105, 107
China Central TV, 106
China's Agenda 21, 85
Chinese characteristics, 79
Citizen suit, 75, 130, 136
City Energy Project, 63-64
City's Water Use Ordinance, 53
Clean Air Act (CAA), 25, 26, 38, 42, 71, 73, 128, 135
Clean Air Action Plan, 43-48, 94
Clean heating pilot projects, 94
Clean Truck Program (CTP), 47, 48
Clean Vehicle Rebate Program, 68, 69
Clean Vehicles, 68, 69
Cleaner coal distribution center, 95
Cleaning the Sources of Electricity, 57-59
Climate change, 20, 25, 29, 35, 48, 78, 88, 124, 142
Coal consumption, 94, 107, 109, 111, 113, 117, 118
Coalition for Clean Air, 48, 73
Collaborative Group of BTH area Air Pollution Prevention and Control, 100
Collective choice, 18
Commercial Lighting Incentive Program, 51, 64
Commercial Solar Incentive Program, 51, 64

Common interest, 126
Common law, 15, 17, 25
Communist Party of China (CPC), 79, 80, 83, 85-88, 131, 132
Community Air Protection Program (CAPP), 31
Community Health Air Pollution Information System (CHAPIS), 70, 124
Comparability, 3-11
Comparative environmental law, 3
Comparative law, 10, 11
Comparison, 2, 114, 119-137
Compliance Assurance Program, 38
Compliance costs, 74
Compulsory end-of-life for automobiles, 96
Conceptual model, 13, 14
Concession agreement, 47
Confucianism, 83, 86
Congress, 100-101
Consensus, 21, 77, 116, 126
Consumer Assistance Program, 37
Cool Roof Ordinance, 52
Cool vegetation, 62
Cooperative efforts, 61
Cooperative federalism, 25
Coordination, 13, 31, 83, 86, 92, 97
Correlated factors, 189
Correlation, 54, 119-121, 123, 125, 126, 136, 140, 141
Cost accounting, 20
Courts, 15, 23-25, 35, 36, 71-73, 78, 90, 104-107, 115, 116, 129, 130, 135-137
Criteria air pollutants, 9
Crude oil, 44, 59
Cultural Revolution, 84
Current price, 20
Currently available technologies, 40
Curve, 28, 29, 89, 110, 122-124
Cutting off excess production capacity, 98

D

Decals, 69
Defeat devices, 72, 75
Democrats, 24, 124
Desire for survival, 125
Deterrence, 20
Development of environmental ethics, 28-29, 89, 122, 126
Diesel exhaust pollution, 39-41
Diesel fuel standard, 39
Diesel Risk Reduction Plan (DRRP), 34
Differences, 1, 3, 72, 75, 120, 123, 135-137
Disciplines of CPC and the Chinese government, 131-132
Discount rate, 19
Driving forces, 122, 124-125, 140, 141
Dual carbon target, 118
Dusts, 10, 59, 93, 98, 100, 101

E

Earth Day, 28, 123-125
Ecological Civilization, 86-89, 124, 125, 127
Ecological economy, 20, 88
Ecological principles, 20
Economic Building Enterprises, 53-54
Economic foundation, 120
Economic growth, 33, 77, 115, 125
Economic policies, 19, 20
Economic structure, 119-121
Effective states, 140, 142
EG Model, 2, 13, 14, 17-22, 25, 29, 80, 83, 115, 126, 127, 137
Elections, 24, 29, 78
Electric cars, 69, 78
Electric passenger vehicles, 35
Electricity source, 58
Emission control zones for ships, 97
Emission equivalent engine, 39
Emission levels, 56
Emission permit, 56-57, 92-93

Emission restrictions, 56
Emissions banking, 26
Emissions inventories, 41, 43
Emissions trading, 26, 66, 91
Employees, 53, 98-99, 102, 116
Energy consumed, 109, 111
Energy Efficiency of Buildings, 51-53, 63
Energy-efficient lighting assessments, 51, 64
Energy Star, 53, 67
Energy structure, 8, 94-95, 107-111, 117, 135
Energy transition plans, 78
Enforcement, 37, 48, 56, 71, 81, 97, 99-102, 128, 135, 141
Engine Manufacturer's Association, 73, 135
Enterprises, 53-54, 72-75, 104-107, 115, 136-137
Environmental awareness, 28, 84, 86, 89, 125
Environmental decision-making processes, 14
Environmental economics, 20
Environmental education, 20, 29, 69-70, 86, 115, 124, 125, 127
Environmental ethics, 14, 15, 17, 20, 27-29, 83-89, 122-126, 132, 140, 141
Environmental impact assessment, 83, 122, 136
Environmental information, 66, 104, 117, 136, 137
Environmental information disclosure, 117
Environmental information labels, 66
Environmental mass events, 123
Environmental mitigation, 46
Environmental performance, 66, 68, 81, 101, 104, 115, 135, 136
Environmental propaganda, 115
Environmental protection, 9, 14, 21, 29, 35, 81, 84, 90, 93, 96, 98, 102, 104-107, 115, 120, 121, 125
Environmental Protection Agency (EPA), 9, 25, 26, 30, 35, 38-40, 44, 46, 47, 49, 62, 66, 67, 71-73, 75, 76, 78, 128
Environmental Protection Law of the People's Republic of PRC (EPL of the PRC), 81
Environmental public interest litigation, 82, 115, 121, 130
Environmental review process, 70
Environmental technologies, 76
Environmentalism, 27
Equilateral triangle, 14-17
Eric Garcetti, 44, 48
Essential feature, 79
Ethical framework, 14, 15, 17, 22, 23, 25-29, 79-89, 119, 121-126, 131, 134, 137, 139
Evolutionary trends, 122-124
Executive branch, 23
Experimental stage, 117
Exposure, 31, 34, 46, 106
External placement, 99
Externality, 18, 20-22, 125, 128

F

Federal ambient air quality standard, 25
Federal Aviation Administration Authorization Act of 1994 (FAAAA), 48
Federal budget, 24
Federal court, 23, 73
Federal enforcement, 71, 128, 135
Federal government, 18, 23, 25, 26, 37, 55, 71, 135
Federal system, 23
Figure, 14, 127, 129
Financial compensation, 99
Financial incentives, 44, 63, 68, 69
Financial penalties, 41
Financial report, 133
First generation of environmental problems, 89, 122

Fleet rules, 38, 73
Forewarning consultation platform for heavy air pollution, 92
Form of organization of the state powers, 23, 24, 80
Form of state structure, 23, 80, 120, 140
Francis Fukuyama, 125, 126, 141
Free interchange of information, 61
Free lighting upgrade, 51, 64
Free rider, 66
Freight efficiency, 45
From-bottom-to-up, 124, 125
From-up-to-bottom, 124
Fuel, 26, 29, 35, 38-40, 42-44, 55-57, 59-62, 66, 73, 77, 78, 97, 135, 142
Fuel-burning utility power plants, 61
Fuel economy and environment label, 66
Fuel evaporation, 59, 60
Fuel nozzles, 60
Function, 20, 63, 124, 133, 135
Funding, 29, 41, 45, 46, 53, 68, 91

G

Gaming, 60
Gas stations, 29, 59-61, 135
Gasoline, 7, 37, 42-43, 62, 76
General pattern, 137, 139, 140
General plan, 55, 58, 70, 124
Geoffrey Brennan, 128
Geographic background, 3-8
Global public domain, 120
Goals and targets, 90-91
Governance, 13-118, 134-137
Governmental failure, 21, 22, 115, 133
Governmental intervention, 18
Great Smog, 34
Green Arts, 63
Green Building Team, 50
Green business, 63
Green Growth, 82, 83, 88-90, 105-107, 124
Green Lodging, 63
Green Seal, 63
Greenhouse gases, 9, 45, 48, 66, 76, 83, 142
Greenpeace, 113
Groundwater pollution, 42
Guideline to Strengthen the Coordination of Legislation and Relevant Legal Research Measures, 83

H

Haze, 1, 90, 123, 124
Health risk assessment, 41
Heavy-duty on-road vehicles, 39
High tax trap, 18, 128
Hotline telephones, 105
Hotspots of air pollutants, 66
House, 23-25, 55

I

Idle reduction technology, 40
Ignorance and apathy, 9
Implementation, 26, 39, 43, 45, 47-49, 53, 68, 71, 73, 76, 81, 90-92, 97, 100-101, 106, 130, 141
Implementation Plan for the Tianjin Emission Control Zone for Ships, 97, 100, 101, 106, 117, 127, 130, 141
Incentive methods, 65
Individual air pollution control districts, 55
Individual behavior, 18
Individual time horizons, 19
Individualized choice, 18
Industrial and utilities sectors, 9
Industrial development policy, 116
Industrial structure, 8, 87, 93, 99, 133, 135
Industrialization, 7, 10, 17, 123, 135
Industry lobbying, 57
Inefficient buildings, 9
Inflation Reduction Act, 25, 36, 78
Inflation trap, 18, 128

Informal institutional arrangements, 13
Information, 2, 19, 20, 23, 29, 30, 51-54, 61-64, 66, 70, 71, 79, 84, 90, 91, 97, 101, 104, 106, 117, 119, 133, 134, 136, 137
Injunctive proceedings, 56
Innovative initiatives, 43
Inspection, 26, 37, 41, 81, 96, 97, 100-104, 135, 136
Integrated Resource Plan (IRP), 58
Internal logic, 21-22
Internal placement, 98, 99
International Council on Clean Transportation, 72, 75
Intrinsic logic, 21
IPPEP, 13, 22

J

James Buchannan, 18, 128
Joint Law Enforcement Action Plan, 99
Joint legislation of the local people's congresses, 83
Joint prevention and control, 83, 90, 91, 97
Joint Research Council on Power Plant Air Pollution Control, 55, 61-62

L

LA Green Business Certification Program, 63
LADWP Commercial Lighting Incentive Program, 51, 64
Law on Prevention and Control of Atmospheric Pollution of the PRC (LPCAP), 81, 92, 100, 101, 105, 107
Law-making, 17
Laws of ecology, 125
Lead, 30, 83
Leadership in Energy and Environmental Design (LEED), 54, 67-68
Legal channel, 15, 141
Legal formants, 10, 11
Legal framework, 14, 25-27, 77, 80-83, 116, 121, 125, 134, 140, 141
Legal remedies, 20
Legislation, 17, 24, 25, 27, 29, 33, 78, 83, 117, 129, 141
Legislative proposals, 24
Legislative reforms, 76
Legitimacy, 126
Litigation for public environmental interest, 20
Local emissions reduction programs, 31
Local framework, 82-83
Local outlines of the economic and social development, 82
Local people's congresses, 80, 82, 83, 100, 115, 116
Local planning and zoning boards, 55
Local regulatory measures, 92-100
Locomotive transportation, 39-41
Long-term goals, 55
Loose coal, 90, 94, 96
Los Angeles Area (LA area), 1-3, 7-10, 23-78, 115, 119, 123-125, 135-137, 142
Los Angeles County Air Pollution Control District (LAPCD), 27
Los Angeles Department of Water and Power (LADWP), 51, 52, 54, 58, 61, 62, 67, 75, 77
Los Angeles Environmental Affairs Department (EAD), 63
Los Angeles Times, 74, 135
Low Emission Vehicles Program, 37-38
Lower-emission vehicle, 38

M

Macro comparison, 119-121
Macro-economic policy, 19
Mainstream social values, 125, 139, 142, 144
Mainstream value of the societies, 134
Major air pollutants, 76
Major air pollution index, 1
Major polluting sources, 96-98

Manufacturing industries, 38, 116
Market failure, 19, 21, 22
Market-based approach, 65, 66
Maximum rate, 56
Measures, 127-134
Measures categorized, 127-134
Media, 15, 20, 74-75, 104, 106, 115, 116, 124, 129, 136, 140
Methodology, 2, 13-22
Metropolitan Transportation Commission, 69
Micro comparison, 119, 121-137
Microeconomics, 17, 18
Middle class, 120
Misdemeanor prosecutions, 56
Model of Environmental Governance, 14
Mohave Generating Plant, 75, 77
Monitoring air pollutants, 30-31
Moral restraint, 17
Motor vehicle pollution control regulation, 36
Motor vehicles, 8, 10, 26, 35-37, 42, 72, 76, 96, 100
Multi-disciplines, 22
Multiple Air Toxic Exposure Study, 46
Municipal garbage collection program, 32
Municipal projects, 53

N

National Action Plan on Prevention and Control of Air Pollution (2013), 81
National Air Quality Standards (NAAQS), 1, 30, 39, 77
National climate policy, 117
National Environmental Policy Act (NEPA), 27, 123, 124
National framework, 81-82
National Measures for Assessment of Implementation of the Action Plan on Prevention and Control of Air Pollution (2014), 81
National Measures for Management of Funds for Prevention and Control Air Pollution (2018), 81
National Peoples' Congresses (NPC), 100
National Programme for Implementation of Cleaner Production Technology in Key Industrial Sectors for Prevention and Control of Air Pollution (2014), 81
National regulatory measures, 90-92
National Report on Air Quality of Key Cities, 9
Natural gas, 37, 62, 69, 82, 94, 95, 110, 111
Natural Resources Defense Council (NRDC), 47, 48, 63, 72, 73
Nature, 16, 17, 27, 84, 86, 87, 120, 125, 131-132
Negative externality, 18
Neo-political economy, 133
Net metering, 51, 64
Net-zero carbon emission zone, 83
New environmental ethics, 27-29, 126
New source construction and operation, 26
Nitrous oxides, 9, 38
Nonattainment area, 35
Nonfinancial incentives, 69
Nonfossil energy, 82, 94
Nongovernmental organizations (NGOs), 15, 47, 48, 63, 71, 72, 75, 78, 104-106, 115-117, 129, 130, 135, 136
Norris Poulson, 32

O

Ocean-Going Vessels Program, 44
Off-street parking plan, 48
Oil refineries, 29, 32, 43, 59-61, 71, 135
Open burning, 99
Operation and maintenance manual, 50

Oral comment, 47
Outdoor Lighting Program, 67
Outline of the 14th Five-Year Plan and 2035 Vision for National Economic and Social Development of Tianjin Municipality (2021), 82
Outline of the 14th Five-Year Plan for National Economic and Social Development of Beijing and the Visionary Goals for 2035 of Beijing (2021), 82
Out-of-state coal-fired power plants, 77
Oversee the enterprises and other polluters, 133
Oversee the government, 133, 134
Ozone, 4, 8-10, 33-36, 76-77, 91, 113, 128

P

Panel discussion, 46
Pareto pessimal, 19
Paris Climate Agreement, 44
Particulate matter, 9, 34-36, 39, 44, 52, 65, 71, 91, 97, 112, 113
Peak times, 122, 123
Per capita carbon emission, 117
Permit, 26, 55-57, 59, 67, 70, 71, 73, 81, 92-93
Personal utilities, 19
Petroleum industry, 59
Petroleum-coke (petcoke) plants, 77
Pie chart, 127-129, 131-134
Plaintiff, 20, 73
Plan for Air Pollution Control in Key Cities, 90
Political pressure, 74
Political process, 14
Political profile, 23-25, 79-80, 119-120, 137, 140, 141
Political relations, 14-17, 23, 25, 29-75, 90-107, 119, 121, 125-129, 133, 134, 137, 139, 141
Political science, 13, 17, 18, 139
Political system, 1, 23, 125
Polluters, 15, 16, 18-20, 29, 65, 71, 74-75, 77, 81, 90, 101, 104-107, 115, 116, 127, 129, 130, 133, 134, 136-135, 137, 140, 141
Pollution Complaints Program, 37
Port, 43-48, 97-98
Port Advanced Vehicle Electrification Project (PAVE), 45
Port of Long Beach (POLB), 43, 46
Port of Los Angeles (POLA), 43-48
Positive crankcase ventilation, 36
Positive factors, 140
Poverty, 109
Power Plant Equipment Improvement, 55-56
Prevention of Significant Deterioration and Visibility Protection, 26
Primary energy consumption, 94
Process of decision, 16
Process of evolving decision rules, 16
Proportion, 8, 9, 19, 82, 87, 107-109, 112, 114
Provisions on Quantitative Accountability for Comprehensive Control and Crucial Actions Air Pollution Control in the Autumn and Winter in the BTH Area (2017), 81-82
Provisions on the Administration of Shore Power for Ports and Ships, 97
Public authorities, 19
Public awareness, 20, 70
Public Choice Theory, 18, 19, 133
Public comments, 46
Public meeting, 47, 50
Public participation, 33, 47-48, 57, 66, 70, 104
Public prosecutors, 102, 105
Public responses, 74-75
Public-debt trap, 18, 128
Public-private partnership, 29, 61-65

Q

Qinhuangdao Fangyuan Packaging Glass Co., 105, 107
Quality of government, 141

R

Railroad, 39-41, 44, 47, 74
Railroad Agreement, 39-41
Reason, 1, 3-11, 18, 19, 79, 111, 117, 120, 125, 128, 130, 135
Rebate program, 67-69
Record-keeping, 39
Refineries, 7, 29, 32, 42, 43, 59-61, 65, 71, 135
Reform industrial structure, 133
Regional approach, 35
Regional Clean Air Incentives Market (RECLAIM), 65
Regulate, 15, 17, 18, 35, 49, 59, 81, 91, 116, 133, 141
Regulator, 15, 16, 18, 21, 29, 60, 68, 69, 71-75, 77, 90, 100-104, 115, 116, 127, 128, 130, 133-136, 140, 141
Regulatory capture, 21
Regulatory functions, 133
Regulatory relation, 16, 29, 115, 127, 134
Relation of supervision over enterprises and other polluters, 16, 19, 74-75, 90, 104, 115, 127, 136-137, 140
Renewable energy, 58, 78, 82, 83, 87, 95, 118
Renewable Energy Ordinance (REO), 58, 59
Renewal processes, 57
Reporting, 39, 47, 74, 105, 115
Republicans, 24, 25, 78, 124
Responsible agencies, 46-47
Retrofitting costs, 39
Review, 29, 30, 43, 56, 59, 70
RFG program, 42
Rice Odell, 27
Richard Nixon, 24
Rio Declaration on Environment and Development, 19
Robert Garcia, 45
Role of government, 69-70, 124, 137
Rubbish burning, 32

S

Sampling procedure, 42
San Pedro Bay Standards, 47
SCAQMD Clean Fleets Program, 38-39
Scientific measurements, 41
Scientific Outlook of Development, 86, 89, 123
Secondary industries, 8, 93
Second-generation environmental problems, 142
Self-employment, 99
Senate, 23-25
Several Provisions on Protecting and Improving the Environment (Draft for Trial Implementation), 84
Sharing the costs of air pollution, 116
Shorter time horizons, 18
Sierra Club, 48, 71, 73, 75
Similarities, 1, 3, 125, 135
Small Business Direct Install Program, 51, 64
Small-scale solar PV, 58
Smog, 36-37
Smog certification, 37
Smog Check Program, 36-37
Smog Index Label, 66, 71, 75
Social conditions, 3-8
Social mobilization, 125, 126
Social-economic background, 79
Socialist country, 79
Socialist market economy, 80
Solar incentive programs, 51, 64-66
Sources of emissions, 96
South Coast Air Basin (SCAB), 30, 34

South Coast Air Basin Multiple Air Toxics Exposure Study (MATES), 34, 38
South Coast Air Management District's Clean Air Incentive Market Program, 76
South Coast Air Quality Management District (SCAQMD), 30, 34, 35, 38-39, 43, 46, 47, 49, 51, 52, 56, 57, 59, 60, 64, 65, 71, 73, 135
Stage of economic development, 123
Stakeholder, 14-17, 46, 52, 63, 68, 121, 137
Standing, 81, 83, 100, 101, 117, 129, 135, 136
State Implementation Plan (SIP), 39, 43, 71
Stationary sources, 43, 56, 65, 70
Steam-electric generating plants, 58
Steven Ferry, 27
Strategy of Sustainable Development, 85
Subject matter jurisdiction, 73
Substantive capabilities, 141-143
Sulfur dioxide (SO 2), 10, 57, 59, 75, 90, 113
Supervision, 71-75, 100-107, 115, 135-137
Supervision over enterprises and other polluters, 16, 19, 20, 74-75, 77, 90, 104-107, 115, 127, 133, 136-137, 140
Supervision over regulators, 18, 71-74, 115, 133-136, 140
Supervisor, 15, 27, 74
Supervisory relation, 16
Supreme Court, 23, 25, 35, 36, 78
Surface mines, 95
Sustainable Design Implementation Program (SDIP), 53
Sustainable Design Task Force, 53
Sustainable development, 21, 85-89, 121, 125
Sustainable economic, 123
System of multi-party cooperation and political consultation under the leadership of the CPC, 80
System of People's Congress, 80
System of political parties, 23, 24, 80, 120, 140
System of presidential republic, 24

T

Tailpipe emissions, 36, 37
Taoism, 83
Tax credits, 51, 64
Tea Party, 24
Technological feasibility, 72
Technology Advancement Program, 44
Technology innovation, 66, 93-94
Telephone "hotline", 37
Tertiary industry, 8, 93
Third party, 16, 67, 130, 136
Third-party verification rating system, 67
Threshold Guide, 70
Total consumption of coal, 82
Total energy consumption, 94, 107-111, 113
Toxic air contaminant, 34, 52, 65
Traditional Chinese environmental ethics, 83-84
Traffic restrictions, 96
Transportation sector, 9, 33-43
Traps, 18, 19, 128
Trash collection program, 33
Trump, 25, 26, 44, 124
Two circles, 14-17, 25, 80
Two-stage combustion, 55, 61

U

UN Conference on Environment and Development, 21, 84-85
Uncertainty, 60
Urban forestry projects, 62
Utility sector, 55-59, 78

V

Value change, 76-77, 115-116, 125-126, 141
Value choice, 17, 20, 21, 77, 126, 134
Value of economy, 16, 17, 20, 77
Value of environment, 16, 17, 20, 77
Vehicle inspections and maintenance, 26
Vessel operators, 44
Viable technologies, 45
VOC (Volatile Organic Compound), 51, 60, 64, 93, 100
Volkswagen, 72, 75
Voluntary energy efficiency programs, 29, 67-69

W

Waste digester project, 58
Water conservation, 48, 49, 54
Water Conservation Ordinance, 54
Water delivery chain, 54
Water use calculator, 54
Wen'an County, 102, 106, 115, 136
Western Oil and Gas Association, 33
Western States Trucking Association (WSTA), 73, 74
Wind power, 58, 95, 110
Wintertime Oxygenates Program, 42
Wood smoke, 52, 65

Z

Zero-emissions, 45
Zoning code, 55

ENERGY AND ENVIRONMENTAL LAW & POLICY SERIES

1. Stephen J. Turner, *A Substantive Environmental Right: An Examination of the Legal Obligations of Decision-makers towards the Environment*, 2009 (ISBN 978-90-411-2815-7).
2. Helle Tegner Anker, Birgitte Egelund Olsen & Anita Rønne (eds), *Legal Systems and Wind Energy: A Comparative Perspective*, 2009 (ISBN 978-90-411-2831-7).
3. David Langlet, *Prior Informed Consent and Hazardous Trade: Regulating Trade in Hazardous Goods at the Intersection of Sovereignty, Free Trade and Environmental Protection*, 2009 (ISBN 978-90-411-2821-8).
4. Louis J. Kotzé and Alexander R. Paterson (eds), *The Role of the Judiciary in Environmental Governance: Comparative Perspectives*, 2009 (ISBN 978-90-411-2708-2).
5. Tuula Honkonen, *The Common but Differentiated Responsibility Principle in Multilateral Environmental Agreement's: Regulatory and Policy Aspects*, 2009 (ISBN 978-90-411-3153-9).
6. Barbara Pozzo (ed.), *The Implementation of the Seveso Directives in an Enlarged Europe: A Look into the Past and a challenge for the Future*, 2009 (ISBN 978-90-411-2854-6).
7. Henrik M. Inadomi, *Independent Power Projects in Developing Countries: Legal Investment Protection and Consequences for Development*, 2010 (ISBN 978-90-411-3178-2).
8. Nahid Islam, *The Law of Non-Navigational Uses of International Watercourses: Options for Regional Regime-Building in Asia*, 2010 (ISBN 978-90-411-3196-6).
9. Yasuhiro Shigeta, *International Judicial Control of Environmental Protection: Standard Setting, Compliance Control and the Development of International Environmental Law by the International Judiciary*, 2010 (ISBN 978-90-411-3151-5).
10. Katleen Janssen, *The Availability of Spatial and Environmental Data in the European Union: At the Crossroads between Public and Economic Interests*, 2010 (ISBN 978-90-411-3287-1).
11. Henrik Bjørnebye, *Investing in EU Energy Security: Exploring the Regulatory Approach to Tomorrow's Electricity Production*, 2010 (ISBN 978-90-411-3118-8).
12. Véronique Bruggeman, *Compensating catastrophe victims: A Comparative Law and Economics Approach*, 2010 (ISBN 978-90-411-3263-5).
13. Michael G. Faure, Han Lixin & Shan Hongjun, *Maritime Pollution Liability and Policy: China, Europe and the US*, 2010 (ISBN 978-90-411-2869-0).

14. Anton Ming-Zhi Gao, *Regulating Gas Liberalization: A Comparative Study on Unbundling and Open Access Regimes in the US, Europe, Japan, South Korea and Taiwan*, 2010 (ISBN 978-90-411-3347-2).
15. Mustafa Erkan, *International Energy Investment Law: Stability through Contractual Clauses*, 2011 (ISBN 978-90-411-3411-0).
16. Levente Borzsa´k, *The Impact of Environmental Concerns on the Public Enforcement Mechanism under EU law: Environmental protection in the 25th hour*, 2011 (ISBN 978-90-411-3408-0).
17. Tarcísio Hardman Reis, *Compensation for Environmental Damages under International Law: The Role of the International Judge*, 2011 (ISBN 978-90-411-3437-0).
18. Kim Talus, *Vertical Natural Gas Transportation Capacity, Upstream Commodity Contracts and EU Competition Law*, 2011 (ISBN 978-90-411-3407-3).
19. WangHui, *Civil Liability for Marine Oil Pollution Damage: A Comparative and Economic Study of the International, US and Chinese Compensation Regime*, 2011 (ISBN 978-90-411-3672-5).
20. Chowdhury Ishrak Ahmed Siddiky, *Cross-Border Pipeline Arrangements: What Would a Single Regulatory Framework Look Like?*, 2012 (ISBN 978-90-411-3844-6).
21. Rozeta Karova, *Liberalization of Electricity Markets and Public Service Obligations in the Energy Community*, 2012 (ISBN 978-90-411-3849-1).
22. Sandra Cassotta, *Environmental Damage and Liability Problems in a Multilevel Context: The Case of the Environmental Liability Directive*, 2012 (ISBN 978-90-411-3830-9).
23. Mark Wilde, *Civil Liability for Environmental Damage: Comparative Analysis of Law and Policy in Europe and US*, 2013 (ISBN 978-90-411-3233-8).
24. Bernard Taverne, *Petroleum, Industry and Governments: A Study of the Involvement of Industry and Governments in Exploring for and Producing Petroleum*, Fourth Edition, 2022 (ISBN 978-94-035-3230-1).
25. Anton Ming-Zhi Gao & Chien Te Fan (eds), *Legal Issues of Renewable Energy in the Asia Region: Recent Developments in a Post-Fukushima and Post-Kyoto Protocol Era*, 2014 (ISBN 978-90-411-4856-8).
26. Sabina Manea, *The Instrumentalization of Property: Legal Interests in the EU Emissions Trading System*, 2014 (ISBN 978-90-411-5420-0).
27. Joseph A. Tolorunse, *Protection of Property Rights in Discovered Petroleum Reservoirs*, 2014 (ISBN 978-90-411-5604-4).
28. Katelijn Van Hende, *Offshore Wind in the European Union: Towards Integrated Management of Our Marine Waters*, 2015 (ISBN 978-90-411-5613-6).
29. Ken'ichi Matsumoto & Anton Ming-Zhi Gao (eds), *Economic Instruments to Combat Climate Change in Asian Countries*, 2015 (ISBN 978-90-411-5408-8).

30. Eduardo G. Pereira & Damilola S. Olawuyi (eds), *Practical Considerations to Negotiate an Enforceable Joint Operating Agreement under Civil Law Jurisdictions*, Second Edition, 2020 (ISBN 978-94-035-0664-7).
31. Ying Shen, *China's Way to Carbon Emissions Reduction: The Choice of Regulatory Instruments and Its Legal Challenges*, 2015 (ISBN 978-90-411-6049-2).
32. Roy Andrew Partain, *Environmental Hazards from Offshore Methane Hydrate Operations: Civil Liability and Regulations for Efficient Governance*, 2017 (ISBN 978-90-411-8730-7).
33. Anton Ming-Zhi Gao & Chien-Te Fan (eds), *The Development of a Comprehensive Legal Framework for the Promotion of Offshore Wind Power: The Lessons from Europe and Pacific Asia*, 2017 (ISBN 978-90-411-8397-2).
34. Tade Oyewunmi, *Regulating Gas Supply to Power Markets: Transnational Approaches to Competitiveness and Security of Supply*, 2018 (ISBN 978-90-411-9869-3).
35. Huseyin Cagri Corlu, *Application of Anti-manipulation Law to EU Wholesale Energy Markets and Its Interplay with EU Competition Law*, 2018 (ISBN 978-90-411-9603-3).
36. Kaisa Huhta, *Capacity Mechanisms in EU Energy Law: Ensuring Security of Supply in the Energy Transition*, 2019 (ISBN 978-94-035-1451-2).
37. Maria João C. Pereira Rolim, *Reconciling Energy, the Environment and Sustainable Development: The Role of Law and Regulation*, 2019 (ISBN 978-94-035-1461-1).
38. Eduardo G. Pereira, Alexandra Wawryk, Heike Trischmann, Catherine Banet & Keith B. Hall (eds), *The Regulation of Decommissioning, Abandonment and Reuse Initiatives in the Oil and Gas Industry: From Obligation to Opportunities*, 2020 (ISBN 978-94-035-0693-7).
39. Rasa Engstedt, *Handbook on European Nuclear Law: Competences of the Euratom Community under the Euratom Treaty*, 2021 (ISBN 978-94-035-2830-4).
40. Cinzia Caporale, Ilja Richard Pavone & Maria Pia Ragionieri (eds), *International Food Law: How Food Law can Balance Health, Environment and Animal Welfare*, 2021 (978-94-035-1761-2).
41. Rafael Leal-Arcas, *Climate Clubs for a Sustainable Future: The Role of International Trade and Investment Law*, 2021 (ISBN 978-94-035-3715-3).
42. Wang Xi & Richard Ottinger, *A Tale of Two Cities: A Comparison of Air Pollution Governance in the Los Angeles Area of the USA and the Beijing-Tianjin-Hebei Area of China*, 2024 (ISBN 978-94-035-4237-9).

www.ingramcontent.com/pod-product-compliance
Lightning Source LLC
Chambersburg PA
CBHW071245230926
51849CB00001B/235
* 9 7 8 9 4 0 3 5 4 2 3 7 9 *